Community Schools in Africa

Community Schools in Africa:

Reaching the Unreached

Co-Editors: *Deborah Glassman*
                Jordan Naidoo
                Fred Wood

Associate Editor: *Kristin Helmore*

Contributor: *Chloe O'Gara*

 Springer

Co-Editors: Associate Editor:
Deborah Glassman   Kristin Helmore
Jordan Naidoo
Fred Wood

Contributor:
Chloe O'Gara

Library of Congress Control Number: 2006932806

ISBN -13: 978-0-387-45106-0
ISBN -10: 0-387-45106-4

e-ISBN-13: 978-0-387-45107-7
e-ISBN-10: 0-387-45107-2

Printed on acid-free paper.

9 8 7 6 5 4 3 2 1

springer.com

Dedication

This book is dedicated to the children, communities and schools who implemented the community school initiative with Save the Children in four countries. Their vision, dedication, commitment, savvy, and hard work to improve their collective and individual futures are the essential heart of each community school.

Contents

List of Photographs..ix

Abbreviations and Acronyms xiii

Summary xvii
Jordan Naidoo

Contributing Authors xxiii

Acknowledgments xxix

Chapter 1... 1
Community Schools: The Solution to Local Needs
Fred Wood

Chapter 2..9
Mali, 1992–2003: The First Experiment
Deborah Glassman and Mamadou Millogo

Chapter 3..37

Malawi, 1994–2003: Training on a National Scale

Amy Jo Dowd and Lester Namathaka

Chapter 4..75

Ethiopia, 1992–2001: Helping Communities Fill the Education Gap

Fred Wood and Mengistu Edo Koricha

Chapter 5..101

Uganda, 1999–2005: Transferring to Government Control

Bonita Birungi, Hadijah Nandyose, Fred Wood and Catherine Kennedy

Chapter 6..133

USAID and Community Schools in Africa: The Vision, the Strategy, the Commitment

Yolande Miller-Grandvaux

Chapter 7..155

Supply-Side Education: Africa's Home-grown Schools

Joe DeStefano

Chapter 8..171

What's Next for Community Schools?

Jordan Naidoo

Index..195

List of Photographs

Schoolchildren in Mozambique at a Save the Children community school.................. 1

The village of Niamou, Mali, site of a Save the Children community school............. 9

Village children in Mali. 11

Girls in Blakala classroom. 13

Girl pounding maize. 14

Bohi village school committee meeting. 16

Classroom in Blakala, Mali. 17

Boys plowing a field... 17

A student leads the class. 19

Teaching in French in Mali. 20

School children in Blakala, Mali. 23

School children at work in a classroom at the Blakala school............................... 24

Blakala classroom, Mali.. 25

School children at the Blakala school.. 27

Malian school children in a race. 28

A girl gets a drink of purified water at the Blakala school..................................... 29

School children in front of their village school. 31

Malawian school children in front of the Malenga primary school, which
   serves 96 pupils. SC is working to provide new classroom blocks, school
   materials and furniture. 37

Children at the primary school in Nikisi stage a drama in English. Their cement block classroom, built by the community with help from SC, accommodates 327 students. *39*

Community members build a new school in Namisi. *41*

A teachers' training workshop. *44*

Students act out a scene to practice their English. *48*

Children study math using the mayerengero in Standard Two. *49*

Community members gather for a meeting while children play with tires. *52*

A teacher in class at the Malenga primary school. *55*

Teaching a large class outdoors at the Namisi school while the new school that Save the Children is helping to build is being completed. *56*

Students act out a scene as part of English class. *59*

A crowded classroom at the Malenga primary school, before the new school was built. *62*

Children attend class outside at the Namisi school until the new school that Save the Children is helping to build is completed. *65*

Teaching in Ethiopia at a Save the Children school that is under construction. *75*

A mother brings her child to the Gode Therapeutic Feeding Center in Ethiopia. *77*

A nomad in front of her home. *78*

School children attend class outside while their new school building is being constructed. *83*

Two girls wait for their PIE school to open. *84*

A teacher in a PIE school uses cut-out letters to teach the alphabet. *86*

Children playing ball outside their school. *87*

A school committee member teaches his children while a new school is being built. *89*

Teaching in a classroom under construction. *91*

A class in session in a sponsorship school. *92*

An Ethiopian boy. *94*

Teaching in a newly constructed classroom.. 97

A six-year-old girl with her exercise book.. 98

Learning English at a Ugandan school. 101

A CHANCE school in the village of Kibuye. 103

Help with the lesson. 106

CHANCE school, Kibuye Village. 108

Teaching at a CHANCE Learning Center. 109

Teaching the digestive system at a CHANCE Learning Center. 112

A class works out a problem at a CHANCE Learning Center.......................... 114

Pupils at a CHANCE school work together to solve a math problem.................. 118

Pupils study human and animal anatomy.. 120

Students work together at a CHANCE school. 123

Help from the teacher. 127

A pupil at a CHANCE school.. 129

Abbreviations and Acronyms

ABE: Alternative Basic Education

ABEK: Alternative Basic Education for Karamoja (Uganda)

ADEA: Association for the Development of Education in Africa

APE: Association des Parents d'Elèves (Mali)

ARSH: adolescent reproductive and sexual health

BEEP: Basic Education and Expansion Project (USAID program, Mali)

BESO: Basic Education Structural Overhaul (USAID program, Ethiopia)

BEN: Basic Education Network (Ethiopia)

BEUPA: Basic Education for Urban Poverty Areas (Uganda)

CAP: Centre d'Animation Pédagogique (the government's teacher training office), Mali

CDA: Community Development Assistant (Malawi)

CEP: Certificat d'Etudes Primaires (sixth grade leaving certificate, Mali)

CEPD: Centre for Education Policy Development (South Africa)

CHANCE: Child-Centered Alternatives for Non-Formal Community-Based Education (Uganda)

COPE: Complementary Opportunities for Primary Education (UNICEF, Uganda)

DEM: District Education Manager (Malawi)

DEO: District Education Office (Malawi)

DFID:	Department for International Development (UK)
EC:	Education Coordinator (Malawi)
ET:	Education Trainer (Malawi)
FENU:	Forum for Education NGOs in Uganda
FPE:	Free Primary Education
GER:	gross enrollment rate
HIPC:	heavily indebted poor country
IEQ:	Improving Educational Quality (Malawi)
IC:	Integrated Curriculum (Malawi)
IIEP:	International Institute for Educational Planning
JCE:	Junior Certificate of Education (Malawi)
MEB:	Ministry of Basic Education, Mali
MIE:	Malawi Institute of Education
MIITEP:	Malawi Integrated In-Service Teacher Education Program
MOE:	Ministry of Education (Mali)
MOES:	Ministry of Education and Sports (Uganda)
MOEST:	Ministry of Education, Sports, and Culture (Malawi)
MOGYCS:	Ministry of Gender, Youth and Community Service
MSSSP:	Malawi School Service System Project
NEF:	Nouvelle Ecole Fondamentale (Mali)
NEU:	Nuevas Escuelas Unitarias (Guatemala)
NFE:	non-formal education
NGO:	non-governmental organization
NRM:	National Resistance Movement (Uganda)
OECD:	Organization for International Cooperation and Development
PASE:	Programme d'Ajustement Sectoriel de l'Education (Guinea)
PEA:	Primary Education Advisor (Malawi)
PIE:	Project for Innovation in Education (Ethiopia)
PISE:	Education Sector Investment Program (Mali)
PLA:	participatory learning and action

PRA: participatory rural/rapid appraisal

PRODEC: Programme Décennal de Développement de l'Education (Ten-year Educational Development Program), Mali

PTA: Parent-teachers' Association

PTC: Primary Teachers' College

PVO: private voluntary organization

QUEST: Quality Education through Supporting Teaching (USAID program, Malawi)

RFA: request for assistance

RH: reproductive health

SC: Save the Children-US

SCOPE: Strengthening Communities through Partnerships for Education (Ethiopia)

SMC: School Management Committee

SNNPRS: the Southern Nations, Nationalities and Peoples Regional State (Ethiopia)

SSA: Sub-Saharan Africa

TUM: Teachers' Union of Malawi

UPE: Universal Primary Education (Uganda)

USAID: United States Agency for International Development

VBS: village-based school (Malawi)

WEO: *Woreda* (Local Administrative Unit) Education Office (Ethiopia)

Summary

Jordan Naidoo

Communities help to realize Education for All

For more than a decade, Save the Children US has been working with illiterate villagers across Sub-Saharan Africa to establish and run community schools, in areas previously unreached by government schools. In contrast to the traditional, colonialist model, community schools are designed to meet the educational needs of students using curricula, language and materials that are familiar to them in their surroundings. They are also planned and run by the communities in which the children live. Moreover, these community schools have been seen to be a low-cost means of ensuring access to education for children who would not otherwise have had the opportunity of attending school.

In general, community schools supported by Save the Children (SC) in Mali, Malawi, Ethiopia and Uganda have served children in grades 1–4 in remote, under-served areas. While SC provided schools with financial and technical support, in most cases the community has been responsible for school construction and maintenance, and is involved in school management and governance. Fundamental to the program is the notion of community involvement in school policy and decision-making: communities identify and recruit teachers locally and promote the adoption of curricula that are relevant to the local setting.

> *Fundamental is the notion of community involvement in school policy and decision-making: communities identify and recruit teachers locally and promote the adoption of curricula that are relevant to the local setting.*

Yet, as Fred Wood, Yolande Miller-Grandvaux and Joe de Stefano point out, community involvement in education in Africa is not completely new. In many parts of Sub-Saharan Africa, communities have traditionally played an important role in providing education in a variety of ways, in particular by offering assistance and contributions for school construction and maintenance.

However, the difference in the past decade has been in the number of new schools established and run by local communities, and in the involvement of international NGOs and donor and funding agencies.

USAID alone, working through NGOs such as Save the Children, CARE and World Education, supports more than 5,000 community-managed schools in Benin, Ethiopia, Ghana, Guinea, Malawi, Mali, South Sudan, Uganda, and Zambia.

As countries confronted the challenge of EFA, community schools, with their flexibility in programming, offered a means to meet EFA goals, improve student achievement, and reach out to remote and disadvantaged populations, while keeping costs low.

In addition, as Wood emphasizes, the influence of the 1990 Education Conference in Jomtien, Thailand, and the international commitment to bring the benefits of Education for All (EFA) to "every citizen in every society" cannot be discounted. As countries confronted the challenge of EFA, community schools, with their flexibility in programming, offered a means to meet EFA goals, improve student achievement, and reach out to remote and disadvantaged populations, while keeping costs low.

Confronted with the deterioration, or absence, of public education, more and more communities across Africa are becoming increasingly active in their children's schooling. In Mali and Malawi, for example, a parallel system of community schools, which provide education of a quality comparable to that offered by government schools, now supplies approximately 10 percent of school places. At least on the surface, community initiatives in education usually seem very desirable, given their potential to help spread the cost and resource burden and increase access to education as well as its relevance and impact.

Acknowledging challenges

Yet while some of the benefits of these community schools are undeniable, critics say that benefits are often based on little concrete evidence, and are reported by those who have a vested interest in community schools. They point out that the sparse literature on community schools in Africa tends to be repetitive and highly descriptive, with endless accounts of how this school or that project was a great success, with little or no sustained critique of practice. To complicate the issue, not only are multiple types and models subsumed under the term "community school," advocates have also tended to define community schools by what they are not rather than by what they are.

This collection of papers and country studies addresses some of these issues by reflecting on SC's experience with implementing the community, or village school model in Sub-Saharan Africa. The case studies are primarily descriptive analyses and are not meant as an evaluation of the experience; but they do point to some of the strengths and challenges of community schools as implemented by SC in partnership with a variety of communities in Mali, Ethiopia, Malawi and Uganda.

Mali

SC first became involved in community schools in Mali in 1988, building schools in four villages and using government-trained teachers and the national curriculum. Realizing early that such an approach would hardly make a dent in helping to meet the EFA challenge or the needs of local communities, SC proposed to share roles and responsibilities with the villages.

The responsibilities of communities involved building a one-room classroom; defining a shorter, locally relevant curriculum and calendar; promoting girls' access; selecting, training, and remunerating teachers from the villages; providing schoolbooks and materials; and training village management committees to oversee the schools.

This involved building a one-room classroom; defining a shorter, locally relevant curriculum and calendar; promoting girls' access; selecting, training, and remunerating teachers from the villages; providing schoolbooks and materials; and training village management committees to oversee the schools. This, then, became the basis of the SC community school model, with some variations in implementation in Ethiopia, Malawi and Uganda. By 1994–1995, the SC Village School Program in Mali had expanded from the four initial schools and 16 teachers serving 240 pupils to 36 village schools and 72 teachers serving 2,160 children. In 1995–1996, there was a leap to 114 schools and 6,840 children in 110 villages.

Malawi

SC's intervention in Malawi was motivated by the challenge presented by the influx of children and the shortage of teachers precipitated by the declaration of free, universal, primary education in 1994. The Malawi Village-Based Schools were different from the Mali Village Schools in that they were not built one to a village, but served several villages. They were closely integrated into the existing school system in terms of curriculum and teacher profiles, and were to be handed over to the Ministry of Education in the short term. Furthermore, both in the initial stages and later as part of the USAID-funded QUEST Program (a broader Ministry of Education Reform Initiative), SC worked closely with the Ministry, to the extent of including Primary Education Officers in its capacity building activities. The emphasis at every level—School Management Committees, teachers, Teacher

The emphasis at every level: School Management Committees, teachers, Teacher Mentors and government education officials, was on training, follow-up, evaluation and more training.

Mentors and government education officials—was on training, follow-up, evaluation and more training. SC partnered with District Education Office staff and communities to establish new school facilities and to meet the needs of teachers who had had little, or only limited exposure to a field-based teacher training approach that promotes active teaching and learning.

Ethiopia

In Ethiopia, SC's community schools were targeted at rural, pastoralist communities far removed from public services. They depended heavily on the close involvement of local NGOs in all aspects of the enterprise, from program conception to implementation. This collaboration formed the basis of SC's involvement in the USAID-funded BESO-SCOPE Program (Strengthening Communities through Partnerships for Education). However, since the program focused on upgrading the capacities of local administrative units, there was only limited application of SC's community school principles.

In Ethiopia, the program focused on upgrading the capacities of local NGOs and administrative units.

Also in Ethiopia, the Project for Innovations in Education (PIE) of 1997–2003, funded by the Banyan Tree Foundation, involved strengthening the capacity of local NGOs to deliver basic education services. It was more in the community school mould. Through this intervention the responsibility for PIE schools was handed over to "strengthened" local organizations capable of managing the schools and raising funds to ensure sustainability. By mid-2004, PIE's support system had reached 27 centers, with a total enrolment of 6,483 (48.5 percent of whom were girls).

Save the Children was also the implementing agency for Ethiopia's Bob Marley Schools. This involved selecting locations; mobilizing communities to construct schools; and providing pedagogical support for teachers. Twenty Bob Marley Schools are now operating in the Oromia and Somali regions, serving more than 5,000 students, of whom almost 40 percent are girls.

Through its child sponsorship program, SC also supports nine schools in the Oromia region (2,410 pupils: 1,245 boys, 1,165 girls), that dovetail with the PIE schools and the Bob Marley Schools in expanding access to education through community involvement.

The latest instance of Save the Children's innovative efforts in basic education in Ethiopia is the Pastoralist Education Project (2002–2004), a relatively small-scale, AID-funded effort aimed at meeting the needs of very inaccessible, cattle-herding and semi-settled groups. The schools operate for the most part in the open air, in the shade of a tree. Overall, PEP reaches a total of 1,323 pupils, 27 percent of whom are girls.

Uganda

Save the Children was one of many NGOs that began working in Uganda when the Museveni government came to power in 1986. In 1999, it chose to focus its efforts on the Nakasongola district to pilot CHANCE, a Ugandan version of its community school strategy. The adaptation of the curriculum and the use of local teachers enabled CHANCE to address the needs of three quite distinct groups in Nakasongola with important cultural and linguistic differences.

A major difference between the Uganda initiative and the others is that from the outset the devastating impact of HIV/AIDS was factored into the design of the CHANCE strategy. Although it began as a purely educational program, it was diversified by adding a preventive health program and ultimately a school feeding program as local pressures made such measures necessary.

> *The devastating impact of HIV/AIDS was factored into the design of the CHANCE strategy, which was diversified by adding a preventive health program.*

As of 2004, CHANCE also operated in Luwero district, with plans in place to expand to Wakiso. Currently, there are 2,211 children in Nakasongola CHANCE schools and 2,721 children in Luwero community schools participating in Save the Children education activities. In addition, 246 School Management Committee members, 68 facilitators, 82 teachers and 13 cluster leaders have been trained to build their skills in planning, basic monitoring, evaluation, communication, analysis and decision making to enable them to identify and respond to children's educational needs.

Conclusions

Despite enormous challenges and variability in implementation and impact, Save the Children's community school experience in these four countries indicates that:

- The costs of primary education can be drastically reduced without significantly reducing quality.
- Any community can provide financial and human resources to deliver relevant education for its own children.
- Community participation is fundamental to the success of schools.

Nevertheless, the SC experience also demonstrates that such alternative provision is not meant to be a substitute for a national education system. Hence, except for the early experience in Mali, the plan from the outset was that the schools that were established would eventually be incorporated into the government's school system.

Contributing Authors

Bonita Birungi is a Social Science Graduate from Uganda's Makerere University and holds a post-graduate diploma in education. Before joining Save the Children in 1999, Bonita worked for an International Consultancy firm (Development Consultants International) as a Researcher.

At SC, Bonita co-designed and implemented the non-formal education project entitled CHANCE targeting hard-to-reach communities in an effort to provide access to education to the most disadvantaged children in the pastoralist and fishing communities. She was also responsible for mobilizing communities, training teachers, providing technical support to cluster leaders, program logistics management and liaison with district departments and other NGOS.

As Social Services Manager, Bonita is responsible for planning, managing and coordinating the implementation of non-formal primary and adult education, early childhood development, adolescent reproductive and sexual health, HIV/AIDS prevention; psychosocial support programs in three districts (Nakasongola, Luwero and Wakiso) and fostering collaboration with district and line ministries. She also provides technical assistance for all programs and assists in the development of new program work in all sectors.

Joseph DeStefano is Vice President of the Center for Collaboration and the Future of Schooling that works across the US supporting urban school districts, communities and foundations in organizing and implementing system-wide education improvement strategies. He is also principal investigator for the Education Quality Improvement Project's research on community-based approaches to providing effective schooling for underserved and disadvantaged populations.

Joe has spent seven years providing technical support to school districts and communities across the US. Prior to that, Joe worked for 12 years on international education reform, primarily in Africa. He was senior policy advisor at the Academy for Educational Development on a number of education reform projects; spent time in the Africa Bureau at USAID developing and purveying Education Reform Support as a comprehensive approach to designing system-wide education reform programs; and worked for several years as an operations officer and researcher at the World Bank.

Amy Jo Dowd holds a B.A. in International Relations and an M.A. in Education, both from Stanford University, as well as a Masters and Doctorate of Education from Harvard University.

She joined Save the Children in 1992 and helped to establish the Education Office and its program, Strong Beginnings. She assisted teams in Nepal, Bangladesh, Thailand, the Philippines, Afghan refugee camps, Egypt, Jordan, the West Bank and Gaza, Mali, Malawi, and Mozambique to establish, enhance and expand their early childhood, primary education and parent education programs. In addition to responsibilities for country program support, Dr. Dowd worked closely with colleagues to devise Save the Children's global education strategy, translate this into locally effective programs and represent it internationally to influence multilateral education funding and policy. She built her dissertation into Save the Children's Malawi program and worked on staff until December 1999 as Education Research Advisor.

Debbie Glassman received her B.A. and M.A. from UCLA and earned her Ph.D. from Yale University in 1982. After teaching at Carleton College and Mills College, she moved to France as Director of the Paris Center for Critical Studies. In 1992, she was invited to become the Education Director of the illfated American Center and then joined the OECD. From 1997–2003, she worked as a consultant for OECD, UNESCO, ADEA, IIEP, the African Development Bank, the World Bank, the Research Network for West and Central Africa and Winrock International. She moved to the US to work at Save the Children where she designed and co-authored the book on community schools. Currently she works as a Senior Research Scientist at the American Institutes for Research.

Kristin Helmore has written about development for twenty years, reporting from Africa, Asia and Latin America. Her articles in *The Christian Science Monitor* garnered numerous awards, including the Overseas Press Club Award, the Sigma Delta Chi Award in journalism, the Population Institute's Global Media Award and the President's End Hunger Award. She has authored two books, *Sustainable Livelihoods: Building on the Wealth of the Poor* (UNDP/Kumarian Press, 2001) and *The World of Christian Children's Fund* (Heartland Publishing, 1993), and edited a magazine, *African Farmer*, published by the Hunger Project. She has conducted mid-career training for journalists in Madagascar and Nigeria and worked as a consultant to magazine editors in Nepal, South Africa, Namibia, Swaziland, Malawi, Zimbabwe, Kenya and Uganda.

Mengistu Edo Koricha received an M.A. in Curriculum and Instruction from Addis Ababa University, School of Graduate Studies, in 1996 and a B.Ed. in Pedagogical Science from Addis Ababa University, Bahirdar Teachers College, in 1980. From 2001 to 2005 he was Regional Education Specialist for Save the Children US, overseeing programs in Somalia and Ethiopia. He was responsible for the overall supervision and technical management of all SC operations in education, including the Basic Education System Overhaul—BESO—a project operating in 1,500 schools. He also designed a standard training program for SC staff and facilitated the implementation of the training. From 1997 he worked in the Ethiopia and Somalia offices, managing and coordinating the education activities of the program office. In Ethiopia he designed, coordinated and managed the Partnership for Innovations in Education (PIE) project.

Catherine Kennedy holds an M.Ed. in Education and Development from Bristol University, UK; a PGCE (British teaching qualification) in Primary Education from Warwick University, UK; and a BA in French and Spanish from Leeds University, UK. She has over twenty years experience in teaching and in development work in the education sector. Prior to taking up the post as Field Office Director (FOD) with Save the Children in El Salvador last year, she spent five years as the FOD of Uganda, during which she designed and managed CHANCE, a non-formal primary education project for hard to reach children, now funded by USAID.

Yolande Miller-Grandvaux is a Senior Education Advisor in the Office of Education at the United States Agency for International Development in Washington DC. She holds a Ph.D. in Romance Languages and Literatures from Princeton University and a Masters in International Educational Development from Boston University. She has extensive field experience with ten consecutive years spent working in Africa as education planner, girls' education specialist, education monitoring and evaluation advisor and chief of party for several USAID-funded education projects as well as projects for other development agencies and NGOs. Her posts include Senegal, Mali, Niger and Benin. She has conducted research on issues related to community schools and the role of non-governmental organizations in education in Africa, resulting in the publication of *The Role of NGOs in Education in Africa* and *A Literature Review of Community Schools in Africa in 2002.*

Mamadou Millogo has over twenty years of education experience. He holds a Master's Degree in Education from the West Sussex Institute of Higher Education. UK. Mr. Millogo has worked for Mali's Ministry of Education as a Pedagogical Advisor. In this capacity he was in charge of conducting teacher-training sessions. This job and his current position of Education Program

Manager at Save the Children helped him establish good inter-personal relationships with the staff of the Ministry of Education, World Education, Africare, local NGOs and other education stakeholders, resulting in increased access and improved quality of education for more than 50,000 children. He participated in curriculum development training at the Academy for Educational Development, Washington, D.C., and co-authored *AMANGELE,* a teacher's guide for teaching English in Malian schools. Mr. Millogo is also well versed in using media in education, including video, language laboratory, and computer assisted learning as well as distance education.

Jordan Naidoo has extensive classroom experience and expertise in policy analysis; program and systemic evaluation and monitoring; community mobilization, decentralization, governance and democratization in education; and implementing school reform. After teaching for a number of years in South Africa, between 1995 and 1999 he worked at the Education Policy Unit at the University of Natal and at the CEPD as a policy analyst. In 1999 he joined the design team for the Turning Points School Reform at the Center for Collaborative Education in Boston. He has been on a number of evaluation teams including a USAID design team on basic education reform in Egypt. Most recently he has been a coordinator responsible for the theme of Decentralization and Education Management in the Association for Development of Education in Africa study, *Improving the Quality of Education,* and has worked at the International Institute for Education Planning (UNESCO) on issues related to decentralization and school evaluation. Jordan Naidoo received his M.Ed. from the University of Natal, South Africa and his Ed.D. from Harvard University's Graduate School of Education.

Lester Namathaka is a Director of Education Programs in the Save the Children, US Malawi Field Office. He is an innovative educationist and writer with a B.Ed. and B.A. in Special Education, a Diploma in Education and certificates in Situational Leadership Administration. Since 1994 he has been working with community members, teachers, government partners and non-governmental organizations to establish grassroots networks that decentralize action to improve the quality of education at the zone, cluster, school and community levels.

Under his leadership, Save the Children's Education Program expanded both programmatically and geographically from a pilot phase of eight village-based schools (VBS) to 63 VBSs that provide learning spaces to over 60,000 girls and boys in remote rural areas where regular primary schools do not exist.

Before 1994 he worked as a Director of the Malawi Special Teacher Education Program funded by the World Bank, training 4,000 teachers through contact and distance learning materials.

Hadijah Nandyose is a graduate with five years experience supporting educational activities at the grassroots level with an emphasis on non-formal education.

She started as a classroom teacher and transferred to the NGO sector in 1999, supporting the design and implementation of educational activities for the children and wives of disabled soldiers with support from the Uganda Ministry of Defense.

She joined Save the Children in 2001 as the Adult Literacy Officer, charged with the roll-out and implementation of the adult literacy program. The program aims to foster the participation of parents and other community members in development initiatives, especially those linked to education.

Currently Education Coordinator, a post she has held since 2002, she supports program management activities for adult literacy and a non-formal primary education project that provides access to basic education for children in hard to reach communities. She is also a trainer in NFE approaches and methodologies.

Chloe O'Gara, Ed.D. is the Director for Education and Early Childhood Development Programs at Save the Children. Dr. O'Gara came to Save the Children from the Academy for Educational Development where she served as Vice President and Director of the Ready to Learn International Center on Child Care and Education. Her work at AED and earlier at USAID, Wellstart International, Stanford University, Michigan State University, and Universidad del Valle de Guatemala emphasizes stakeholder engagement, multidisciplinary collaboration, and gender analysis as approaches to generate new solutions to problems in education and the lives of communities, families, and children. She has lived and worked in Latin America, and done extensive project development, management and consulting in Africa, Asia and the former Soviet Union.

Fred Wood was Director of Education, Save the Children US between 1991 and 2004. Prior to that he was, in reverse order, a Research Fellow at Harvard University, Deputy Executive Director at the Bernard van Leer Foundation, Research Associate at the Commonwealth Secretariat and Education Officer for the government of Uganda. He is the author of numerous publications on education and community development. He holds an M.A. (with honors) from the University of Aberdeen, a Masters in Philosophy and a PhD from London University.

Acknowledgments

We would like to express our appreciation and gratitude to the people in Save the Children and other partner organizations who worked on the design and implementation of these community schools. An anonymous donor supported innovations and operations and funded the studies in this compilation. We thank them for their vision, and thank the many sponsors and donors who have transformed the lives of children through community schools.

Chapter 1

Community Schools:
The Solution to Local Needs

Fred Wood

Schoolchildren in Mozambique at a Save the Children community school.
Photo credit: Carolyn Watson

The 1980s and 1990s have been labeled "years of crisis" in education in the countries of the developing world. National budgets for education did not grow in response to rising demand, spurred by the international commitment to Education for All (EFA). Public goals and practical realities on the ground became separate and occasionally contradictory worlds. Donors found education to be increasingly frustrating as an area for investment and, in many instances, backed away. The major US foundations, such as Ford and Carnegie (which had made innovation in education in Africa a priority in the 1960s), typified this trend. At a time when the accent in development switched to "hard," measurable outcomes, investment in what seemed to be the softest sector was not appealing.

Community schools: education, participation, social change

> *School can be both the product of community efforts and the formative source of community change.*

In a sense, then, the rebirth of the community school approach—the notion that school could be both the product of community efforts and the formative source of community change—seemed to be an idea whose time had come at last. The 1990 Jomtien Conference, proclaiming the goal of Education for All but with an emphasis on cost effectiveness (interpreted frequently as cost sharing and cost reduction) seemed to underscore this. As national agendas for education grew, community schools, with their flexibility in program and their constant search for educational forms that were more cost effective and pertinent to social needs, were perceived as the vehicle which could cut fixed costs, increase relevance and address newly emerging issues. Such issues had been beyond the scope of conventional schooling but nonetheless impinged on schools—both on what was taught, who did the teaching, and on the structures available for basic education of a reasonable standard.

One new issue in the 1990s was that major donor agencies were prepared to invest to some extent in communities' efforts to organize around the issue of access to education. The goal, somewhat obscurely stated, was not only to generate a new and different model of basic education but also to promote a wider social development agenda: increasing girls' access to schools and addressing a range of "newfound" social concerns, e.g., awareness of HIV; addressing preventively children's immediate health needs; and, indeed, building grassroots "democracy" through new, local management structures.

> *The goal was not only to generate a new and different model of basic education but also to promote a wider social development agenda.*

The underlying hypothesis was that communities could be motivated to take the task of delivering an expanded primary school system on their own backs and, strengthened by this success, move on to address other concerns. The recent flourishing of support for basic education, and in particular for the community school, has involved a systematic scrambling of agendas, or "cross sectoral action." In that sense it is a reversion to some earlier attempts to build relevance into whatever educational experience might be available to "the poor" as a way of furthering their "development."

To the cynics, the community school movement of the 1990s, principally in Africa but also elsewhere, is an exercise in the delivery of very basic (poor) services: a stripped-down curriculum, a shortened basic education cycle, drumming up local support for schools so that poor people expend much of their limited financial resources on the development and delivery of basic education services. At times this is viewed as letting government off the hook or, somewhat more ponderously, as a denial of the child's basic right to education as formulated in the 1990 Convention on the Rights of the Child.

The only game in town

But cases such as the Mali Village Schools have become legendary. Schools are built with community labor, controlled by a community management committee, staffed by local community volunteers and funded by communities' own contributions and efforts, in cash or in kind. Whether this is releasing the government from its obligations is a moot question. What is indisputable is that the effort of rural Malians to bring basic educational services to their communities through their own endeavors is the only way in which significant access to basic education services could be attained in these areas within this generation, and probably several to come.

The result in Mali—a school that costs a tenth of what the conventional government primary school costs[1]—is claimed to make a major inroad into the need for rural children to have, first, a basic education that covers the essential skills and, second, an educational experience that is close to the children's daily life, addressing real needs and motivating the coming generation towards change for the better.

A tradition of educational reform

The desired outcome mainly harks back to the idealistic era of Julius Nyerere and "Education for Self-Reliance" which, it was hoped, would provide the skills and motivation to lead to the transformation of Tanzania's rural areas, both economically and politically. This idea rested on a stereotype of a somewhat idealized Africa in which rural people would come together and pool their resources and strengths to build a different, more positive rural environment. This approach goes back to earlier traditions in educational reform—to late 19th century America's Tuskegee Institute, to the 19th century Ruskinite tradition in England, to the Jeanes Schools in Kenya in the 1920s, to Gandhi's Basic Education in India. Together, these amount to a stream of attempts to deliver education that would not only impart book learning but would also convey the skills and attitudes that change society. It would provide a skilled workforce which would feed the process of industrialization, or lead the way in collectivizing agriculture, or provide the critical building blocks at the local level for the development of democratic government.

Save the Children community schools in Mali, Ethiopia, Malawi, and Uganda can be viewed as one more instance of this search to produce graduates who do not simply add to the nation's stock of literate unemployed. Where the Save the Children community school movement is slightly different, and may have something to add to the long tradition, is in its concentration on local responsibility for the delivery of the basic service. It has shown that launching such programs does not need to wait for the arrival of the missionary with the urge to do things differently or the progressive-minded administrator from the central government.

Local responsibility, local ownership,
increased access to education

Arguably, the reason for the relative failure of some of the historic attempts to change education in the developing world—for example, Tanganyika's efforts in agricultural education in the 1950s and Tanzania's efforts to build rural socialism in the 1970s—was that those who developed the central body of ideas were seeking to persuade the mass of the population to accept a "product" which these same people regarded as in some ways second best.

The Save the Children community school movement is different in its concentration on local responsibility for the delivery of the basic service.

The contradictory circumstances of today are, first, an understanding that in many instances where community schools are emerging, they represent the only educational opportunity on offer. We are not dealing in one product as against another. It is this one or none. Secondly, the community school idea originates in community organizing, in communities themselves coming to their own awareness of their options for education and, primarily, in their response to those options. What emerges in practice is a blend of conventional schooling and curriculum content that is needs-based. Only in a very few instances do community schools serve the variety of clienteles in different ways, as was advocated by the pioneers of the community school approach. The underlying notion is to keep the technology simple and within the capacity of village people to organize. The Save the Children cases that follow seek to illustrate these principles.

The community school idea originates in community organizing, in communities themselves coming to their own awareness of their options for education and in their response to those options

It is at least arguable that the beginning of the 21st century is revealing a new refinement of an old idea. The key to this refinement is local control: the local conviction that what is achieved is owned by local people, rather than being the result of capital city policy-making or brief visits by experts from other ends of the earth. If it wishes, the community can have a circular or a square school; can have their children taught in their mother tongue or in the recognized language of the state; can address practical matters such as terracing or composting; or can stay with the basic learning areas.

In increased access alone, whether we are talking about the efforts of the Harambee movement in Kenya in the 1970s or the Village Schools in Mali in the 1990s, there can be no disputing the fact that organized community effort, coupled with modest external support, has gone far towards making an important contribution towards

The key is local control: the local conviction that what is achieved is owned by local people.

providing children with basic education. That communities generated 800 schools in Mali in a decade is testimony enough.

Systematic capacity-building for

School Management Committees

In order to achieve this, there had to be a systematic effort to build capacity and new institutional structures at the community level. Working with parents and other interested adults through a School Management Committee is central. The committee, in turn, presents a series of training needs over time which must be met to the point where it is fully autonomous in decision-making and, indeed, increasingly takes the form of a local NGO, able to conduct its own external negotiations, apply pressure to politicians and decide on its own future evolution. Without this effort in systematic capacity-building, the schools would not have happened or would have been abandoned along the way.

Quality more difficult to achieve than access

On the other hand, insufficient effort has been made to couple the act of creating a school with the equally crucial process of ensuring that teachers working in that school have support, guidance and materials. Thus, access has not always been coupled with "quality." Communities can mobilize to address successfully the access issue; improving quality in the classroom environment, in children's learning, in support for teachers on the job is a slower, far more difficult process. The QUEST program in Malawi, with its close attachment to one of Anglophone Africa's more progressive ministries of education and its links to academia, is perhaps the outstanding exception.

The notion that the community-based school, dependent on community efforts and mobilization, would have benefits for that community other than those defined in conventional education terms, has still to be proven. Schools are also being promoted as centers for improved health, hygiene and economic production. The effect of these strategies, which again revert to much older issues in education in Africa, will not be seen for years to come.

Impact on national policy

Can this experience convey a set of lessons for national ministries to the effect that community partnership and strengthened quality are linked?

Where, then, does this leave the latest recurrence of the theme, "school in the service to the community"? Is this another indication of determined local action with minimal resources serving as a temporary stop-gap with no long-term prospects? Have the village schools and their offshoots had an impact at the level of national policy? Is reconciliation with, and absorption into, the government service the inevitable end, the only way to sustainability? Can this experience convey a set of lessons for national ministries to the effect that community partnership and strengthened quality are linked?

Four important developments provide at least partial answers to these questions. First, some governments have clearly heard the message and made their own efforts to rethink the costs of basic education and develop an educational structure and content that meets local needs—the *Nouvelle Ecole Fondamentale* in Mali, the Mubarak Schools in Egypt, and the various efforts to emulate the BRAC schools of Bangladesh are examples. These are the obvious showpieces ever on display for foreign visitors. The question is whether these experiences have wider implications for policy and practice for community-led initiatives. In this respect, perhaps more important in the long run are the shifts that are going on in government, particularly the widespread trend towards decentralization of services, including education.

In recent years both Ethiopia and Uganda have not only gone through profound changes in basic education policy, they have also linked this with systematically transferring the responsibility for the delivery of basic education services to much lower levels of local government than was the case heretofore. Placing the responsibility at the base of society can validate community school efforts and strengthen the government's own rhetoric about EFA in critical, practical ways. Yet all of these initiatives are small relative to the scale of the needs.

All of these initiatives are small relative to the scale of the needs. This shortfall provides the real case for educational partnerships.

This shortfall provides the real case for educational partnerships between the state and interested agencies outside the state. The record would suggest that only by working together will they achieve the goal of Education for All.

Indigenous NGOs take the lead

Secondly, there has been a switch on the part of many large NGOs away from direct service at the grassroots level to working through third parties,

If these ideas are to last, to continue to spark innovation and therefore guarantee quality service, it will be through local action by local entities.

usually indigenous NGOs. The large, mainly international NGOs take upon themselves direct responsibility for building the capacity in these local organizations to deliver services. If these ideas are to last, to be more than a stop-gap set of measures, to continue to spark innovation and therefore guarantee quality service, it will be through local action by such local entities. Significantly, in Ethiopia, one of Africa's most challenging physical and educational environments, it is the local NGOs, trained and motivated to be sure, that are tackling the problems of those who are left behind—the small linguistic minorities; the groups that are physically hard to reach; the culturally marginal nomadic cattle keepers; and groups unconvinced of the virtues of girls' education.

Thirdly, some NGOs have approached with unusual seriousness the issue of measuring impact and learning achievement with a view to elucidating the degree of external effort that is needed to bring about improvements in quality and attainment. The first sets of results point clearly to the possibility that conventional curricula in primary schools in Africa may be overloaded on the one hand and may make inappropriate assumptions of how much children can learn on the other. In other words, comparable levels of achievement can be reached through less input, less time devoted to matters not central to the curriculum. Yet cutting back on hours of schooling is a decision which no one in power in the public education sector has so far been willing to make.

Comparable levels of achievement can be reached through less input, less time devoted to matters not central to the curriculum.

School committees demand the best

Fourthly, although there are no clear indicators of change in villages engaged in the community education process, there are instances, especially in +, of community education associations exercising their newfound muscle and deliberately insisting that the basic village school model be expanded. Indeed, it is becoming very clear that whereas some NGOs may still be living in a Nyererean dream world, School Management Committees are demanding even more for their children: not an abbreviated curriculum but the full measure; not a local paraprofessional teacher but a full-fledged qualified or certified teacher; not a locally contrived test of learning accomplishment but the full national standard for the completion of primary school. In short, the new cycle of community schools may in their turn be following the path of their predecessors in the search for what communities regard as a proper education. But what this illustrates, as in Kenya in the 1960s, is that the community, once mobilized and with a taste for success in the provision of education, will not be satisfied with what is perceived to be second best, however cost effective or innovative it may be. They will demand more and better.

In this sense, the community school as now conventionally perceived may not be a permanent feature of the educational architecture in many Third World countries. It may, if resourced and sustained, be a transitional phase to solid, basic Education for All. Insofar as this is true, this book provides some examples from the Save the Children portfolio of education projects that demonstrate moments in the discussion of how to educate the world's children in ways that are effective, affordable, and sustainable.

In each country, the approach was relatively similar and the problems, similarly, relatively homogenous: making education relevant, attractive, available to people whom the government could not reach using intermediaries; and integrating the community schools or building a bridge from them to government schools so as not to reinforce the marginalization of rural populations. Yet in every case, the goal of having an education

> *The community school may be a transitional phase to solid, basic Education for All.*

system that produces enough people well enough educated to meet the nation's needs remains unmet; all the more difficult, then, the effort to train enough people to be the country's educators.

In addition to the four case studies reflecting decades of effort made possible by generous funders, two other writers address some of the same questions from different perspectives: Joe DeStefano, Vice President of the Center for Collaboration and the Future of Schooling, meditates on the lessons to be drawn for policy-makers from the community school successes around the world that he has seen first hand. Yolande Miller-Grandvaux, USAID Africa Regional Advisor, provides an historical canvas for the expectations of the decades of support for community schools on the part of the US government. Together these essays and case studies provide a story whose ending is not yet written on the ground. Yet while many questions remain unanswered, many answers are offered in Save the Children's community school experiment to be part of the Education for All endeavor.

Notes

[1] Velis, Jean-Pierre. *Blazing the Trail: the Village Schools of Save the Children USA in Mali.* UNESCO, Paris, 1994. "The villagers themselves were to build their schools … for a total cost of … about thirty times less than the cost of an official primary school." P. 10; Peter Laugharn, who ran the field office in Mali while the program was being developed, says ten times less (cf. Mali article in this publication).

Chapter 2

Mali, 1992–2003[2]: The First Experiment[*]

Deborah Glassman and Mamadou Millogo

The village of Niamou, Mali, site of a Save the Children community school.
Photo credit: Michael Bisceglie

---

[*] This chapter benefited from Dana Burde's earlier research in Mali, and the report she submitted entitled 'Save the Children Community Schools in Mali: Exploring Perceptions of Access, Quality, Opportunity, and Participation,' July 2003. Westport, CT: Save the Children Education Unit.

More than a million unschooled children

In 1962, educational reform in Mali mandated schooling for all children. Yet 30 years later, barely 2,000 primary schools existed for the 12,000 villages in this largely rural country. Only about 500,000 of the 1,533,000 7- to12-year-olds in the country went to school. The overall enrollment rate of 32 percent, when disaggregated, showed that only 26 percent of school-age girls were in school.[3] Enrollments varied between rural and urban, poor and less poor, and the north and the south. Insufficient numbers of classrooms meant that student-teacher ratios of 100:1 were not (and, indeed, are still not) uncommon.[4]

Save the Children US (SC) came to Mali in 1986 in response to the Malian government's request for urgent relief. A series of droughts in the mid 1970s and '80s had driven large numbers of Dogons from the Bandiagara Cliff and the area around Mopti to Sikasso, a cotton-growing region that also serves as a corridor for migrant labor traveling to Côte d'Ivoire directly to the south. Children were dying in large numbers. In response, SC initiated a child survival program based broadly on the UNICEF GOBI model (Growth Monitoring, Oral Re-Hydration, Breast-Feeding and Immunization).

To manage this program, village committees were created. These, in turn, led to adult literacy programs in a few villages where volunteers and village leaders were trained to read and write their mother tongue so that they could participate in, and manage, the development activities in which SC was engaged: food security, water and sanitation and micro-finance. The centers used a curriculum of health and agriculture as the basis for their training. They were manifestly interesting to children who watched their parents learn to read and write.

The success of the village-managed health and literacy programs coalesced around the need for schooling.

"Though it was nighttime, there were lots of children, especially boys, looking in at these lessons through the windows. The lessons were a curiosity because in most villages there was no school at all."[5] The success of the village-managed, NGO-sponsored health and literacy programs coalesced and converged around the need for schooling for children in the rural villages of southern Mali.

Launching community schools in Sikasso

In the Sikasso region, where infrastructure was generally poor, enrollment rates were particularly low. In 1991, the gross enrollment rate in Kolondieba district, where SC built its first community schools, was around 14 percent—8.5 percent for girls.[6] Schooling in the district was concentrated in urban areas: of the 29 primary schools serving children in 207 villages, 24 were located in five administrative centers.[7] The government provided virtually no education for village children.

The SC school program in Mali was inaugurated in response to a concatenation of international, national, and local events. In 1990 in Jomtien, Thailand, the international community had designated Education for All as a goal for the year 2000. At the time, the Malian government was investing heavily in secondary and higher education and "was pointed to as a paragon of inefficiency and wasted resources."[8] In 1991, Moussa Traoré's regime ended in a coup d'état. When Alpha Oumar Konaré took office, he became acutely aware of the difficulty of responding to popular expectations for more basic education while at the same time maintaining support for higher education.

Village children in Mali.
Photo credit: Sara Carpenter

A new Ministry of Basic Education (MEB) was created, indicating a belief in the need to expand basic education and make the school system more responsive. The minister worked to "bring the school back into the community and to bring the community back into the school,"[9] one of many educational reforms and innovations that were to stud the next decades. USAID, to support the government's efforts to decentralize basic education in this newly "democratic"[10] African nation, supported Save the Children's[11] community school program.

By 1988, SC had built government schools in four villages using concrete building blocks, government-trained teachers, the national curriculum and a traditional teaching methodology. Government primary schools in Mali, like those in other former French colonies, bore the stamp of their heritage: the French language, a French curriculum, textbooks published in France, the sequence and numbering of classes, diplomas based on year-end exams, the Baccalauréat. If the plan was to provide greater access to rural populations, it quickly became apparent that the construction costs and time required to build the schools would prevent the achievement of EFA goals by the year 2000—always an explicit objective of the endeavor.[12]

A new Ministry of Basic Education was created, indicating a belief in the necessity of expanding basic education and of making the school system more responsive.

Villagers take the lead

SC, therefore, proposed sharing roles and responsibilities with the villages: building a one-room classroom; defining a shorter, more relevant curriculum taught in the local language; selecting, training, and remunerating teachers from the villages; selecting equal numbers of girls and boys to go to school according to a calendar based on the harvest and planting seasons and on children's chores; providing schoolbooks and materials; and training village management committees to supervise the enterprise and the schools. These proved to be fruitful innovations.

SC drew on the Bangladesh Rural Advancement Committee (BRAC) model that took a community-management approach and significantly increased enrollments, particularly those of girls. In its Kolondieba pilot schools, SC made three basic assumptions about the capacity and value of community parparticipation in education:

The costs of primary education could be drastically reduced without significantly reducing quality.

Each community, with proper training, could contribute the financial and human resources to provide highly relevant primary education for its own children. Community participation in, and engagement with children's education is a fundamental and often unmeasured index of the success of these schools.

Moreover, the political climate in Mali was conducive to decentralizing education and developing a dynamic, government-NGO-community partnership.[13]

Girls in Blakala classroom.

Photo credit: Michael Bisceglie

SC sought to engage with communities so that they could participate actively in defining and providing an education that they found appropriate and relevant.

SC sought to engage with communities so that they could participate actively in defining and providing an education that they found appropriate and relevant, even if the government did not or could not. SC also made gender equity a high priority, proposing that equal numbers of boys and girls be enrolled—something which was not typically the case in Mali, where girls often stay home to help their mothers with household chores and women's crops. SC discussed in detail with community members the reasons why their daughters were less frequently enrolled in school, and more often removed from it, in order to devise a more "girl-friendly" school.

Gradual changes in attitude about educating girls are illustrated by an incident that took place one hot afternoon in Kolondieba. An SC vehicle passed a farmer pulling a heavily laden cart packed with newly picked cotton.

"You have a heavy load. Where are you taking it?"

"To the agent who will buy the crop."

"Can you not find someone to help you?"

"But I already have someone. My daughter," he says, pointing to a small eight-year-old girl by the roadside.

"But she is very small and your cart is very big. How can she help you?"

"She is a pupil at the school in our village. She will tell me whether the agent is cheating me. She can write and she can count."

Girl pounding maize.
Photo credit: Michael Bisceglie

Access was the obvious mission of the enterprise, but quality was also an essential goal. The curriculum's objectives were to prepare villagers to better live in their environment; to achieve gender parity in enrollment; to be flexible regarding children's ages; to serve a determined number of children; to conduct triannual enrollments; to maintain viable student-teacher ratios; to employ recently literate, somewhat schooled teachers attuned to village needs; and to practice child-centered pedagogy using the local language and materials produced for the local context. Many, if not most of these objectives meet the criteria of quality education.

Criticized by some as "poor education for poor people," village schools in fact provided access to local schooling at affordable fees, and overcame most of their shortcomings (or short cuts), such as low-cost classrooms, poorly qualified teachers and fewer materials. "What is given up to assure lower costs, i.e., higher teacher qualifications and more elaborate materials, is made up for by an environment of higher community, teacher and student commitment."[14] Communities' engagement in managing these schools reflected their desire to have their children educated and to be involved in that education despite their own lack of schooling. It also reflected their confidence in the model.

Selecting villages

The villages in which SC sought to undertake community school collaboration were selected according to a number of criteria, including a minimum number of children and distance from existing schools. Initially, a "school map" helped determine which villages had at least 60 school-age children, (the initial cohorts also included older children) located at more than "walking distance"

> *Communities' engagement in managing the schools reflected their desire to have their children educated and to be involved in that education.*

from public primary schools. (In remote villages, this can mean up to two hours each way.) *Medersas,* or Koranic schools, were not included. SC staff visited the potential villages to engage in a Participatory Rapid Appraisal with the traditional leaders, to determine why the children did not go to public schools and whether the village wanted a school. Above all, a consensus had to exist in the village to build and manage its school.

> *Above all, a consensus had to exist in the village to build and manage its school.*

In 1992, 20 villages were visited. Three of these, and later a fourth, appeared particularly favorable to starting a school. (The fourth school, located in a poorer village, ultimately failed.) Villagers wanted schools in their villages because distance was a strong disincentive to school attendance, especially for girls who were vulnerable if they walked long distances to school, and because boarding children elsewhere was expensive.

School Management Committees

Traditional village leaders were asked to designate representatives for a five-member School Management Committee (SMC) that included two women and two literate people. The SMC structure was based on the Bambara tradition of *tons,* task-oriented community organizations guided by traditional leaders.

The site chosen for the initial classroom was often a temporary shelter so that the SMC and other villagers could determine where to situate the "permanent" classroom, with technical advice from SC.

Building took place at the end of the rainy season (October, November) using local mud bricks. SC provided doors and roofs.

Bohi village school committee meeting.

Photo credit: Christine 'Spee' Braun

Classrooms were outfitted with student desk/benches (two students per bench), a blackboard and chalk. In 2000, "flip charts" made from salvaged cement bags, wall maps and a "library" or box of books, most in Bamanakan, were added. SC provided all school supplies until 1998 when it began to gradually reduce its contribution. In 2002, parents became responsible for purchasing pens, notebooks, and slates.

The SMCs compiled a list of all 6-, 7-, and 8-year-olds to be enrolled, respecting the SC rule of parity between boys and girls. In the larger villages, an initial cohort of 60 children was chosen for the first single-classroom schools, divided into two groups of 30 (half boys, half girls) for two sessions, morning and afternoon.

Calendar

The village school annual calendar followed the agricultural seasons. School opened in October, after the maize harvest, and closed at the end of May before the onset of the rainy season, so that children could help plant and harvest. The three-hour school day allowed children to do their chores (primarily girls' household chores and babysitting) and therefore did not disrupt daily life.

Classroom in Blakala, Mali.

Photo credit: Michael Bisceglie

Boys plowing a field.

Photo credit: Michael Bisceglie

Reducing the curriculum to basic lessons that could be covered in three-hour sessions gave the school a better chance of surviving because the interruption of village life was minimal.

The day was divided into two sessions for two teachers. Reducing the contents of the curriculum to basic lessons that could be covered in three-hour sessions gave the school a better chance of surviving because the interruption of village life was minimal. On the other hand, a school year of six days per week, 28 weeks per year, with no holidays and no student or teacher strikes made it possible to cover the curriculum effectively, and even to add grades 4–6 in 1996.

Teaching in the local language

From the outset, SC decided that classes would be conducted in Bamanakan, the most widely spoken language in Mali and in the Sikasso region, rather than in French, which many Malians learn to speak in school as a second or third language. The choice had significant implications: children could understand what their teachers were saying in the classroom from day one, and learned more quickly for not being forced to learn in a foreign language. SC also developed its own materials in Bamanakan.

Children could understand what their teachers were saying in the classroom from day one, and learned more quickly for not being forced to learn in a foreign language.

Curriculum

The curriculum was organized around village life, agriculture and natural resource management, health and basic business skills.

The initial three-year curriculum was developed and adapted from the adult literacy curriculum, with its focus on agriculture and health, and was designed to meet the local needs of a rural setting and an agricultural economy.[15] It grew out of a regular consultative process between SC field staff and local development committees—the lowest level of local government representing the traditional village leadership. The curriculum was organized around village life, agriculture and natural resource management, health and basic business skills, in addition to the "three Rs," history, geography, and observation of nature. Functional literacy and numeracy skills were combined with life skills and with knowledge that would enable village children to make better use of local resources and improve their health and their ability to function effectively in the village setting and in the commercial world.

Each teacher received a teaching guide in Bamanakan for the subjects taught in the local language: civics, agriculture, natural science, history, geography, health and math, as well as a reader created by SC for its curriculum.

In addition to structured learning materials, teachers and students use local materials such as leaves to teach medicine, cement bags for flip charts and clay for pottery. They also use local human resources: for example, the village chief teaches the history of the village.

A student leads the class.

Photo credit: Michael Bisceglie

Each school has two classes, one of young children (6–10 years) who might still have the possibility of joining the formal education system after three years in the community school, and one of adolescents (11–15 years). They would not normally enter the official school system, but they would be able to participate in village health, agriculture, and credit committees upon graduation from the community school.

Selecting, training, and supervising teachers

SC's child-centered, active approach to pedagogy seeks to develop pupils' imagination and creativity; to engage students in speaking, rather than re-legating them to the more common "choral response" role where the authority of the teacher goes unquestioned and where learning involves mere memorization by rote.

SC's child-centered, active approach to pedagogy seeks to develop pupils' imagination and creativity; to engage students in speaking.

Initially, teachers were drawn from the villages. SC took a pragmatic approach by selecting neo-literates (mostly men) who usually had at best 6th grade educations but whose understanding of their communities offset their lack of education. Interested candidates were tested and trained by SC staff, with support from the Ministry of Education (MOE), for four weeks during a period of three months (July, August, and September). The month-long training program included child psychology, pedagogy, reading, writing, basic mathematics, health, agriculture, civics and local history. It specifically taught teachers to be sensitive to girls. Initial training was reinforced by annual, two-week refresher sessions; when teachers moved to higher grades, they again received two-week, specialized training from local ministry staff.

In 1996, dissatisfied parents requested more schooling for teachers. They wanted their children to be able to take the CEP, the national sixth grade leaving exam, and become civil servants—an expectation that was no longer realistic but was a vestige of a previous era. Since the CEP was administered only in French, French and the fourth grade were introduced, and fifth and sixth grades were subsequently added. SC worked with the national ministry to expand the curriculum,[16] drawing it closer to the national curriculum and providing a means for village school students to go on to junior high school if they were able. The calendar and approach remained innovative and local. Intensive French was progressively introduced as an optional class in third grade. Today it is introduced in the second grade.

Teaching in French in Mali.

Photo credit: Michael Bisceglie

Teaching French and adding grades 4, 5, and 6 meant hiring and training teachers who could speak French, which usually meant going outside the village to recruit them. More skills—francophone teachers typically had 9th grade educations—raised salaries, and required a different kind of teacher management. Trained teachers stayed with their classes as they progressed through the grades, while new first and second grade teachers were recruited and trained on an ongoing basis.

Training required reinforcement and supervision. Local teacher supervisors from the *Centre d'Animation Pédagogique* (CAP) provided pedagogical supervision and received remuneration from SC. Later, as the network of schools grew, another level of management was required. Scaling up was possible thanks to the dynamic partnerships established among the SMCs, the *Académies Éducatives* (regional education authorities responsible for the CAPs), USAID, and implementing local NGO partners. The numbers of local NGOs who managed the relationships on the ground between the teachers, SC, and the CAP[17] grew from four to as many as 16 as the network of schools grew.

Scaling up was possible thanks to the dynamic partnerships established among the SMCs, regional authorities, USAID and local NGOs.

These partners benefited from the capacity building, institutional development and technical and financial assistance provided by SC.[18] With different degrees of success, they oversaw the village schools in their areas, serving as a link among all the administrations involved. As they demonstrated more skills, the NGOs became involved in strategic planning. From 2001–2003, in preparation for the end of USAID funding, local NGOs became entirely responsible for their part of the project, having developed a plan for supervising teachers in the area where they worked and for promoting relationships with the CAPs and the communal councils.

In preparation for the end of USAID funding, local NGOs became entirely responsible for their part of the project.

Costs

Costs were low. A typical, government-built, three-room, cement schoolhouse cost approximately US $10,000 to build and outfit with student desks, a blackboard, and a teacher's desk.[19] By contrast, "schools built from local materials could be constructed at about a fifth of the cost of the prevailing concrete model. Not only did this make the construction of a school financially affordable by a typical village, but it also made the school seem less of a foreign body within the community."[20]

Similarly, "Teachers were paid FCFA 3,500 (US$12.80) per month out of school fees and a general village association contribution, compared to national salaries of about FCFA 30,000 (US$110)."[21] The largely symbolic salaries were supplemented by support in kind—cereals, labor, and other services. SMCs collected 100 CFA per student per month, but encouraged communities to raise 1,000 CFA per household, regardless of the number of pupils in a family, to make the school a community-wide concern.

Table 2.1: Costs of running a village school [22]

Category	$ per school year	$ per student per year	% total cost
School startup	423	7	13
Development (5 years, allowing for curriculum updating and revitalizing community support)	173		
Capital costs (10 years, or estimated lifespan of a school building)	250		
School operations	1471	25	45
Teacher salary	103		
Materials and supplies	1254		
Maintenance	105		
PTA operations	9		
School support	911	15	28
Teacher (ongoing in-service training)	123		
Inspection (by MOE)	28		
Committee/PTA training	263		
Committee/PTA monitoring	497		
NGO development	13	22	< 1
Startup	4		
Operations	8		
Supervision	1		
PVO management (SC management costs not allocated elsewhere, business costs, and costs of maintaining institutional identity)	417	13	
Totals	$3,235 per school	$54 per student (based on 60 students per school)	100

Source: Save the Children US Sahel Office

SC proposed that the village association that managed cash crops earmark 2 percent of cotton revenues to cover recurrent school costs.

Families with no children in school, like taxpayers who do not benefit from the schools in their local communities, did not want to pay. SC proposed that the village association that managed cash crops earmark 2 percent of cotton revenues to cover recurrent school costs, including teachers' salaries.

Most villages accepted, and the revenues provided a major source of funding until the cotton crisis in 2000.[23] Alternatives such as collective field, market gardening, and per capita gain taxes were used to support the schools after that.

School children in Blakala, Mali.

Photo credit: Michael Bisceglie

Expansion, evaluation, improvement

Three years after they were introduced in Sikasso, SC village schools were flourishing. "In its third year of operation, the project had grown to become the main provider of formal education in grades 1 through 3 in Kolondieba district."[24] The four initial schools of 1992–1993 had served 240 pupils and 16 teachers had been trained; the following year, 22 schoolrooms were serving 1,320 pupils in 22 villages and 44 teachers had been trained. In 1994–1995 there were 36 village schools

In its third year of operation, the project had grown to become the main provider of formal education in grades 1 through 3 in Kolondieba district.

with 2,160 children and 72 teachers. In 1995–1996, there was a leap to 114 schools and 6,840 children in 110 villages.[25] The estimated cost for teachers of 1,000 to 1,200 CFA per month was based on the numbers of teachers and pupils projected for school year 1999–2000, and a 7-month salary of 8,000 to 8,750 CFA.[26]

School children at work in a classroom at the Blakala school.

Photo credit: Michael Bisceglie

In 1997, five years after it had initiated funding, USAID wanted to know what was working and what needed to be improved, and to assess and compare the costs of the alternative schools it was supporting with government schools.[27] USAID's report noted that while it was relatively easy to recruit students, the first schools experienced high dropout rates, especially among teenagers. A 13 percent dropout rate meant 32 dropouts, 27 of whom were boys who migrated to work outside the village or girls who got married; the rest left because they could not pay the fees.[28] Today's dropout rates are far lower at 2.4 percent.

Student achievement had not yet been systematically evaluated but there were plans to do so. Promotion rates were far higher than in government schools, because village schools do not fail any students, and they teach in Bamanakan. The USAID report noted the introduction of French in third grade and that students were doing "at least as well as students in the regular state schools."[29]

It was clearly a positive thing for children to attend school in their own villages, eliminating the risks and costs of their going elsewhere for school. Education was perceived to be relevant; parents felt involved in school management; and the relationship between the school and the community was sufficiently strong to have "changed the basic paradigm under which primary education is provided in Mali."[30]

The USAID evaluation made powerful claims for the impact of SC's model beyond Kolondieba, stating that the "appearance on the Malian scene of a successful village school model has helped alter the trajectory of education sector reform."[31] Given the success of the model, USAID Mali made a "decided effort" to have the MEB overcome its reluctance to recognize non-official schools, since the ministry had imposed standards that prevented communities from establishing schools. USAID lobbied hard to promote what became a legal framework for non-government schools, enabling them to be officially recognized.

> *The relationship between the school and the community was sufficiently strong to have changed the basic paradigm under which primary education is provided in Mali.*

This was a "first step in establishing a mechanism whereby the state can provide funding for non-governmental schools."[32] The USAID view was that "village schools have illustrated that quality basic education can be delivered in buildings that are locally constructed, with teachers who are less qualified and not civil servants, in languages other than French, and in a management environment determined and directed by private citizens (not MEB officials)."

Blakala classroom, Mali.

Photo credit: Michael Bisceglie

Impact on government policies

The resulting sectoral policy led to the government's *Nouvelle École Fondamentale* (NEF) project that introduced "local language in grades 1 through 3; a consolidated number of subjects; local recruitment and training of teachers; and greater community involvement in school management—all strategies drawn from the village school model."[33]

How would civil servants, reluctant to lose their job security or salaries, welcome local language teaching and different curricula?

However, USAID was concerned with some critical issues. If NEF incorporated "many of the lessons from village schools into its definition" and if the new schools were to be bilingual, could existing schools be converted? How would civil servants, reluctant to lose their job security or salaries, welcome local language teaching and different curricula? The USAID evaluation was prescient about the problems that PRODEC, the decade-long (1999–2009) education reform program that supplanted NEF, would face.

The USAID report also addressed the changes facing village schools that added French to their curriculum. Where would they find the teachers and how would villages react to curricula that were less focused on their needs? Would the village model be considered second rate? Would it change in order to conform to the standard model? There was also some concern about a segmented primary education system in Mali, divided along rural and urban lines, the latter financed by the state and the former financed by the villages: an inherently inequitable provision of basic education.

There was concern about a segmented primary education system, divided along rural and urban lines: an inherently inequitable provision of basic education.

The only solution, it was argued, was to "develop a mechanism through which the state would funnel resources to village schools—without subverting the essential element of community control, oversight and management of the schools— in order to equalize disparities between villages in different regions of the country."[34] This has been done to some extent, but the prescient concerns remain relevant today. USAID provided another five years of support, 1997–2002, and the SC schools continued to spread and to be evaluated by the MOE.

Preparing for national exams

Pupils educated in the village schools had acquired new skills and could participate in new ways.

SC strengthened some of the weaknesses pointed out in the mid-term evaluation (1997–2002),[35] such as teacher training and supervision and student testing. The expansion of the curriculum and the expectations of parents meant that pupils needed to take the CEP exam. To prepare them and to assess their achievement, SC investigated testing techniques. In 1999, a consultant was hired to begin designing and evaluating a test, and in 2000, SC and MOE staff were trained in testing and began to develop test materials for teachers to prepare pupils to take exams in unfamiliar formats. Teachers were subsequently trained to design and administer tests and were taught to define short-term goals that pupils could demonstrably acquire (*objectifs pédagogiques opérationnels*).

School children at the Blakala school.

Photo credit: Michael Bisceglie

SC was also interested in knowing whether pupils were contributing more to their villages as a result of having gone to school. At the end of 1999, it therefore conducted a study to verify levels of out-migration as one measure of effective schooling. The study confirmed that pupils educated in the village schools had acquired new skills and could participate in new ways.

Strengthening the SMCs

The role of the SMCs was also changing. From mobilizing the community and getting the school built and running, SMCs were learning to manage more effectively—organizing meetings to discuss student and teacher attendance, girls' education, the provision of books and school supplies, maintenance and equipment. Their responsibilities grew, in part,

SC strengthened the capacity of SMCs to develop community action plans, to understand the community's civic rights and to advocate for its needs

to prepare for the end of USAID funding. SC strengthened the capacity of SMCs to develop community action plans, to understand the community's civic rights and to advocate for its needs. As the government decentralizes more and more responsibility for education to the communes and to the CAP without providing the resources, SMCs will have to work harder to advocate for themselves. SC encouraged the organization of federations of SMCs, known as SMC/APE, to give them more weight in promoting community schools, but these remain relatively timid about approaching government authorities.

Sustaining the community schools requires dynamic partnerships among all education stakeholders. Partnerships with local NGOs and others had been

Sustaining community schools requires dynamic partnerships among all education stakeholders.

nurtured on an on-going basis and had helped SC to capitalize on a range of capacities to achieve significant results. These partnerships were reinforced to ensure that all stakeholders participated in the operation, financially and otherwise. Various education actors were invited to *cadre de concertation* meetings. SC provided organizational development support to the implementing NGO partners, based on analyses of their institutional needs.

Malian school children in a race.

Photo credit: Michael Bisceglie

The problem of teacher retention

Paying teachers had always been an issue. In 2001, the World Bank and USAID encouraged the government to include the salaries of community schoolteachers in their Education Sector Investment Program (PISE), using HIPC debt forgiveness. The PISE program negotiated a US $45 million loan for 2001–2004, of which US $34 million was earmarked for basic education, including building schools and providing textbooks.

The government agreed to finance a portion of community schoolteacher salaries, but the money has not been paid regularly or to all teachers. Therefore, 40–50 percent of the communities have continued to pay their teachers, who often wait months for their payments. Community school teachers' salaries continue to be low compared to the salaries of civil servants, which may help to explain why teachers leave their jobs.

A girl gets a drink of purified water at the Blakala school.

Photo credit: Michael Bisceglie

Looking ahead

The decade of USAID funding ended, as planned, in 2003. The future of the community schools in Sikasso without that funding, without SC's oversight, and without support for the network of local NGOs, remains to be seen. The indicators of the success of the village schools rarely include the community engagement and ownership that must be retained if the schools are to endure.

Table 2.2: SC Teacher Retention, 1992–2000

Initial year of service	Still teaching	No Longer Teaching	% Still Active
1992	2	6	25.00
1993	3	18	14.29
1994	9	48	15.79
1995	26	168	13.40
1996	60	357	14.39
1997	97	564	14.67
1998	160	491	24.58
1999	163	318	38.89
2000	162	241	40.20
2001	306	186	62.2
2002	422	7	98.37

Source: Save the Children US Sahel Office, Annual statistics 2002–2003 (October)

> Community schools in Mali serve approximately 18 percent of all elementary school pupils.

Education reform has already benefited from the experiments in the community schools; the process of decentralizing the management of education to the communes should also draw upon the experience of these last years. Sustainability requires using the experience gained in these village schools in southwest Mali to help implement the decentralization of education that will itself help to determine the future of the community schools in Mali.

Community schools (established by SC and others) provide an important part of basic education in Mali,[36] serving approximately 18 percent of all elementary school pupils. Several issues must be addressed as the government considers what to do with the existing schools:

How to continue the process of integrating community schools into the national system, when only teachers' salaries are being paid by the government, without losing schools that were supported with much more than salaries until 2003?

How to strengthen the acknowledged weaknesses (teachers, number of grades, construction) so that the schools can be integrated into the national system?

How to maintain the innovations that have worked? In a word, can the government use the experience in southern Mali to help decentralize its school management, integrate the community schools within the national system and maintain the successful innovations that set these community schools apart?

Community school teachers are, typically, less well trained than professional teachers and will continue to be perceived as inferior unless they receive more and better training. This requires time and money, but will benefit the education system as a whole. A medium-term plan to train these teachers should be linked to salary increases in order to consolidate the experience and retain the teachers who have already proven themselves in these schools.

A planned transition to communal schools will take time, and may well be preceded by a government assessment of all community schools in Mali. Some interim support is likely to be needed to keep the teacher attrition and school closure rates to a minimum during this period.

School children in front of their village school.

Photo credit: Michael Bisceglie

Long-term impacts

Certain innovations promoted by the village schools—such as initial local language teaching—have affected national education reform, which today promotes bilingual education. Other reforms—a flexible calendar, enrollment parity—have helped to make the community schools attractive. Can these innovations that heighten the attractiveness and quality of education in Sikasso be retained as the community schools become communal schools? This would suppose system-wide standards and norms, designed as part of the regulatory support and framework that should be provided by the decentralization process, and a negotiated deviation from tradition. Maintaining the innovations will be important for sustaining the enterprise.

The most effective innovation of the SC village schools is, arguably, local commitment and management: community engagement and governance made these schools a part of village life. Decentralization will work if this local management and governance are effectively maintained. The experience is embodied in the communities that have mobilized to educate their children; the trained School Management Committees that run the schools; the local NGOs that have been trained by SC and have worked closely with the committees—these are all well positioned to help implement the decentralization of education management and should remain vital links in the decentralized system.

> *Decentralization will work if local management and governance are effectively maintained.*

Notes

2 As originally presented at the ADEA Biennale, Mauritius, 2003.

3 Les écoles communautaires (écoles du village) dans la région de Sikasso/Mali: 1992–1997: Bilan et perspectives, Rencontre de Bougoni, 16 décembre 1996, Save the Children Sahel Field Office, p. 2.

4 Personal observation of classrooms in Kalana. MOE statistics suggest an average ratio of 80:1.

5 DeStefano, Joe. Community-Based Primary Education: The Experience of the BEEP Project in Mali A Collaborative Effort USAID/Mali Save the Children USA. (April 1995) Numbers vary slightly on these figures but none are higher than 20%. Laugharn, p. 15, probably the most reliable source, cites "under 20% for girls."

6 Laugharn, Peter, Negotiating 'Education for Many:' Enrollment, Dropout, and Persistence in the Community Schools of Kolondieba, Mali., (Ph.D. Dissertation: University of London : July 2001) p. 15.

7 At the end of the 1980s, access to formal basic education in Mali was stagnant if not declining. Government capacity to provide basic schooling was severely constrained because of the persistent patterns of resource allocation that favored secondary and higher education, coupled with an overly centralized, supply constraint dominated approach to sectoral development. That is, the government's ability to expand access was constrained by the rate at which it was willing and able to allocate funds, organize the installation of schools, and hire teachers." Ibid. p. 2.

8 Christensen, et al. p. 69.

9 "Under the Fourth Education Project, in conjunction with which the BEEP (Basic Education Evaluation Project) project was developed, the World Bank, French Cooperation, USAID, and other donors made funds available to the education sector for expansion and improvement of basic education. School construction was to be jointly funded, 75% by the ministry, with the Fourth Education Project funds, and 25% by the communities.... USAID's emphasis was on trying to increase access by improving the quality and efficiency of the system, thus allowing more children to be served by the existing structure...." DeStefano, pp 2–3.

10 USAID also supported the community schools of World Education whose emphasis is parent-teacher associations. In all other ways, however, WE community schools were identical to government schools.

[11] With "funds…for one such construction per year… it would have taken almost two centuries to have a school in every community." Laugharn, p. 15. DeStefano also remarks, "In 1990, Save the Children began working with the Ministère de l'Education de Base (MED) to help communities share the cost of school construction according to the Fourth Education Project formula. The three classroom school model has a total cost of US\$ 30,000…..only one official school was constructed in 1991, and another in 1992." p. 2.

[12] Laugharn, p. 17.

[13] DeStefano, p. 3.

[14] Laugharn, p. 19.

[15] To design the expanded curriculum, between 15–20 participants attended a series of five workshops (\$1000/workshop) to develop new modules that were then tested, corrected, validated and used.

[16] AID Mali, AADEC, AMPJ, ASG, CRADE, GADS Mali, GRADE Banlieue, GRAT. Local NGO partners were added in groups of 4 starting in 1994–1995; by 1999, the 16 NGOs were reduced to 12 after budget cuts; in 2001, a mid-term review suggested further cuts, leaving eight.

[17] In 2003, after funding had ended, many NGO partners were interviewed to give a disinterested view of their work with SC. Their appreciation of the training, and in particular, greater autonomy during the last two years of the program, were cited.

[18] Velis, Jean-Pierre. Blazing the Trail: the Village Schools of Save the Children USA in Mali. UNESCO, Paris, 1994 "…the cost of building permanent, three-classroom schools in accordance with current standards (the cost per classroom was about US\$10,000)…" Blazing the Trail, page 9.

[19] Laugharn, p. 17.

[20] Blazing the Trail, p. 11.

[21] Cotton is the primary source of income in the Sikasso region, and the second largest export for Mali after gold. Pointing to the contradiction of development investments being given to countries whose exports are blocked by the US and the EU, Nicholas Kristof (NY Times, May 27, 2003) cites US agricultural subsidies of roughly \$2 billion yearly to farmers as causing a deep crisis in world cotton markets and Oxfam (2002) points out that "while the US advocates free trade and open markets in developing countries, its subsidies are destroying markets for vulnerable farmers… For the region as a whole [sub-Saharan Africa], the losses amounted to \$301m, equivalent to almost one-quarter of what it receives in American aid… Mali lost 1.7 per cent of GDP and 8 per cent of export earnings." Subsistence single-crop farmers like those in Sikasso are vulnerable to shifts in world market prices and unable to lobby against them. Education, however, at least enables them to read the contracts or the scales weighing their crop.

[22] Tietjen, Karen. Community Schools in Mali: A Comparative Cost Study, USAID SD Publication Series Technical Paper No. 97, (June 1999), Taken from Table 7, page 61. Note that the data was collected in late 1996 and 1997.

[23] Tietjen, Karen. Community Schools in Mali: A Comparative Cost Study, USAID SD Publication Series Technical Paper No. 97, (June 1999), Taken from Table 7, page 61. Note that the data was collected in late 1996 and 1997.

[24] Les Ecoles Communautaires (Ecoles du Village) Dans la région de Sikasso/Mali: 1992–1997: Bilan et Perspectives, Rencontre de Bougoni.

[25] Cissé, Morifing, et al. Les ecoles communitaires au Mali. (IIEP, Paris, 2000) pp. 220–221, annual per child cost to pay for teachers.

[26] DeStefano.

[27] Ibid. p. 5.

[28] Ibid. p. 6.

[29] Ibid. p. 7.

[30] Ibid. p. 8.

[31] Ibid. p. 8.

[32] Ibid. p. 9.

[33] Ibid. p. 11.

[34] Sicotte, Alfred, Djoume Sylla, and Laladou Soumare. Evaluation a mi-parcours du Programme Education 97–02 (Mali, April 2001)

[35] In 2000, the late payments came in two chunks: each teacher was paid 300 000 CFA, or an annual salary of 25000 CFA/month. In 2001, more teachers were paid but only for 10 months. In 2002, teachers were paid for 9 months; in 2003, teachers received 5 months of their salary through July 2003. This situation discourages teachers and makes SMCs less able to manage their schools partly because teachers paid under this system tend to consider themselves more accountable to the CAP than to the SMC. This situation led SC, World Education and Africare to call a forum to discuss suitable and appropriate mechanisms of payment that ensure the employer's role of SMC. This mechanism was used the first year but the CAPs gradually kept the NGOs and the SMCs away. For example, SMCs were paid directly the first year and they paid the teachers in turn. Now radio broadcasts announce that salaries are ready for distribution by the CAP, whom some teachers consider to be their employers.

[36] The 2002–2003 MOE statistics (vol. 1 p 18), counts 2437 community schools and 3441 public schools for a total of 7200 elementary schools. Community schools therefore count for one-third of the national infrastructure of basic education, and serve approximately 18% of Mali's pupils (231,302 of the 1,294,672 pupils).

References

Boukary, Hamidou, The Community Schools of Save the Children in Mali. (Ph.D. Dissertation: 1998)

Christensen, Philip, Aly Badra Doukouré, Peter Laugharn, Talaat Moreau, Jeanne Moulton, Joshua Muskin, and Michel Welmond, *Kids, Schools and Learning: A Retrospective Study of USAID Support to Basic Education in Sub-Saharan Africa* Technical Paper No. 56, (USAID Office of Sustainable Development, Bureau for Africa: July 1997)

Cissé, Morifing, et al. *Les écoles communautaires au Mali* (IIEP, Paris, 2000)

DeStefano, Joe. *Community-Based Primary Education: The Experience of the BEEP Project in Mali A Collaborative Effort USAID/Mali-Save the Children USA* (April 1995)

Esquieu, Paul et Serge Péano. *Fonctionnement et financement de l'enseignement fondamental malien,* Rapport de Recherche No. 106, (UNESCO-IIEP, Paris, 1996)

Fomba, Cheick Oumar. *La gestion communautaire de l'école, une solution alternative a la problématique d'une éducation de base de qualité pour tous au Mali.* (CNE Ministry of Education, Bamako, Mali, 1999)

Fomba, Cheick Oumar, et al., *Les écoles communautaires de l'ONG Save The Children/USA et partenaires au Mali: fonctionnement et qualité.* (Pour le Ministère de L'Education de Base, IPN, Mali, July 1999)

Haidara, Youssouf Dr. *Informations sur la Pédagogie Convergente* (MEN, Bamako, Mali, 2003)

---- *Module de Formation des Maîtres en pédagogie convergente, Niveaux I, II, III* (Bamako, July 2001)

Laugharn, Peter. *Negotiating 'Education for Many' Enrollment, Dropout, and Persistence in the Community Schools of Kolondieba, Mali.* (Ph. D. Dissertation: University of London: July 2001)

Miller-Grandvaux, Yolande and Karla Yoder. *A Literature Review of Community Schools.* (USAID Office of Sustainable Development, Bureau for Africa, Washington, DC, February 2002)

Obanya, Pai. *Revitalizing Education in Africa.* (Printmarks, Nigeria, 2002)

Samba Traoré. *La Pédagogie Convergente: Son expérimentation au Mali et son impact sur le système éducatif.* (UNESCO, 2001)

Save the Children USA, *Les Ecoles Communautaires, Ecoles du Village dans la région de Sikasso,Mali, 1992–1997: Bilan et Perspectives.* (Rencontre de Bougouni: Dec. 1996)

---- *The Impact of Community Participation on the Quality of Learning.* Subregional Education Workshop. (Feb. 1995)

---- *Curriculum des Ecoles Communautaires*

Sicotte, Alfred, Djoumé Sylla, and Mamadou Soumare, *Evaluation a mi-parcours du Programme Education 97–02.* (Mali, April 2001)

Tietjen, Karen. "Community Schools in Mali: A Comparative Cost Study," *USAID SD Publication Series Technical paper No. 97* (June 1999)

Tounkara, Brehima, et al., Evaluation de la Qualité de l'éducation dans les écoles communautaires gérées par World Education et ONG Partenaires. (ROCARE, Bamako, July 2000)

Chapter 3

Malawi, 1994–2003: Training on a National Scale

Amy Jo Dowd and Lester Namathaka

*Malawian school children in front of the Malenga primary school, which serves 96 pupils.
SC is working to provide new classroom blocks, school materials and furniture.*

Photo credit: Carolyn Watson

Coping with a flood of children

In 1994, the United Democratic Front won Malawi's first multi-party, democratic elections. In his June inaugural speech, President Bakili Muluzi announced a policy of Free Primary Education (FPE). School fees were abolished and, as a result, Malawi's schools were flooded. Over one million pupils enrolled in October; more than two-thirds of these children were in the first three grades of primary school.[37]

The Ministry of Education, Sports, and Culture (MOEST) was caught unprepared. There were neither enough schools nor enough trained teachers to cope with such an influx of students. Moreover, the teacher/pupil ratio had grown from 1:80 in 1994 to 1:108 in 1995, an increase of almost 30 percent.

"Parents were extremely eager to send their children to school, especially when this was framed as an essential component of a new set of democratic entitlements."[38]

In response, the government of Malawi hired 22,000 academically qualified "teacher candidates" between October 1994 and October 1995. The trainees had either gone to school for ten years and passed the Malawi Junior Certificate Examination (JCE), or for twelve years and had passed the Malawi School Certificate Examination (MSCE). In addition, the candidates attended a two-week crash course to "provide them with preliminary skills and knowledge in teaching, lesson preparation, classroom management and interpersonal relations"[39] before schools opened.

However, in 1995 MOEST and the World Bank estimated that 22,000 *more* teachers were needed to bring the classroom ratio down to the national goal of 1:60.[40] But by 2000, some 30,000 teachers in the Malawi school system—20 percent of the teaching force—were still untrained.[41] It is against this background, and the fact that many children in remote rural areas did not attend school owing to the long distances from their villages to conventional government schools, that Save the Children's Village-Based Schools (VBSs) were introduced in Malawi.

SC's Village-Based Schools in southern Malawi: 1994–1998

SC moved to southern Malawi's Mangochi District in October 1994 from the central and northern regions where it had worked for the previous decade. The government of Malawi and USAID, SC's major funder, felt that the needs were greater in the southern region where the government had not effectively targeted or served the rural Muslim and Chiyao-speaking population. In 1994, fewer than half of Mangochi's approximately 1,500 teachers in 231 schools had received professional teacher training.[42] The area was also particularly hard hit by the influx of children into the schools with the declaration of Free Primary Education. In every grade, the average number of pupils per teacher in Mangochi was higher than in Malawi as a whole.

SC had already developed its Malawi Village-Based School (VBS) pilot in January 1994, before the FPE declaration. The Malawi VBSs, adaptations of the village schools launched in 1992 in Mali, were different in that they were not built one to a village, but could serve several villages. They were also "more closely integrated into the existing school system in terms of curriculum, teacher profiles, and expectations of phase-over to the MOE in the short term."[43] As in

Mali, USAID also funded the Malawi pilot from 1994–1997. Eight schools opened in October 1994, each consisting of two blocks of two classrooms.

Children at the primary school in Nikisi stage a drama in English. Their cement block classroom, built by the community with help from SC, accommodates 327 students.

Photo credit: Carolyn Watson

VBS schools were built and managed by the communities, who also helped to recruit and select teachers. Typically, the teachers had only eight years of education (primary school). VBS teachers were trained in the field for two weeks before the beginning of each term and attended in-service

On-going teacher support and supervision and active student participation in learning were VBS hallmarks.

courses every other month. In addition, an SC-trained and paid supervisor resided in the area of the schools and visited each teacher at least once a month. School materials—textbooks for the national curriculum, distributed by MOEST—were in most cases available and class sizes were kept at, or near, 60 pupils drawn from a few villages near the VBS. The national curriculum was taught in these schools, but in creative ways.

Initially, SC designed the schools to offer three years of schooling, with the end of the third year serving as a target for anchoring literacy and numeracy[44] rather than being merely a cut-off point. This approach included on-going teacher support and supervision and active student participation in learning. These became VBS hallmarks.

Community mobilization and training

The strategy for poverty alleviation adopted by the new government of Malawi and supported by donor agencies and international, national and local NGOs included harnessing community forces as full partners in education.[45] Hence, many of these organizations, including SC, engaged communities on behalf of FPE.

Community mobilization, from SC's perspective, meant flexibility, openness to discussion and negotiation and a strong, consistent commitment to the quality of teaching and learning. SC's approach to inaugurating community schools was to go to communities to ensure their commitment and involvement in decision-making from the outset.

> Community mobilization, from SC's perspective, meant flexibility, openness to discussion and negotiation and a strong commitment to quality.

SC's education staff met with the eight communities in Mangochi to decide how SC could best accommodate the needs for building, running, and maintaining schools. Parents wanted their children to be educated, to study the national curriculum (with emphasis on Chichewa, math, and health issues) in schools close to their villages with local teachers whom they trusted with their children, especially their girls. They would assist in building a schoolroom but resisted paying teachers' salaries as they could not afford to and because of the promise of FPE.

SC decided to pay teachers' salaries for a year, with the expectation from the start that the teachers would be integrated into the national education system and become civil servants. To ensure that MOEST would accept the VBS plan, SC involved the Ministry from the beginning, including district level participation of Primary Education Advisors (PEAs), or school inspectors. The Mangochi PEA responsible for the area in which the new VBSs were established even attended SC training sessions.

Community members build a new school in Namisi.

Photo credit: Michael Bisceglie

Two school blocks with two classrooms each were built in eight communities between April and September 1994. SC monitored the construction to ensure basic quality and safety standards, and provided tin roofs. (VBS supporters saw sharing costs as an immediately useful response to the overwhelming demand for primary education; detractors noted that VBS buildings were not permanent and would ultimately require more maintenance than the more expensive alternatives.)

SC, the community and the teachers (once they were selected) then met to determine the structure of the PTA and the school committee, and the relationships, responsibilities and expectations of parents and teachers. During the pilot phase the community had many responsibilities. They were expected to erect the school structures; elect a school committee; choose teachers; hold monthly meetings on children's school life; discipline teachers and students for punctuality and per-formance [46] by tracking absenteeism; work with families to avoid dropouts and set an appropriate school timetable and calendar. (While the communities made some changes to the school timetable, eliminating classes that conflicted with religious education in the mosques, the calendar was the same as the national calendar.)

Initially, community members were more readily mobilized to build classroom blocks than to monitor and handle dropouts or teach local history to pupils.

Community members needed time to warm up to some of their new responsibilities. Initially, they were more readily mobilized to build classroom blocks than to monitor and handle dropouts or teach local history to pupils.

School committees had been institutionalized in Malawi as early as 1962 by the Education Act, but most were unaware of their roles and responsibilities.[47] SC, therefore, trained communities, school committees and teachers to promote collaborative efforts and to reinforce basic lessons. Community training was practical, participatory and used diverse methods and local materials. It "stimulat[ed] community participation and train[ed] community members for school management roles" that went beyond the "old meaning" of community participation as defined and dictated from above. It introduced a "grass roots-up" model that SC staff, District Education Office (DEO) staff and communities continue to refine.[48]

Teachers' roles and the interaction between teachers and committees were also addressed. Teacher training included practical sessions on involving the community in the classroom or calling on the PTA to address the problem of drop-outs. School committees had three days of training to learn what their roles were and what officers did, as well as leadership, project management (such as constructing school blocks or generating income for school supplies), conducting meetings, and taking minutes. SC also encouraged committee members to monitor children's learning and behavior and to work with teachers to resolve absenteeism and child health issues. Day-long follow-up training sessions every other month reinforced the lessons and use of these skills.

Teacher training included practical sessions on involving the community in the classroom.

When two separate studies of the communities' efforts found that the communities were anxious to take on roles beyond the preliminary vision,[49] SC intensified its efforts, advocating to all local stakeholders the extension of teacher-community partnership activities. SC also organized additional training sessions for teachers, head teachers and community members alike.

The communities were anxious to take on roles beyond the preliminary vision.

By 1998, the communities had taken on more roles, including monitoring the headmaster and his records; reporting on teacher punctuality to supervisors; addressing conflicts among teachers; responding to school problems; being involved as curricular resources and monitoring pupil hygiene, performance, punctuality, attendance and drop-out rates.[50] The VBS committee members also became local education advocates, bringing needs and concerns to the attention of local authorities.

Recruiting and paying VBS teachers

SC involved communities in hiring community members to train as teachers for two reasons. Giving communities a role in selecting teachers reinforced their sense of ownership, and teachers from the community did not need housing. (National policy required housing for teachers posted from elsewhere: a cost that thwarted the expansion of primary education throughout Malawi.[51]) A local teacher was also less likely to resign or cut class. However, in Mangochi, parents and teachers did not accept the proposition that a local literate person could be trained to teach children an alternative (non-national) curriculum. Communities wanted the national curriculum and an educated teacher, even though they could not afford to pay the salary.

> *Communities wanted the national curriculum and an educated teacher, even though they could not afford to pay the salary.*

Communities worked with SC and the DEO (who had to approve all candidates) to recruit and hire teachers from among local young men and women with JCEs, or who had at least completed primary school (eighth grade).[52] The community nominated candidates, and SC and the DEO examined their general knowledge of English, math and Chichewa; ranked them and let the community make the final selection. The community generally chose candidates with the best scores, although reputation and trust also influenced selections.[53] Salaries were based on the 1994 civil service standard that varied according to education levels.

VBS teachers with a primary education earned less than half of what a JCE-holder earned. Hence, two additional years of formal education doubled the recurrent teacher salary expenditures: "the cost of a child-hour of instruction in a VBS with a PSLC (Primary School Leaving Certificate) holder is approximately eight times less than in a government school with a JCE holder."[54]

From the outset, SC envisioned that VBS teachers would be integrated into the civil service and negotiated with the government to have it accept them as MOEST teachers. When the government insisted that VBS teachers needed JCEs, SC helped them to become certified by facilitating their registration in neighboring secondary distance education centers and mentoring and tutoring them on weekends. This was a way of sustaining the system, ensuring that the teachers could be integrated into the national system and be paid as civil servants.

> *The VBSs are a much better investment [than government schools] in terms of outputs per dollar spent.*

The relative costs of VBSs versus government schools were debated by evaluators (who described them as "not cheap") and SC staff. In fact, "a reading of the three comparisons…of training costs, teachers' salary costs, and supervision costs does not seem to show the VBSs as being much more expensive in the absolute, and indicates that the VBSs are a much better investment in terms of outputs per dollar spent. …when …eight schools … are running at full capacity (50 pupils per class times eight classes per school) they will enroll 3,200 pupils per year ….cost per pupil per year will be substantially lower than …US $95…. …the VBS model stands to be fairly comparable to GS costs."[55]

Intensive teacher training

In October 1994, prior to the start of the academic year in the communities around Chilipa in Mangochi, SC and Primary Education Advisors (PEAs) trained VBS teachers during two intensive weeks (14 days).

Active, child-centered teaching methods were promoted. The team taught teachers to diversify their teaching approaches during a single lesson. For

> *Active, child-centered teaching methods were promoted VBS schools.*

example, the teacher would make the main point of the lesson using writing, then music and then have pupils role-play with the teacher to drive it home. The teacher would then switch to a physical activity to introduce a new concept, reinforce it with copying or chanting and review it with drawing in the sand outside the classroom. Variation and activity kept children attentive. Teachers learned to use familiar objects to present new material to children in ways that invited their participation.

A teachers' training workshop.

Photo credit: Carolyn Watson

An initial seven-day training session covered the national curriculum, as well as subject planning; activity-based lesson planning and daily planning; instructional methods; creating teaching aids using the local environment; classroom and school management; progress reporting; assessing and testing children and basic child psychology. Training between the longer holiday workshops took place on weekends every other month and reflected the observed difficulties and issues that had arisen during the supervisory visits of the preceding weeks.[56]

The SC-MOEST partnership on the ground began in the VBS… cooperation and collaboration were sought at all possible meetings.

From the initial phases of the pilot, the PEA responsible for that part of Mangochi where the VBSs were located assisted during the introductory training and in-service courses. Hence, the SC-MOEST partnership on the ground began in the VBS. SC met with MOEST repeatedly to design the pilot, involving the DEO in Mangochi and the PEA in the target zone in the hiring and initial training of the VBS teachers and during their support and professional development. An SC supervisor who supported the schools resided and worked in the PEA's zone of pedagogical influence; cooperation and collaboration were sought at all possible meetings.

A system of intensive pre- and in-service training and support came to define SC's field-based teacher training.

Teachers were closely supervised during the first term of 1994. They were brought together for a second one-week workshop during the holidays and continued to be monitored and supervised through the second term. A third training session was held during the holiday break. The second and third training workshops reviewed instructional methods, planning and classroom management skills and the use of music, art and physical education during math, English, Chichewa and general studies lessons. To perpetuate the process, SC trained a strong leader from each VBS to become a headmaster who would supervise teachers, coach, keep records, report on administrative and attendance issues and oversee community relations, income generation and fund-raising. This system of intensive pre- and inservice training and support came to define SC's field-based teacher training.

Teachers were required to try out the methods on each other and on groups of school-aged children and to be creative in using local materials.

Through this effort, SC developed and tested "Survival Skills for Teachers in Village Based Schools" that used MOEST teacher training but focused on practical skills, student participation, diverse methods and local materials. SC's training sessions were practical; pupils participated and a diversity of methods and local materials were used. During training sessions, teachers were required to try out the methods on each other and on groups of school-aged children (micro-teaching and peer teaching) and to be creative in using local materials.

By 1996, despite being local, the VBS teacher training system had become more expensive on a per capita basis than MOEST teacher training.[57] However, since 1996, the MOEST training colleges had failed to meet the dire need for trained teachers. Therefore Malawi's Integrated In-Service Teacher Education program (MIITEP), together with MOEST, mounted other projects, but their impact has been less than desired.[58] However, their costs have not been compared to the current teacher training scheme under USAID's QUEST program, (Quality Education through Supporting Teaching) so it is not known whether this approach is as expensive as existing MOEST teacher training schemes or not.

Teacher supervision

Since VBS teachers were less academically qualified, they needed to be supervised on an ongoing basis.

Since VBS teachers were less academically qualified than teachers hired by MOEST, they needed to be supervised on an ongoing basis. SC supervised and supported VBS teachers closely, even during classes. One supervisor based in Chilapa oversaw the teachers at the VSB, visiting them once or twice a month. (Government school supervisors often covered from ten to 15 schools in a given zone and visited them one to three times a year.[59]) A VBS supervisor received a higher salary and more resources for transportation and training than a government inspector; nevertheless, the cost of an SC supervisory visit was one-fifth that of a visit in the government system.[60]

A typical classroom visit began with a review of lesson plans, observation of teaching and a discussion about the lesson. Sometimes a hypothetical suggestion, "Suppose you did it this way?" was made. The teacher and supervisor would conclude by agreeing on the most suitable presentation method and the supervisor would promise to return and review the classroom at a later date.[61]

Within the first year, local, frequent, relevant supervision was perceived to be essential. Indeed, in 1996, evaluators noted, "we are fairly certain that without the supervision, the [test] results in the VBS schools might have been even lower than those in the government schools."[62]

At the close of the VBS pilot, educational quality was on the government policy agenda.

At the close of the VBS pilot, educational quality was on the government policy agenda. A national commission was named and resources mobilized to enhance teaching and learning. The MIITEP aimed to train teachers while the Malawi School Service System Project (MSSSP) planned to support them at the zone level. With four years of VBS groundwork, SC had the experience and the resources to assist MIITEP with its field-based study and help extend the MSSSP system of teacher support into the cluster (three to four proximate schools) and into individual schools.

The Integrated Curriculum

The VBS early primary school curriculum divided the national curriculum into core subjects—Chichewa, English, math and general studies. Subsidiary subjects—art, music and physical education—were used as vehicles for the core subjects. For example, pupils jumped while counting, sang in English, acted out skits in Chichewa and drew objects from nature. This "Integrated Curriculum" (IC) enabled teachers to spend more time per week on core subjects, teach more than one short period of a core subject per day, and review and follow up on difficult areas of a subject on the same day.[63] It also responded to the concerns of parents and professionals that the early primary years were too full with eight subjects.[64] But most importantly, it made the lessons more dynamic and kept children focused on learning.

Classrooms were adorned with "charts made by teachers from local materials and fixed to mud brick walls using sticks," as compared to "the walls in government classrooms (that) were generally bare."[65] Classrooms had flash cards; sentence strips; bamboo counters; nature tables made of sticks and covered with stones, leaves, and vegetables used in teaching language and math; and shopping areas with empty cartons and wrappers marked with prices so that pupils could buy and sell to practice mathematics. The *mayerengero*—a piece of bamboo, clay beads and string—was a ubiquitous, locally-made teaching and learning aid that works like an abacus.

Evaluators, donors and other visitors to the VBS pilots have remarked that these classrooms "felt different," that teachers and communities were involved here in ways that were different. Policy makers and practitioners explained the VBS success in various ways.[66] One example of success was that second grade pupils in the pilot schools had "learned more over the course of the 1997 school year than did their government school counterparts" and that the teaching in these schools was "well-prepared, interactive, pupil-centered teaching [with] on-going opportunities for improving teaching through supervision."[67]

> *These classrooms "felt different" … teachers and communities were involved here in ways that were different.*

However, MOEST officials, researchers from the University of Malawi's Center for Research and Training (CERT) and donors hotly debated many of these innovations. It was seductive to believe that "given that amount of money per school" the MOEST system could provide the same quality of education. The challenge then was: could some, or any, of these innovations be implemented in the government system?

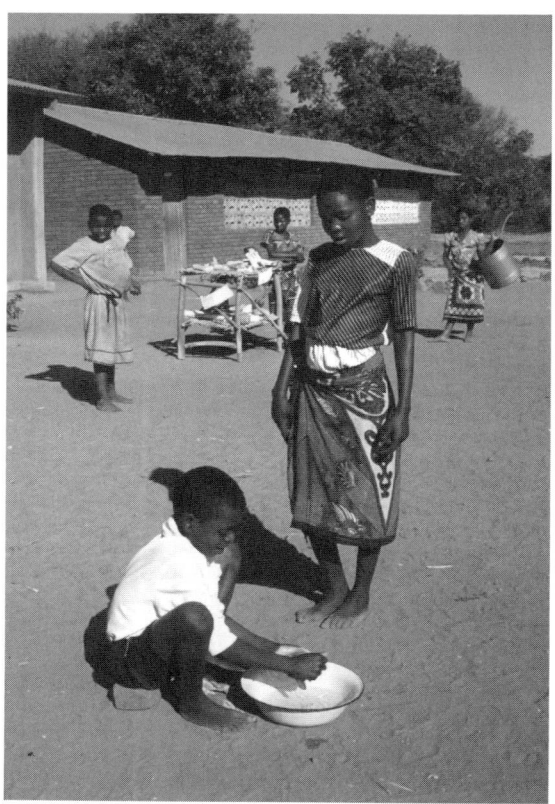

Students act out a scene to practice their English.
Photo credit: Carolyn Watson

Expansion and impact

Some pieces of the pilot were replicated in partnership with other NGOs and/or MOEST during the pilot phase. Others were adapted or dropped, as in SC's collaboration with USAID's QUEST, and when the pilot was expanded to a district-wide approach in 1998.

In 1996, SC implemented some VBS innovations in eight developing primary schools south of Mangochi, in neighboring Machinga district, funded by Redd Barna (Save the Children Norway). This was done in partnership with the DEO and involved collaboration between SC trainers and supervisors and the Machinga PEAs. In Mangochi, SC partnered with the DEO and the Muslim Association of Malawi in 12 additional schools, for a total of 20 schools. The VBS pilot also affected policy, in that the MOEST showed greater interest

The VBS pilot affected policy in that the MOEST showed greater interest in community mobilization and a commitment to educational quality.

in community mobilization and a commitment to educational quality. The Zambian government was also interested in the pilot and sent three paramount chiefs to Malawi to learn about VBS.

The VBS pilot produced a USAID-funded teacher training guide consolidating the four principles of SC teacher training—that teaching should be participatory, practical, diverse, and local. The guide informed SC's teacher training and support efforts in the QUEST program and was used by government teacher trainers and NGOs throughout the country. In 2000, the SC education team in Malawi produced a teacher training resource handbook with the MOEST and other agencies including UNICEF, the creative centre for community mobilization that influenced SC education staff around the globe[68]. SC also helped the Muslim Association of Malawi in Mangochi, UNICEF in the central region and churches supporting schools in the northern region to train cadres of PEAs and teachers. With HIV/AIDS and other factors contributing to soaring teacher deaths, this training system helped many newly appointed, untrained teachers—beyond the VBS pilot—to cope in their classrooms.

Children study math using the mayerengero in Standard Two.

Photo credit: Carolyn Watson

QUEST: 1998–2003

When Save the Children's VBS initiative was expanded through participation in USAID's QUEST program, VBS provided the model and QUEST the means for expansion. SC's collaboration with QUEST focused on how to use VBS lessons in partnership with government to better meet the learning needs of teachers, communities and pupils in Malawi.

With HIV contributing to soaring teacher deaths, this training system helped many newly appointed, untrained teachers to cope.

The VBS pilot drew to a close in 1998. In order to distill what it had learned, SC assessed the pilot's strengths and capacity as well as the needs and status of pupils and teachers. The major challenge was to have government schools adopt the best practices of VBS:

- manageable classes;
- teachers with hands-on practice in creative, participatory and diverse teaching methods;
- regular supervision;
- in-service training;
- locally available materials used as teaching and learning aids;
- teachers trained to stimulate community participation and train communities for school management roles beyond the traditional meaning of community participation.

In addition, concerns about pedagogy and teacher training raised questions about how much ongoing support would be needed to keep teachers motivated.

SC's needs assessments indicated that districts had unequal numbers of pupils and teachers. For example, one had far too many second grade pupils; another had an unusually low number of first grade pupils. One school was overwhelmed with un-certified teachers, while another had experienced teachers who had never received in-service training. MOE recruited teachers nationally and assigned them based on enrollment. All this, and the variety of staffing needs in Mangochi and its surrounding

QUEST focused on how to use VBS lessons in partnership with government to better meet the learning needs of teachers, communities and pupils in Malawi.

districts, led SC to suggest a decentralized approach to supporting teaching and learning based on the VBS experience.

SC designed the QUEST for Learning program with MOEST and the Ministry of Gender, Youth And Community Service (MOGYCS) in a way that involved all the players: primary education advisors (PEAS); teachers and head teachers; Community Development Assistants (CDAs) at MOGYCS and community members in order to increase access, enhance quality and maximize efficiency.

Teacher training and support and working collaboratively with communities were expected to increase learning test scores by 20 percent, and reduce dropout and repetition rates by 10 percent. While SC continued to focus on schools and classrooms, the initiative included "skills-building" of government partners at the zonal (15–25 schools proximate enough for one PEA), cluster (three to four proximate schools) and school levels to ensure that officers made more than one perfunctory annual supervisory visit. In the meantime, 33 new VBSs in three districts (Mangochi, Balaka and Blantyre-rural) with 132 classrooms (providing spaces for over 16,500 children), and 33 boreholes for safe water were created.

SC suggested a decentralized approach to supporting teaching and learning based on the VBS experience.

Community capacity building again involved partnerships, but this time it had a district-wide focus, with the participation of the CDAs, SC and the PEAs interacting in a community dialogue about quality. It included a focus on training school committees to help manage and maintain schools and promote effective teaching and learning. Student and teacher performance data were added to the agenda for local discussions.

SC also instituted the "QUEST Term Plan for School Improvement," which required community members and teachers to collaborate on quality improvement projects each term in order to enhance teaching and learning. SC aimed to develop a sustainable, decentralized system that improved education in each district in two years. The figure below illustrates the cycles of training and support for communities and teachers at the school, community, cluster and zone levels.

SC aimed to develop a sustainable, decentralized system that improved education in each district in two years.

Measuring results

Each district where QUEST was implemented represented "a laboratory for innovation." Starting in 1999, extensive data was collected and analyzed to examine the impact of various VBS components on pupil learning. A partnership with the Malawi Institute of Education (MIE), a quasi-governmental curriculum, teacher training and research institute, and with the Improving Educational Quality (IEQ) project[69] funded by USAID, broadened the effort and enabled SC to produce more, richer documentation and policy statements. The partnership offered access to curriculum designers, local research expertise and links to policymakers helping to set the MIE agenda at MOEST.

Community members gather for a meeting while children play with tires.

Photo Credit: Michael Bisceglie

For example, an experiment in Balaka district conducted by SC in 2001 in partnership with MIE found that pupils using the QUEST Integrated Curriculum scored significantly higher than pupils in schools where there were only QUEST interventions. The same is true for pupils using the QUEST Integrated Curriculum for mathematics.

> *Pupils using the QUEST Integrated Curriculum scored significantly higher than pupils in schools where there were only QUEST interventions.*

In 2000, QUEST was extended to Balaka and Blantyre-rural districts. In 2003, it was operating in three districts: Mangochi, Balaka and Blantyre–rural. In June 2003, SC turned over teacher and community support to the well-trained DEO staff. And at the national level, SC tried to ensure that MOEST understood its work. Accordingly, it organized one national and three district advisory teams (one per district) that included regional, division and national MOEST officials who visited project activities periodically to assess progress and review plans.

The QUEST project provided classrooms for 336,111 primary school pupils in 436 schools in which 4,403 teachers taught and were supervised by 28 PEAs for an approximate cost of $10.48 per student. This amount covered three years of community and teacher training, community and teacher support, research and construction costs. Extending the project without additional budget further lowered real costs.

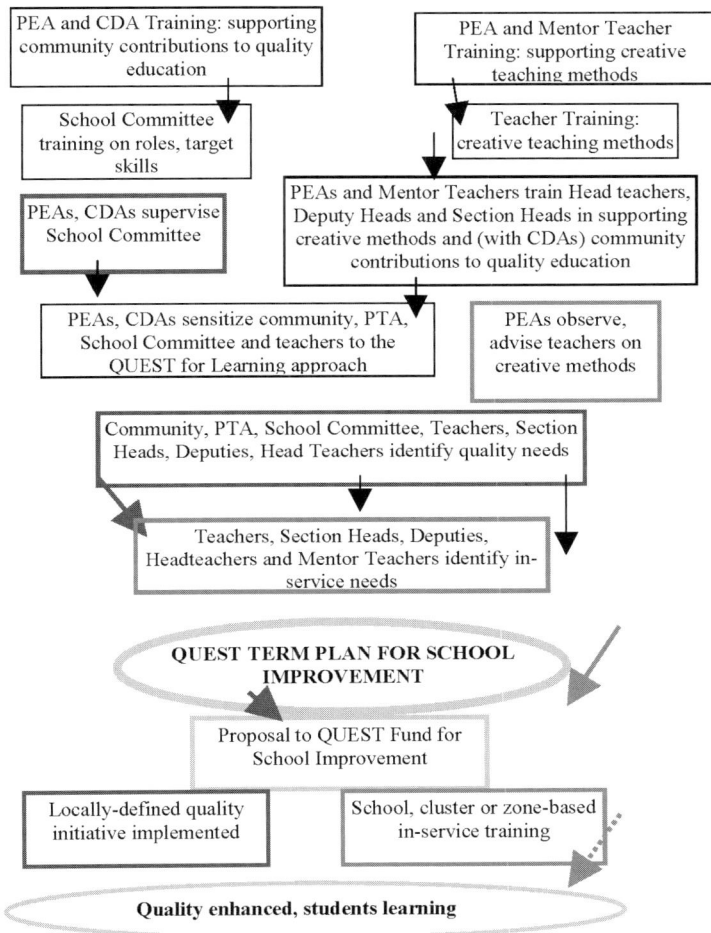

Figure 3.1: QUEST for learning: addressing quality through action at the zone, cluster and school levels.

What changed with QUEST?

In QUEST, Research and response to the HIV/AIDS crisis and other recurrent challenges were added.

Some VBS components were adapted in QUEST for greater program and policy impact, while research and response to the HIV/AIDS crisis and other recurrent challenges were added. When SC began to plan for QUEST in January 1998, Malawi had made some progress towards universal primary education, but isolated rural areas without schools, facilities or supplies still existed. And elsewhere, classrooms were so over-crowded that more schools were needed. The government's 2000 Policy and Investment Framework called for an additional 40,000 classrooms by 2012 to enable children to learn close to their homes.[70]

During QUEST, the DEO worked with SC on a school mapping exercise, consulting communities about their educational needs. QUEST schools were more complex than the four-room VBS schools. They also had four classrooms but included a storage facility for books and administrative materials; a borehole for fresh water and concrete pit latrines (two blocks of six toilets for children, to make it easier for students, especially girls, to stay in school from 8 am to 1 pm; and one block of two toilets for teachers) and a head teacher's house and office for non-local teachers. All facilities were built with community labor and SC provided imported cement and roofs. The DEO provided teachers and instructional materials for the new schools. SC lost the battle to establish head teachers who had low academic qualifications but who were highly trained and supported as educational leaders in the larger MOEST system in Mangochi.

QUEST teacher training and support

SC trained teachers, head teachers, and supervisors in participatory, diversified pedagogical strategies and in the use of locally available, relevant teaching materials. SC and the DEO also organized schools into clusters and trained local Mentor Teachers to provide ongoing, professional, local support, as well as developing the professional supervisory skills of PEAs and cluster mentor teachers.

Mentor Teachers

Mentor Teachers constituted a new layer of support for a cluster of three to four schools, designed to make participatory training more manageable and frequent. Mentor Teachers could observe teachers and provide feedback between PEA visits. Finally, and perhaps most importantly, QUEST wanted to further the development of peer groups in each cluster and encourage sharing.

QUEST wanted to further the development of peer groups in each cluster and encourage sharing.

SC and DEO partners selected Mentor Teachers for their organizational, training and communication skills, their classroom performance and peer judgment. Training was organized in March of 1999. Mentor Teachers were trained in the teacher training curriculum and in the organization of local workshops and given a bicycle for their visits. Seven months later, 36 of 180 teachers under study had been trained by a Mentor Teacher and 55 teachers had been observed in the classroom.

A teacher in class at the Malenga primary school.

Photo credit: Carolyn Watson

By October 2000, the end of the second school year of implementation, SC staff saw that Mentor Teachers were more effective in training and supporting teachers than the over-extended PEAs and better able to sustain their support. Retention rates seemed to bear this out: only two of 63 Mentor Teachers in Mangochi left their posts in the 1999–2000 school year; both to become PEAs. Their mastery of teacher training and support strategies would now serve larger numbers of teachers above the cluster level. Not surprisingly, some Mentor Teachers complained about the additional work and lack of incentives, and their bicycles often broke down. SC began to repair bikes, and in new target districts, to purchase better bicycles until June 2003, when QUEST ended. Today, all Mentor Teachers are still using their old bicycles.

> *The Mentor Teachers' mastery of teacher training and support strategies would now serve larger numbers of teachers.*

QUEST teacher training

> *HIV/AIDS, retirement and new opportunities were increasing the rates of teacher attrition.*

Initial teacher training in QUEST was similar to VBS training of unqualified teachers in Mangochi, Machinga and Balaka districts between 1995 and 1998. It consisted of four seven-day sessions during the school year for groups of no more than 30 teachers. But in 2000, HIV/AIDS, retirement and new opportunities were increasing the rates of teacher attrition in all three districts where QUEST was working. The combination of FPE and HIV/AIDS had created a vicious cycle: more and more teachers needed training, yet many trained teachers were dying every year. Even though all the teachers in the district had been trained during the first year, by year two approximately 35 percent of teachers were new to the classroom. Above all, it was very difficult to plan for cohorts of trainees. As a result, thousands of teachers in Malawi were classified as "serving, untrained."[71] QUEST therefore changed its strategy for training 2,104 untrained teachers in Mangochi, Balaka and Blantyre-rural by training in groups, or clusters, and at the work place. Workshops were held at the zone or cluster level or in individual schools where sufficient numbers warranted it.

Teaching a large class outdoors at the Namisi school while the new school that
Save the Children is helping to build is being completed.

Photo credit: Carolyn Watson

Evidence shows that QUEST directly impacted teaching in the classroom. For example, Mr. Odala, Deputy Head Teacher at Namitambo Primary School in Mangochi district, said his teaching "has improved dramatically." He cited specific improvement in his ability to lay out schemes of work and lesson plans, to assist pupils and to conduct conduct continuous assessment of pupil performance. Techniques for conducting continuous assessment are an area that is emphasized in the QUEST training, enabling teachers, parents and pupils to monitor progress on an ongoing basis.

The Deputy Head Teacher cited specific improvement in his ability to lay out schemes of work and lesson plans, to assist pupils and to conduct continuous assessment of pupil performance.

In the Namitambo school alone, the drop-out rate declined by 8 percent, demonstrating the impact of the training and continuous assessment on pupil attendance.

Education Trainers and Primary Education Advisors

SC implemented a program to improve teaching quality in Malawi by employing experienced Education Trainers who understood, supported and demonstrated the desired approach to teaching.

By 1999 MOEST and the donor agencies had begun to question whether the staff who were ostensibly supporting MIITEP teacher trainees (PEAs, head teachers, and senior school staff) actually agreed with and were competent in interactive teaching approaches.[72] For one thing, only 20 percent of the MIITEP trainee supporters had ever taught primary school. SC therefore implemented a program to improve teaching quality in Malawi by employing experienced Education Trainers who understood, supported and demonstrated the desired approach to teaching. Each PEA was supported for two full years by an SC Education Coordinator (EC) and an Education Trainer (ET) who had taught primary school. Each EC or ET was responsible for three or four PEAs, an approach that complemented MIITEP in target districts.

In December 1999, the lead-up to the second year of QUEST, three MOEST representatives from above the district level attended the PEA training session to prepare for the initial teacher training and the start of school. One of them suggested taking the SC training manual to the Principal Secretary for Basic Education to inform policy and practice elsewhere in Malawi. This resulted in the Teacher Training Resource Handbook that SC produced in 2000, which systematized the approach for all trainers. MOEST management was pleased with the product and asked SC to further distribute it and share skills with teacher trainers. Copies were distributed to all teacher training colleges and to the Malawi Institute of Education. By 2004, more than 200 college lecturers were using it, though its effects have yet to be measured. SC's receptivity to MOEST continues to bear fruit and its effectiveness in training supervisory colleagues and teachers continues to attract attention at the highest levels.

QUEST teacher supervision

The 1999 baseline survey indicated that QUEST schools were not adequately supervised. Some had not been visited for up to two years. Teachers were not being adequately supported or guided and the quality of teaching suffered. QUEST, therefore, established a supervision model that used a "narrow lens" approach focusing on key areas where teachers needed the most improvement, rather than the "wide lens" approach of PEAs, which covered all areas of teaching. QUEST organized cluster Mentor Teachers and provided training in supervisory skills. PEAs, head

Copies of SC's Teacher Training Resource Handbook were distributed to all teacher training colleges.

teachers and SC Education Trainers were also trained in the same skills and encouraged to work as a team in the cluster and zone.

During a supervisory visit, the team would observe a teacher, engage him or her in dialogue on strengths and weaknesses and elicit feedback for future training. The team assessed pupils' performance by sampling their abilities in reading, writing and numeracy. After supervising a number of teachers in a school, the team conducted an all-staff meeting for cluster training needs assessment and feedback. The visit also aimed at identifying outstanding teachers to serve as peer educators in cluster trainings. Finally, the supervision team assessed the performance of the head teacher, the school committee and the PTA, as well as the support of local leaders to the school. Mentor Teachers, PEAs and/or SC Education Trainers made, on average, five to nine supervisory visits per year.

> *Outstanding teachers were identified to serve as peer educators in cluster trainings*

Community training and support

MOEST had long advocated community participation in, and support for education, calling upon the community to make FPE a reality. The MOEST 2000 Policy Investment Framework envisioned greater autonomy of school committees, but offered strategies only for school construction, maintenance and furniture building.[73] The community was primarily, and for some, exclusively, seen as a resource for building and maintaining schools and teacher housing, despite being touted as an important stakeholder in local school planning and decision-making. Moving beyond molding bricks and building and maintaining schools was a challenge for officials, teachers and community members alike.

QUEST training, therefore, focused on increasing the capacity of school committees, PTAs and local leaders to support the development and management of schools and the implementation of school curricula. PEAs, CDAs, selected head teachers, cluster Mentor Teachers and SC education trainers conducted one- to three-day training sessions in four cycles for members of school committees, PTA chairpersons, executive committee members, secretaries and treasurers, development committee chairpersons, head teachers and local leaders. A total of 8,968 stakeholders received training in such areas as:

- roles and responsibilities;
- school development, management, and curriculum implementation;
- planning, implementing and monitoring QUEST Term Initiatives and other school project activities;
- fundraising and community mobilization;
- conflict resolution and coordination between school committees, PTAs and head teachers;

- monitoring pupil learning;
- and strategies to address absenteeism and dropout rates.

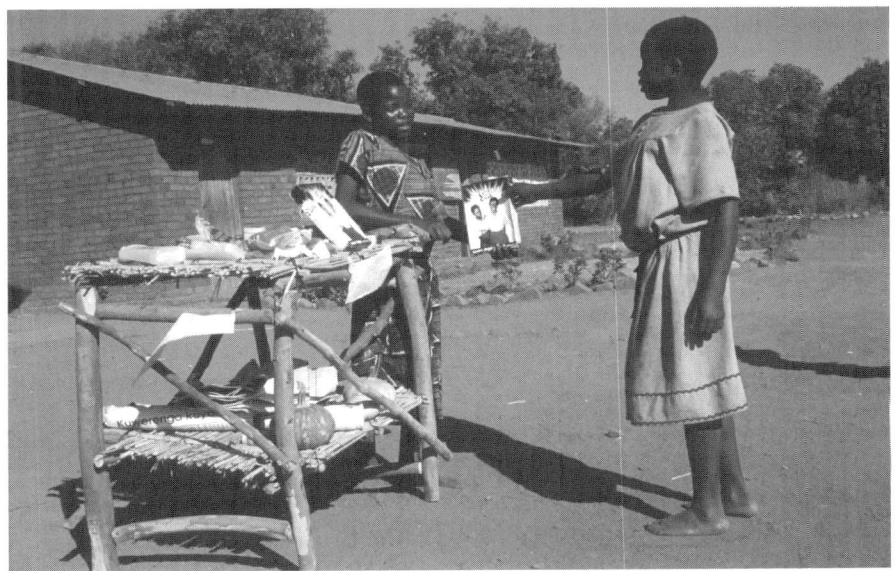

Students act out a scene as part of English class.
Photo credit: Carolyn Watson

The training was essential and was well received. In particular, school committee and PTA members learned about the importance of collaborating to support school development, management and curriculum implementation. They are now able to dialogue and work together to improve education for their children.

QUEST Term Initiatives

QUEST training focused on increasing the capacity of school committees to support the development and management of schools and the implementation of school curricula.

QUEST Term Initiatives were designed to create a platform for dialogue among education stakeholders from the district and community levels in order to plan school improvements to enhance quality. They involved a community needs assessment and prioritization, project design, implementation and project monitoring and evaluation conducted by community members. A total of 1,025 QUEST Term Initiatives were implemented in 466 primary schools in Mangochi, Balaka and Blantyre-rural.

The process began with a meeting of the head teacher, school committee and key members of the PTA at which the concept of the QUEST Term Initiative was described. A large community meeting was then organized to brainstorm about the activities that members wanted to implement. Once needs were identified, community members delegated a technical committee composed of teachers and parents to prioritize and cost the activities, which they then described to PTA members at a meeting. The PTA had to agree on the initiative if it was to be carried out. The cluster Mentor Teacher helped them write out the initiative on the appropriate QUEST fund form.

The average initiative for school improvements cost US $170 and included such items as buying portable chalkboards; improving fixed chalkboards; lowering chalkboards for the initial grades; gardening; zone, cluster and school-based trainings and workshops to improve teaching and learning; organizing open days; seminars for PTAs and school committees; securing teaching and learning materials; purchasing plastic sheets for roofing; cement to repair broken floors and walls; lime and paint to improve the walls; and soccer and netballs for recreational activities.

Each zone had a QUEST Fund Appraisal Committee composed of the PEA, CDA, SC/US Education Trainer and a member of the Teachers' Union of Malawi (TUM) who reviewed initiatives to ensure that they would:

- help to improve quality, particularly in teaching and learning,
- not include activities outside school premises,
- be of high quality,
- be planned by the entire community,
- be signed by the chairperson and secretaries of school committees and PTA executive committee and two parents (a man and a woman),
- be written on the QUEST Term Initiatives form,
- be approved one at a time from each school and only if the previous one was completed.

The committee signed and forwarded the initiative form for final approval to the District Board of Trustees which verified the process and contents, approved the initiatives and use of QUEST funds and dispatched the approved initiative forms to the Zone Appraisal Committee for transmission to the schools.

Although few initiatives focused on in-classroom quality as had been anticipated, schools and communities were united around their children's learning and took action to contribute to its improvement. Term Initiatives created a new forum for dialogue, and space for communities to turn concerns into actions in collaboration with school personnel and members of the wider community.

Term initiatives created a new forum for dialogue, and space for communities to turn concerns into actions.

Assessing the Integrated Curriculum

Beginning in 2000, QUEST worked with MOEST approval on developing and field-testing materials for the Integrated Curriculum and assessing the approach in Balaka district. An Integrated Curriculum team, which included staff from SC and MIE, a PEA, and representatives from MOEST and the Teacher Training College, visited Ghana in January 2000 to learn about its experiment in Integrated Curriculum. The team learned three important principles for Malawi:

- involve all teacher development institutions in the process;
- promote collective responsibility;
- assess children at baseline and in non-IC districts to establish gains and comparisons.

Following this visit, the team developed teacher training support materials to broaden the VBS approach with adaptations of the QUEST teacher training materials and supervision forms. To assess the new materials, SC set up an experiment, implementing QUEST using the traditional curriculum in some zones of Balaka district and the integrated approach to the national curriculum in others. SC and MOEST partners helped four first grade teachers in Balaka district (half of all the first grade teachers) to implement the traditional curriculum while the other half taught using SC's proven, integrated methods to enliven lessons and promote learning.

Second grade pupils in rural, urban and semi-urban classrooms were tested in May 2000 and in June 2001 to compare their progress. A third group was tested in Mwanza, where QUEST activities were not yet being implemented, to compare QUEST and non-QUEST schools. The results for mathematics showed that pupils in QUEST-only and QUEST IC schools performed better than pupils from Mwanza. Those in QUEST IC schools performed best of all. Similarly, in English and Chichewa, pupils in QUEST IC schools performed better than those in QUEST-only schools.

QUEST conducted a third follow-up survey and added another comparison group, Machinga, which does not have QUEST interventions. This survey demonstrated that pupils learning under the QUEST IC program showed great improvement in mathematics as compared with pupils in each comparison district, with girls and boys in QUEST IC schools outperforming children in all comparison schools. And Balaka pupils in QUEST schools learned more Chichewa than their counterparts in Machinga.

Although pupils learning under the IC approach have a comparative advantage in mathematics and Chichewa, they are not outperforming the comparison schools in English. The teaching of English, therefore, needs strengthening across many districts in Malawi.

The Integrated Curriculum study can be a viable model to inform the national curriculum implemented in primary schools in Malawi.

A crowded classroom at the Malenga primary school, before the new school was built.
Photo credit: Carolyn Watson

Although QUEST IC pupils scored significantly higher in all subjects than QUEST-only pupils, the approach requires more time for developing and pre-testing materials, implementation, regular supervision and guidance of the teachers before any evaluation can take place. Nevertheless, the IC study can be a viable model to inform the current national curriculum implemented in primary schools in Malawi.

Research

SC received funding for QUEST from USAID to research teacher, school and community factors influencing learning in Mangochi district; assess the new curriculum in Balaka district; and assess an additional policy or practice-related study in Blantyre-rural district to be determined by challenges such as HIV/AIDS. SC had already agreed with MIE to collaborate closely on the IC in Balaka. At the suggestion of USAID, SC began discussions with the implementers of the IEQ project regarding the research and its extension to gather data to address policy and practice issues that MOEST and MIE considered to be their priorities.

SC saw this as an opportunity to expand its audience and its research skills. The partnership would engage local, national and international policymakers in analysing the progress and impact of QUEST. In addition, IEQ would lend technical assistance in research approaches—curriculum-based assessment and qualitative research skills—that would upgrade SC staff skills and the documentation describing these efforts. IEQ placed its project within MIE and joined with SC to extend the instruments to be used in Mangochi and to include third and fourth grade pupils in the original cohort of second grade pupils proposed by SC.

In February 2000, after the partnership's first year, SC and MIE convened a national workshop on educational quality at which they presented findings from the 1999 school year data and invited colleagues from other DEOs and NGOs to present their experience and ideas. This was the first workshop of its kind in Malawi to bring together teachers, head teachers, school committee members, Mentor Teachers, PEAs, MOEST representatives and NGOs as well as donors and staff from teacher training colleges and universities. Seventy-two participants met to hear presentations, discuss issues, suggest action for improving quality and for extending implementation of "what works" and to raise issues for additional research by IEQ partners.

> *This was the first workshop of its kind in Malawi to bring together teachers, head teachers, school committee members, Mentor Teachers, PEAs, MOEST representatives and NGOs as well as donors and staff from teacher training colleges and universities.*

The IEQ partnership in Malawi led to the development of an assessment manual and instruments to measure factors that could affect learning among pupils, classes, teachers, schools and in the community. These instruments were developed to address the research agenda in Mangochi in1999–2001, but were adapted for use in Balaka and Blantyre-rural and used in SC field offices as a basis from which to begin a dialogue about instrumentation for programmatic or policy-related educational research questions. Importantly, the SC staff members involved in QUEST now have experience in devising, implementing and adapting these instruments.

HIV/AIDS and quality education

> *SC understood that it had to make HIV/AIDS part of the curriculum in its next phase of training and support for Malawi's teachers.*

HIV/AIDS affects education by killing disproportionate numbers of teachers.[74] MOEST and DFID estimate cumulative deaths among primary teachers at between 6,158 and 18,948 from 1999 to 2006. Between 13 and 40 percent of primary school teachers are infected[75] and therefore often absent. Replacing absent teachers on a short or long-term basis diminishes the quality of teaching and learning in all classrooms. By late 2000, SC understood that it had to make HIV/AIDS part of the curriculum in its next phase of training and support for Malawi's teachers.

After consultations with various partners, including SC/US Malawi programs implementing HIV/AIDS interventions, QUEST designed a concept paper/training proposal for a school-based approach to preventing and mitigating the impact of HIV/AIDS. Education staff then developed a results-oriented framework for HIV/AIDS in schools to monitor and evaluate the intervention. Lastly, QUEST developed a training curriculum that included basic information on HIV/AIDS, current beliefs and perceptions, psychosocial counseling, guidance and care, life skills and monitoring. The participatory approach and methodology were intended to motivate teachers to learn about and teach HIV/AIDS information in and outside the classroom and to monitor progress. When QUEST II produced the Malawi Education Support Activity (MESA) in 2003, SC was responsible for Teacher Professional Development which includes life skills to mitigate the impact of HIV/AIDS.

Measuring the impact of QUEST

In order to collect solid data on its impact, QUEST had built data collection, analysis and program and policy feedback into its agenda from the outset.

Impact on pupils

Mangochi pupils learned the new QUEST-based mathematics curriculum in 1999. A math test of 80 curriculum-related items was devised and field-tested by the IEQ partnership, then administered by teams of trained assessors from among SC, MIE and MOEST staff. After just one year, pupils' mathematics scores for grades 2 and 3 had risen by the objective of 20 percent. Pupils of teachers who used participatory and child-centered teaching techniques and young teachers with higher academic certificates had higher math scores during the 1999

Pupils of teachers who used participatory and child-centered teaching techniques had higher math scores.

school year. Moreover, community support for education—monitoring teacher punctuality and absence, and taking follow-up action—similarly raised pupil math learning.

In a vast array of community, teacher and pupil factors, this set of rudimentary, but new actions (and not building construction) enhanced second grade math learning. Teachers, plus community support for teaching, had an impact on pupil learning in 1999.[76] At the end of the 2000 school year, Mangochi pupils continued to do well in math.[77]

On the other hand, in Mangochi, reading in Chichewa and English improved less than math during 1999 (12 percent or less). In English, reading accuracy was below 25 percent for standard third grade and below 5 percent for second grade repeaters by October 2000. Comprehension scores for these groups were below 5 percent and 2 percent, respectively.

Support for reading

These findings led to a more specific study of support for learning to read in the classroom, implemented in Blantyre-rural district in 2001. SC hypo-thesized that teachers needed more training in how to teach reading skills and/or how to identify and assist slower learners, as it became clear that the backgrounds of the pupils and their parents and the parents' support for learning to read were influencing progress. The reading study collected pupil, parent and teacher information, including classroom observations, to try to discern what influenced learning to read and the implications for SC action.

Children attend class outside at the Namisi school until the new school that Save the Children is helping to build is completed.

Photo credit: Michael Bisceglie

The study was carried out in Blantyre beginning in February 2001 in six schools. The study was adapted and tested, and refined survey instruments were used in selected Blantyre city and rural schools. Data collectors were trained to administer the baseline survey at six QUEST schools, six QUEST control schools and six non-QUEST control schools—18 schools in all. After completing a baseline, the training content was prepared for six reading skills teachers who were trained four times beginning in May 2001.

Teachers, plus community support for teaching, had an impact on pupil learning.

Changing teachers' attitudes to use participatory methods for reading instead of simply reading in chorus is a big challenge.

Supervision of the teachers began between May and June 2001 and again in July 2001 with one PEA, the District Education Coordinator and one SC Education Trainer supervising the reading skills teachers. After this, the DEM, PEAs, head teachers, cluster Mentor Teachers and SC Education Trainers from the district were briefed on the study. Supervision did not continue in the third term of the last school session that ended in November 2001 because all primary school teachers were on strike. One round of supervision was conducted in February to establish how the teachers were using the improvised reading materials. Changing teachers' attitudes to use participatory methods for reading instead of simply reading in chorus is a big challenge. More supervision occurred before a follow-up survey in October 2002.

The findings show that children read better when teachers use interactive methods in class.

The findings show that children read better when teachers use interactive methods in class. Pupils participating in the reading skills intervention made tremendous gains between baseline and follow-up. Boys show a clear advantage over their counterparts in the comparison schools. The girls also increased their scores considerably in Chichewa and English, albeit less than the boys. Both still understand English passages only with difficulty. Once again, it is clear that the teaching of English still needs to be improved.

SC disseminated these results in two national conferences, one for practitioners and one for policymakers. Both groups expressed interest in using the interactive methods to enhance pupils' reading skills. QUEST also initiated the reading campaign in 93 schools in Blantyre-rural using some of the proven methods from the study. More concerted reading interventions should enable children to read well and develop permanent literacy skills.

In an assessment in October 2000 of pupils in Mangochi and Salima, a control district with no QUEST interventions, third, fourth and fifth grade pupils in the QUEST schools outperformed their Salima counterparts in English reading and comprehension on the same IEQ-generated exams. In Chichewa reading and comprehension, QUEST pupils in third grade outperformed Salima pupils by more than 35 percentage points, while in grades 4 and 5, the pupils were more comparable (3 to 7

The grade 4 and 5 scores indicate that QUEST is helping all pupils read well.

percentage points apart), with Salima pupils dominant in grade 4 and QUEST pupils dominant in grade 5. Salima has more homogeneous communities than Mangochi and mostly Chichewa-speaking people; hence children in Salima are learning in their mother tongue while more than half the pupils in Mangochi are learning Chichewa as their second language. Given this linguistic background, the grade 4 and 5 scores indicate that QUEST is helping all pupils read well.

When these results were given to the schools and communities, they ignited discussions of quality as well as plans for further local action to improve reading.

Impact on teachers

QUEST teachers were observed more often, received more frequent in-service training and experienced greater improvements in their classroom teaching practices than non-QUEST teachers.

In 1999, the first year of QUEST, a Mangochi teacher was observed in his/her classroom 2.49 times, compared to 1.89 times in 1998. A system of local planning for in-service training and school improvement at the cluster and school levels increased the frequency of participation in in-service training sessions. In February 1999, teachers reported having attended an average of one in-service session during the previous three years, whereas by October, they had attended more than three on average. QUEST staff and DEO partners conducted training and displayed and shared teaching and learning materials in teacher development centers (of the MSSSP program) in the QUEST target districts that had such centers.

QUEST teachers were observed more often, received more frequent in-service training and experienced greater improvements in their classroom teaching practices than non-QUEST teachers.

More important, perhaps, than the frequency of teacher observation and in-service training was their impact. In its first year, QUEST demonstrated that the classroom practices of 185 teachers had changed.[78] Trained raters observed and rated the teachers on a variety of skills used in teaching math, Chichewa and English. The performance of Mangochi teachers improved significantly between the baseline of February 1999 and follow-up in October in using varied teaching approaches, pupil participation, effectiveness of teaching methods, and locally available teaching and learning aids. While some progress had been made in promoting certain types of methods such as group work, role play, and the integration of other curriculum subjects into the lesson, these typically received low ratings (poor or weak) and SC noted that teachers needed additional work to be able to use these techniques effectively in 2000 and beyond.

The performance of teachers improved significantly in using varied teaching approaches, pupil participation, effectiveness of teaching methods, and locally available teaching and learning aids.

Impact on communities

In 1999, QUEST helped to mobilize and retrain the 15 percent of school committees in Mangochi district that were not functioning, and provided training to all 231 committees in the district. It also worked to establish PTAs in the 55 percent of schools where there were none; by year's end, only 10 percent of schools had no PTAs. While communities continued to make bricks, they also enhanced their efforts to monitor pupil learning and absenteeism, and several communities began to participate in teaching. In 2000, QUEST spread these community mobilization efforts into Balaka and Blantyre-rural, beginning with school mapping, establishing VBSs and school committee elections and training as they had done with the DEO in Mangochi in 1999.

Communities enhanced their efforts to monitor pupil learning and absenteeism, and several communities began to participate in teaching.

Proposing, funding and implementing local (school and cluster-based) plans through the QUEST Term Initiatives for school improvement were valuable for SC and the communities alike. In the first two terms of 2000, 106 school committees from Mangochi had school improvement projects funded. These included teacher training in various subjects (developing teaching and learning materials, math, English and physical education); school gardening; teacher and community first aid training; materials provision (globes); and improved chalkboards. Projects cost K 6,320 (US $82.02; 45 Kwacha = $1) on average, and a total of K 669,948 (US $8,700.62) was allocated in Mangochi district for these improvements.

SC also honed its approach to diversifying community roles in supporting education through training and ongoing dialogue. At the beginning of QUEST, Mangochi communities primarily made bricks (81 percent) and monitored their pupils' learning (73 percent) and absences (70 percent); very few (3 percent) were involved in teaching. By October 1999, after just one year of implementation, 81 percent of the communities were still molding bricks, but 81 percent now monitored how well their pupils learn, 82 percent monitored absences, and a whopping 80 percent of the communities were involved in teaching. The October 1999 reviews of the head teachers in Mangochi echoed this report of enhanced community involvement; 90 percent noted that school committees were functioning differently and that there was an increase in school improvement projects undertaken jointly by teachers and community members. In 2000, communities came into the classroom more often and got involved in homework and mobilizing against teacher and pupil absenteeism.

At the beginning of QUEST, 3 percent of Mangochi communities were involved in teaching. After one year of implementation, 80 percent were involved in teaching.

While QUEST had an impact on communities, communities were also beginning to have an impact on MOEST policy. During the late fall of 2000, as school schedules were being set for 2001, Mangochi community leaders voiced many complaints about dropouts due to culturally inappropriate school schedules. DEOs, village chiefs, the Minister of Education and two principal secretaries from MOEST met at a national meeting convened on the subject to discuss the details. The problem was a mismatch of school holidays with harvest and initiation rights, during which times children were absent for a number of weeks and often dropped out. These officials promised to consider the input of these community leaders and discuss it further at MOEST.

Handbooks for teacher training and community mobilization

SC's Teacher Training Resource Handbook: *An Innovative Approach to Teaching and Learning* comprises 34 chapters of training topics with very specific objectives, materials, and varied activities and suggested assignments for the teacher trainees. (See appendix for the Table of Contents.)

In 1996, SC, in partnership with UNICEF, had begun drafting a manual entitled *Community Participation in Primary Schools* in both Chichewa and English for training PTA and school committee members and local leaders in their roles in school support. The Chichewa version was printed and is used nationally.

SC also produced a handbook on the effectiveness and impact of cluster school mentorship in response to MOEST's request for documentation on this best practice. This practical document explains how to develop a cluster system and describes the impact of cluster school mentorship and challenges and lessons learned based on the QUEST experience. The handbook describes a cluster, defines how it is organized and who is involved and outlines mentor roles and responsibilities. It also describes the Mentor Teacher's relationship to the head teacher, PEA, DEM, the trainer head teacher, CDA, and the communities and outlines content for training and motivating mentor teachers.

National impact

The VBS and QUEST experiences in Malawi illustrate workable solutions to the urgent needs of preparing teachers and of stimulating communities to become more active in support of local schools. These programs also honed their ability to undertake research and documentation and began to address the HIV/AIDS crisis. SC partnered with DEO staff and communities to establish new school facilities and to meet the needs of teachers for training in a field-based, initial teacher training approach that promotes active teaching and learning. It partnered with PEAs to increase the frequency and improve the content of their supervision visits to schools. It also partnered with PEAs on:

The VBS and QUEST experiences in Malawi illustrate workable solutions to the urgent needs of preparing teachers and of stimulating communities to become more active in support of local schools.

- how to select and train Mentor Teachers to work with PEAs to support teachers within a cluster of schools with observations, feedback and in-service training that promotes active teaching and learning;
- how to mobilize communities in partnership with CDAs and PEAs to take on roles beyond the molding of bricks and the building and maintenance of schools;
- how to encourage and support collaboration between teachers and communities to plan together for school improvements and even request funds for such; and

- how to assess pupils to adjust teacher and community training and insert pupil performance information into local discussions and planning for improving quality.

These experiences and achievements and the people involved in them are invaluable resources for Malawi and SC alike. The partnership with PEAs and CDAs and with the DEO on policy and implementation indicates that the government has adopted some of the experiments introduced by the Village Based Schools.

Notes

[37] Government of Malawi, Ministry of Education, Sports and Culture, *Basic Education Statistics.* (Lilongwe. 1996).

[38] Mundy, Karen. *The Implementation of Educational Reform in Malawi.* (USAID, Washington D.C., 1999) p. 10.

[39] Mwale, J.B.K. *Levels and Patterns of Education Expenditure and Quality of Education in Malawi.* (Center for Education Research and Training, Zomba, 1998) p. 19.

[40] World Bank. *Third Education Sector Credit Project Preparation Mission Aide Memoire,* (World Bank, Washington DC, 1995).

[41] EFA 2000 Assessment Report.

[42] Strickland, Bradford H. and James H. Williams. *Communities and School: A Research Report on Save the Children's Village-Based Schools in Mangochi, Malawi.* (USAID, Washington DC, 1997).

[43] Laugharn, Peter. *Southern Africa Trip Report.* (May 1997) p 2. Peter Laugharn was Field Office Director in Mali and inaugurated the village schools there.

[44] Save the Children. *Survival Skills for Teachers in Village Based Schools.* (Mangochi, Malawi, 1994).

[45] Mwale.

[46] Dowd, Amy Jo. *Teaching and Learning in Mangochi Classrooms: Combining Quantitative and Qualitative Information to Study Twelve Primary Schools in Malawi.* (Creative Associates International, Washington D.C., 1998) Dowd reported that even as the community and School Committee members "had no supervision skills," the SC staff reported that "their presence at the school was enough to make the teachers work." Dowd, *op. cit.*, p. 20.

[47] Dowd, Amy Jo. *Training and Support for Paraprofessional Teachers and School Committees;* Mwale; Tizora, A.

[48] Strickland and Williams, pps. xvii and 60.

[49] Dowd, *Training and Support for Paraprofessional Teachers and School Committees;* and Strickland and Williams.

[50] Dowd, op. cit.; Hyde, Karin L. et al. *Determinants of Educational Achievement and Attainment in Africa: Village-Based Schools in Mangochi, Malawi, an Evaluation.* (Institute for Policy Reform, Washington DC, 1997); Miske, S. Dowd, A.J., *Teaching and Learning in Mangochi Classrooms: Combining Quantitative and Qualitative Information to Study Twelve Primary Schools in Malawi.* (Creative Associates International, Inc., Washington, D.C., 1998); Strickland and Williams.

[51] This policy also led to high rates of teacher transfer, absence and mobility.

[52] At the time, the JCE was the minimum MOEST qualification for teachers. Few teachers hired to teach in the VBS had a JCE when they began teaching.

[53] Dowd, *op.cit.*

[54] Strickland and Williams, p. 42.

[55] Laugharn *op. cit.*, Appendix one, 28 April 1997, p. in response to the Strickland and Williamns report.

[56] Dowd. *Training and Support for Paraprofessional Teachers and School Committees.*

[57] Ibid.

58 Evaluators and observers noted that MIITEP is neither functioning properly nor being fully implemented, that trainees are infrequently visited, supported or given any feedback after they attend the three months of residential training. Further, only an estimated 12,800 of the 16,000 trainees are certified, as trainee dropout and failure on the final exam for certification have raised further challenges. (Sandhaas *et al.*; Dowd, *Training and Support for Paraprofessional Teachers and School Committees*; Mundy; Government of Malawi, Ministry of Education, Sports and Culture, and UK Department for International Development.).

59 Dowd, *op. cit.*; Miske and Dowd.

60 Strickland and Williams.

61 Ibid.

62 Hyde *et al.*, p. 53.

63 Miske and her Malawian research observation team saw this in action.

64 The subjects are those listed plus religion, which was left out in agreement with the primarily Muslim communities which had a separate infrastructure and schedule for teaching religion. Several class schedules were altered to meet these needs in agreements negotiated between communities, teachers, and SC.

65 Hyde *et al.* p. 24.

66 One hotly debated point not noted here previously was class size. SC attempted, with mixed results, to keep the classes at or below 60 pupils per VBS teacher compared to government classes of between 84 and 100 pupils per trained teacher. Miske and her team in early 1998 saw a great difference between enrollment and attendance in the government classrooms so it is not clear that SC's limited ability to cap class size the and actual attendance at the government schools did not moot the differences in class size. All teachers struggle with large classes, a problem that continues to plague Malawian primary schools.

67 Miske and Dowd, p. 2.

68 The handbook was translated into French for the Haiti community schools and is being distributed to the different field offices for testing and adaptation in other countries where SC trains teachers.

69 IEQ was a USAID project aimed to improve educational quality in target countries via research and partnerships between governments, researchers and practitioners. In this sense, it brought similar resources to bear from the US-government perspective: links to research expertise and policy makers.

70 Government of Malawi, Ministry of Education, Sports and Culture, *Policy and Investment Framework*. (Ministry of Education Sports and Culture, Malawi, 2000).

71 Lester Namathaka, telephone conversation with author, 25 January 2000.

72 Sandhaas *et al.*, Government of Malawi, Ministry of Education, Sports and Culture, and UK Department for International Development.

73 *EFA 2000 Assessment Report*; Government of Malawi, Ministry of Education, Sports and Culture Policy and Investment Framework.

74 Government of Malawi, Ministry of Education, Sports and Culture, and UK Department for International Development.

75 Ibid.

76 Dowd, Amy Jo. *Learning Requires Qualified Teachers, Good Teaching and Community Support in Malawi.*(Ed.D. Dissertation, Harvard University, 2001).

77 Standard 3 and 4 girls improved more on average than their male colleagues: QUEST was effectively closing the gender gap or lower scoring girls were dropping out, or both.

78 Namathaka, Lester, Francis Mabeti and Amy Jo Dowd. *Report on Drop Out, Repetition, and Pupil Performance 1999–2000* (Paper presented at the Community Schools Program Learning Group meeting of Save the Children, Kolondieba, Mali, June 2001).

References

Dowd, Amy Jo. *Learning Requires Qualified Teachers, Good Teaching and Community Support in Malawi*. (Ed.D. Dissertation, Harvard University, 2001)

---- *Teaching and Learning in Mangochi Classrooms: Combining Quantitative and Qualitative Information to Study Twelve Primary Schools in Malawi*. (Creative Associates International, Washington D.C., 1998)

---- *Training and Support for Paraprofessional Teachers and School Committees*

Government of Malawi, Ministry of Education, Sports and Culture, *Basic Education Statistics*. (Lilongwe, 1996)

---- *Policy and Investment Framework*. (Malawi, 2000)

Namathaka, Lester, Francis Mabeti and Amy Jo Dowd. *Report on Drop Out, Repetition, and Pupil Performance 1999–2000* (Paper presented at the Community Schools Program Learning Group meeting of Save the Children, Kolondieba, Mali, June 2001)

Miske, S. and Amy Jo Dowd. Teaching and Learning in Mangochi Classrooms: *Combining Quantitative and Qualitative Information to Study Twelve Primary Schools in Malawi*. (Creative Associates International, Inc., Washington D.C., 1998)

Mundy, Karen. *The Implementation of Educational Reform in Malawi*. (USAID, Washington D.C., 1999)

Mwale, J.B. Kuthemba. *Levels and Patterns of Education Expenditure and Quality of Education in Malawi*. (Center for Education Research and Training, Zomba, 1998)

Save the Children. *Survival Skills for Teachers in Village Based Schools*. (Mangochi, Malawi, 1994)

Strickland, Bradford H. and James H. Williams. *Communities and School: A Research Report on Save the Children's Village-Based Schools in Mangochi, Malawi*. (USAID, Washington DC, 1997)

World Bank. Third Education Sector Credit Project Preparation Mission Aide Memoire, (World Bank, Washington DC, 1995)

Appendix: Malawi Teacher Training Resource Handbook: An Innovative Approach to Teaching and Learning

Table of Contents

1. Who is an effective Teacher 2
2. How Children Learn 6
3. (A) Schemes of Work...11
    (B) Records of Work... 15
4. The Lesson 19
5. Effective Methods of Teaching 22
    (A) Demonstration Method...35
    (B) Pair Work Method...38
    (C) Group Work Method...42
    (D) Role Play Method...46
    (E) Focus Group Discussion Method......................................51
    (F) Games 56
    (G) Songs and Rhymes...61
6. Effective Beginning of a Lesson..65
7. How to Reinforce Learning...68
8. Variation Technique..72
9. Questioning Technique 76
10. Effective Ending of a Lesson..80
11. Effective use of a Chalkboard..84
12. Illustration Technique...88
13. Teaching and Learning Materials with Emphasis on Locally
    Available Materials 98
14. Effective Lesson Presentation.. 103
15. Guidelines for Successful Teaching 107
16. Integration of Subjects 112
17. Creating a Conducive Environment for Learning................... 118
18. Creating Learning Centers 125
19. Assessment of Pupils Achievement 130
20. Marking Pupils' Work... 135
21. Supervision of homework by Teachers and Parents................ 139

22. How to Assist Slow Learners 144

23. Improving Teaching through Clinic Supervision 149

24. Life Skills... 155

25. Interactive Reading Skills 163

26. Writing Skills 168

27. Achieving Permanent Numeracy... 175

28. Community Participation in Curriculum Design and
    Implementation... 179

29. Community Participation in Curriculum Design and
    Implementation Follow-up Practice 183

30. Quality School Management 187

31. Introducing Beginners to School Life.. 191

32. Community Empowerment.. 195

33. Water and Sanitation.. 199

Appendices.. 204

 Appendix A: Sample Record of Work.. 205

 Appendix B: Appraisal Guide for the Skill of Introduction 206

 Appendix C: Appraisal Guide for Skill Reinforcement............................. 207

 Appendix D: Appraisal Guide for the Variation Technique 208

 Appendix E: Appraisal Guide for the Questioning Technique 209

 Appendix F: Appraisal Guide for the Skill of Closure................................ 210

Chapter 4

Ethiopia, 1992–2001: Helping Communities Fill the Education Gap

Fred Wood and Mengistu Edo Koricha

Teaching in Ethiopia at a Save the Children school that is under construction.
Photo credit: Michael Bisceglie

Education challenges in Ethiopia today[79]

The national education system in Ethiopia has experienced tremendous stress in recent years. With more than 13.6 million children of primary school age—a population larger than that of many African nations—of which some 85 percent are rural, it is difficult to create the conditions to meet the challenge of Education for All. Indeed, in 1998 the Ethiopian government released this depressing statistic: "...only 30 percent of school age children were enrolled in school....less than half the average of sub-Saharan Africa."[80]

The effort to attain EFA has caused schools to be overfilled without a concomitant growth in available teachers and schools. First grade classrooms have as many as 150 children. Many school buildings are old, poorly ventilated and lit, and structurally fragile, which may contribute to a low demand for education. Only 22 percent of children who begin first grade actually complete eighth grade, which concludes primary education. Dropout rates between first and second grade are often as high as 28 percent. High dropout and repetition rates contribute to educational inefficiency, as does inefficient public expenditure in the education sector.

Enrollment rates outpace growth in educational inputs

Since 1996, when 4,468,294 children were enrolled in primary schools, primary school enrollments have grown at an average annual rate of 11.8 percent. Six years later, there were 8,743,265 children enrolled. Schools had to accommodate 4.3 million more children in six years but even this increase belies the overall low enrollments, high gender and regional disparities and poor quality of education. In 2002, the gross enrollment rate (GER)[81] was 64.4 percent, far below the sub-Saharan average. Still, this figure represents a growth rate of nearly 96 percent in primary education in just six years. Disaggregated for gender and region, the figures show that girls and children in rural areas, particularly in the Afar and Somali regions, are the most disadvantaged in terms of access and achievement. The 2002 GER for boys was 74.6 percent and for girls 53.8 percent, a gender gap of 20.8 percent in favor of boys.

Table 4.1: Ethiopia's Widening Gender Gap in Enrollment

Year	Boys: GER	Girls: GER	Total	Gender Gap	Gender Parity index
1994/95	31.7	20.4	26.2	11.3	0.64
1995/96	36.6	22.7	30.1	13.3	0.62
1996/97	43.2	26.0	34.7	17.0	0.60
1997/98	52.2	31.2	41.8	21.8	0.60

Source: Improving Retention with Special Focus on Girls, MOE/BESO, 1999, page 4.

While primary school enrollments grew at nearly 12 percent a year between 1996 and 2002, the number of teachers increased on average by only 4 percent a year, while the number of primary schools grew at an average annual rate of 3.1 percent a year. Consequently, the pupil/teacher ratio increased from 57/1 to 73/1. Such ratios tend to hamstring teachers and, hence, the quality of education. What's more, at second cycle level (the last four years of primary school, grades 5–8) few teachers are qualified. In 2002/2003, only 30.9 percent of the 46,872 second cycle primary school teachers were trained. Finally, textbooks and other materials necessary for education quality are scarce.

A mother brings her child to the Gode Therapeutic Feeding Center in Ethiopia.
Photo credit: Michael Bisceglie

The experience of Save the Children

Save the Children first got involved in Ethiopia during the drought and famine of the mid-1980s, with an emphasis on relief work. As the famine slowly abated, the agency chose to move away from general development work towards promoting specialized, sector-focused skills. The themes for the new sector-focused plans—health and education—seemed to fit well with Ethiopia's changing needs and stated interests. The road was open for moving forward with the new strategy.

The goal of involving local NGOs was to build local capacity to sustain the enterprise once the international funder and implementer had left the scene.

Save the Children's efforts on behalf of education in Ethiopia have taken multiple forms, including targeting rural, pastoralist communities far removed from all public services. Central to all these efforts is the engagement of local NGOs in the various aspects of the enterprise, from program conception to implementation to the federation of the NGOs into a lobbying group. The goal was to build local capacity to sustain the enterprise once the international funder and implementer had left the scene.

For example, Save the Children had embarked in the early 1990s on a small-scale community development effort in what was to become the Afar Region. The nomadic life-style of many Afar communities, the evident poverty and the constant threat of renewed drought and famine attracted Save the Children at a time when education was barely on the agenda. The work with the Afars was interesting, but at a time when a new, radically different federal education policy was taking shape, it was peripheral to the main educational debate.

A nomad in front of her home.

Photo credit: Michael Bisceglie

Apart from the rural Afar work, Save the Children was also working in Addis Ababa with a project to address the needs of street children. The project sought to rehabilitate them after life on the street and to convey more positive behaviors as well as usable skills. The project was in due course transferred to an Ethiopian NGO and continues to this day.

The Basic Education Structural Overhaul (BESO)

In 1995, USAID issued a request for assistance focusing on the "structural overhaul" of basic education. The goal was to strengthen the Federal Ministry of Education by putting into place the systems necessary to support reform. This provided an opportunity to test a new, decentralized structure focused on local administrative units (*woredas*) in the vast, poor and culturally diverse region known SNNPRS (the Southern Nations, Nationalities and Peoples Regional State) and Tigray Regional State. This area had an abundance of local languages and, certainly at the outset, very little capacity to provide quality education.

A central element of the new education strategy, called BESO (Basic Education Structural Overhaul) was community mobilization. Merely legislating decentralization was insufficient. This would have to be complemented by equipping the rudimentary *woreda* offices and devising training and capacity building systems for the *woreda* officials, for the schools and for the parents' groups—without whose efforts the resources available to achieve the goals of reform would be inadequate. Obviously, the questions of the language of instruction and the accompanying materials were critical. The widening gender gap in education was also a concern.

> *Training and capacity building were needed for the woreda officials, for schools and for parents' groups.*

The BESO study on girls' retention pointed out that the problem differed by region: Addis Ababa had achieved parity of enrollment in 1993, Tigray had not greatly changed but "….in other regions for which current data is available, the gap is widening.[82]

There were promising efforts to address this problem elsewhere in Africa. SC's work in southern Mali was attracting widespread interest due to its low cost, successes in community engagement and ability to attract equal numbers of boys and girls. The BESO pilot project in Awassa district, in the SNNPRS, was itself demonstrating what could be accomplished by local councils to support access, at least in areas that were relatively accessible. The clear message was that there was little chance of realizing the EFA goals by warming over the old ways of doing things while delivering them in greater quantity. A different strategy was required.

All of this gradually led to a second phase of the BESO program, with a component, BESO II-SCOPE (Strengthening Communities through Partnerships for Education), implemented by Save the Children. The underlying idea was that if the basic education system in Ethiopia was to move forward, the main emphasis had to be on increasing community participation in education management and building the *woredas'* capacity to perform their stated task. Also important would be an expanded search for low-cost, alternative methods of providing basic education services, and educating and training government officials, as well as reaching out to include other regions and working with state and federal governments to change a number of fixed practices.

> *If the basic education system in Ethiopia was to move forward, the main emphasis had to be on increasing community participation in education management and building the woredas' capacity to perform their stated task.*

A second Education Sector Development Program was launched in 2001/2002, with the aim of bringing the federal government and the interested NGOs together around the concept of Alternative Basic Education (ABE): combining funding and putting aside some of the traditional resistance from the education hierarchy to practices such as using uncertified teachers and training them on the job.

Save the Children and its fellow NGOs were already pointing towards important new policy trends, even before the Dakar Forum of 2000. The final Dakar document did, however, state quite bluntly that "….by 2015, all children, particularly girls, children in difficult circumstances and those belonging to ethnic minorities [shall] have access to and complete free and compulsory primary education of good quality."

The repercussions in Ethiopia's education and training policies were straightforward. An immediate doubling of children attending school, from 3.1 million to 7 million, was foreseen. Girls, especially those living in rural areas, would increase their attendance from 38 to 45 percent. Textbooks in core subjects would be supplied to every child. Facilities and teacher training would be improved. As ever, the problem lay not in the perception of the problem, but much more in the preparedness to do something about it.

Communities would have to be engaged in a stronger, more structured way than before.

The Federal Ministry of Education was committed to these goals, but it did not have the resources to take on the EFA task alone. This would have to be a shared task and communities would have to be engaged in a stronger, more structured way than before. Hence the Ministry's guideline of 2001 hits hard: "It has now become crucial to amend the existing organization of educational management to include representatives of the community, education professionals, directors, teachers and supervisors, clearly indicating their respective power, responsibility and accountability in the system … to create a conducive atmosphere whereby communities, particularly parents, can actively participate in educational activities." [83]

BESO II-SCOPE: 2002–2007 Supporting local administrations

The Ministry's determination to ensure that the burden of expansion was shared had already been reflected in various NGO efforts to launch "community schools." In these, the responsibility for delivering the service was shared between the *woreda*, the NGO and the local community, or *kebele*. The BESO II-SCOPE project had already begun to address one central issue, strengthening community-government partnership.

One of the new project's first efforts was to set out its view of how BESO II-SCOPE would complement the Ministry of Education's training strategy, particularly the Ministry's manual on *School Organization, Community Participation and Financial Management*, highlighting the emerging role of Parent Teacher Associations. Close relations with these were "….critical for improved pupil retention, achievement and greater gender parity……the vital goals of BESO II."[84] The content of the training program over a three-year period was set out as follows:

Table 4.2: BESO II Training for Woreda Education Offices and PTAs

Content	Activities
Decentralization of the school management system	<ul><li>New Education and Training policy and its implementation strategy</li><li>Decentralization of education management</li><li>The roles of the community in the education system</li><li>The roles and responsibilities of PTAs, Village Education and Training Boards and others as stated in the MOE paper</li><li>Concepts and practices of PTAs' accountability to the community and local Education and Training Board</li><li>The concept of gender equity in the decentralization of education management</li></ul>
Action plan development and gender mainstreaming in schools	<ul><li>Gender PLA/PRA techniques in actively engaging the community in gender planning, implementation and monitoring of school activities</li><li>Designing school gender policy</li><li>Designing school action plan</li><li>Writing grant proposals</li><li>Gender responsive participatory monitoring and evaluation</li></ul>
School finance and management of materials	<ul><li>Income-generating activities. Organizing local fund-raising events and encouraging income-generating practices in the school</li><li>Basic skills in financial record keeping/book keeping and budgeting</li><li>Property management (store keeping, recording, procurement)</li></ul>

Source: BESO II Training for Program Development

BESO II-SCOPE was launched with the understanding that its main task was capacity-building and its main target was the WEO, the new, localized governance system for basic education. The outcomes of the training program aspired to reflect this. The intended outcomes were:

1. Participants will share information on the New Education and Training Policy and Strategy and be able to explain the new role of communities, especially of PTAs, in education.
2. Participants will work with community members, carry out administrative and organizational communications tasks and explain their needs and aspirations.
3. Participants will be able to develop and implement community-defined action plans and activities in support of basic education.
4. Schools will be able to develop and implement annual operational plans reflecting the principles of the gender equity policy statement.
5. Participants will act as change agents by advocating gender equity in basic education.
6. Participants will develop skills for cooperative group decision-making.

7. Participants will be able to mobilize human, financial and material resources and be able to design strategies for the sustainability of school-based practices; and

8. Participants will be able to discuss existing social problems, relate them to their settings and suggest potential solutions.

The initial vision of BESO II-SCOPE in trying to work with the *woreda* structure to put in place a cadre of motivated and alert leaders who would drive the "overhaul" forward is very clear. It certainly added an important dimension to what BESO II sought to do, supplementing "policy" work in Addis Ababa and limited field work with an across-the-board effort with those basic institutions and individuals essential to the implementation of the new structure of education.

The justification for BESO II-SCOPE's prioritizing capacity-building at the community and *woreda* level was the speed at which the expansion program proceeded. In BESO II-SCOPE's first cohort, 459 schools were associated with the program, serving 257,000 children. In the second wave, a further 540 schools were added. By mid-2004, approximately half a million children were being served. When the third cohort joined (mid-2005), a further 541 schools were added, with an estimated 750,000 additional children. BESO II-SCOPE's target in terms of coverage has therefore been achieved.[85]

Responding to a food crisis, 2002

Achieving the numerical targets is all the more remarkable since, as the project began to move ahead, Ethiopia was revisited in 2002 by another in the cycle of periodic droughts that afflict the Horn of Africa, necessitating immediate food relief. During the severe droughts of the 1980s, heavy criticism had been leveled at both Ethiopia and the relief agencies for their tardiness in responding to the crisis, and, in some cases, their inability to deliver food to the neediest communities. In 2002, the response was very different. Food was to some degree pre-positioned. USAID was committed to using all available "tools" to make sure that accurate information on the drought situation was known at the right levels and that all the structures with which USAID was engaged at the grassroots level were adapted swiftly as feeding points for hungry children.

> *The woredas were able to respond to urgent human need and to prepare and deliver a warm meal to all attending students twice a day.*

BESO II-SCOPE, which was focused on building the *woredas* to deliver basic education services, was soon facing a new role: working through the *woredas* to ensure that children were fed, with USAID increasing its support substantially to cover additional food supply. It is to the great credit of BESO II-SCOPE and the *woredas* with which it is working that they were able to handle this major switch of purpose in response to urgent human need, and to prepare and deliver a warm meal to all attending students (and a few others besides) twice a day.

It is also significant that, in accommodating the need for a vast expansion of school feeding, BESO II-SCOPE still maintained its basic educational purposes: expanding the schools network through community involvement; strengthening school committees and efforts to refurbish schools; increasing the capacity of teachers and parents to address their shared problems; and that it remained on course to achieve its numerical targets.

School children attend class outside while their new school building is being constructed.
Photo credit: Michael Bisceglie.

The final word on BESO II-SCOPE is not yet written, but since its inception in 2002 it has shown itself capable of building PTA and *woreda* capacity; supplementing the range of purposes which schools can address (such as emergency feeding) and expanding the network of schools. It is an example of the wider application to broader ends of the community school principles—local participation, local management, and local contributions towards capital costs—with which Save the Children has become identified. The sight of newly-built school kitchens staffed by local women delivering a warm meal twice a day to long lines of students at the end of a completed school session powerfully illustrates what SCOPE has accomplished.

> *BESO II-SCOPE is an example of the wider application to broader ends of the community school principles—local participation, local management, and local contributions towards capital costs—with which Save the Children has become identified.*

Yet arguably, the real test of SC's principles, its insistence on organized community action as the core of what it seeks to do, could not be demonstrated in a program as generously funded and supported as is the case with BESO II. BESO II takes demonstrated principles and brings them to scale to serve wider ends, while drawing upon substantial external assistance. The real issue is the degree to which the principle can be used to attain the same ends without the kinds of donor support that BESO II has enjoyed. From this standpoint, the PIE Project offers a more pertinent illustration to those (governments, organizations) struggling with the cost issue in their response to the EFA goal.[86]

The real issue is whether the principle of community action can be used to attain the same ends without substantial external assistance.

Two girls wait for their PIE school to open.

Photo credit: Michael Bisceglie

The Project for Innovations in Education (PIE) 1997–2003

PIE came about following USAID's decision to concentrate BESO I on reinforcing and restoring the Ministry of Education and its satellites, while limiting field work on the role of communities in developing basic education. At the same time, Save the Children was convinced that the problem of access to education needed to be treated with a greater degree of urgency and originality, since Ethiopia was still relatively shaky. Although the civil war had ended in 1992, occasional outbreaks of fighting still occurred on the Eritrean border. The country could not live comfortably with large numbers of youth who had had virtually no exposure to education.

Save the Children was able to respond by negotiating with its long-standing supporter, the Banyan Tree Foundation, which has a particular interest in supporting non-governmental action to bring about change in education. Outwardly, Ethiopia was wide open to such a strategy. The issue at the planning stage was whether the Ethiopian non-governmental sector, at that time in an early stage of development, could support the kinds of initiatives needed to meet the country's needs. The goal at the end (2003) was to assess the degree to which community-generated institutions—schools, parents' committees, other support systems and new entities—could stand on their own feet, main-

The goal of PIE was to assess the degree to which community-generated institutions—schools, PTAs, etc.—could stand on their own feet, and even aim for other targets of community action.

taining both staff and structure and even aiming for other targets in the area of community action. Hence, PIE became a six year exploration (1997–2003) of aspects of the conundrum of "sustainability" in development action.

The initial three-year task (1997–2000) was to identify and strengthen 15 selected local NGOs, gradually weeding out those that clearly would not be able to survive without external support. The second phase was to progressively disengage, transferring responsibility to autonomous local NGOs deemed to be viable in their delivery of basic education services. As the end of a second three-year period approached, Save the Children would be able to move away and transfer the responsibility for PIE schools into the hands of local organizations capable not only of managing the project but, crucially, of raising funds to ensure that the work would continue. This, at least, was the aspiration.

SC worked to build in the Ethiopian NGOs the skills needed to become self-reliant; developing NGO capacity by training trainers in programmatic and institutional development, experience-sharing, mentoring and coaching.

To help this process on its way, PACT, an international NGO operating in Ethiopia since the 1980s, offered an initial assessment of NGO organizational capacity. Save the Children worked systematically to build in the Ethiopian NGOs the skills needed to become self-reliant, developing NGO capacity by training trainers in programmatic and institutional development, experience sharing, mentoring, and coaching. For organizational training, Save the Children collaborated with the Ethiopian Management Institute. A series of workshops concentrated on fund-raising, including proposal-writing, public relations and speaking skills.

A teacher in a PIE school uses cut-out letters to teach the alphabet.

Photo credit: Michael Bisceglie

This process was later reinforced by the emergence of BEN (the Basic Education Network) which took on the task of mutual support initially within, but ultimately beyond, the PIE group of projects. BEN was in fact a PIE creation and has itself been quite successful in attracting its own funding from international donors as well as offering paid services to members. BEN now appears to have an assured future as a force for basic education complementing the support efforts of the federal ministry.

A community moves toward self-reliance

PIE takes many forms and has a variety of focal points. One of the most significant examples is the effort of the small community group in Guraghe (the Guraghe People's Self-help Development Organization), part of the first generation of PIE schools. Seven schools fall under the organization's umbrella, each comprising a small citizen's-based organization.

Guraghe lies just over the boundary between southern Oromia and the Southern People's Region. The contrast with neighboring Oromia is very marked. Local resources are almost all agricultural. The prospects of a local community group generating the resources to maintain a four-unit primary school, let alone, as they confidently state, expand it to complete the full primary cycle, are indeed challenging. Yet on closer inspection, there are distinct signs that the Guraghe school is not about to expire quietly.

Children playing ball outside their school.

Photo credit: Michael Bisceglie

The school is well made, purely from locally materials, and is in good order. Students show the usual enthusiasm despite overcrowded classrooms, over one hundred to a class (an exception to the average class size of Save the Children community schools of 50 pupils), rudimentary desks and shared work books. Teachers, none "certificated," appear determined to follow whichever course will lead them to full certification. They are confident in class, aware of their task and open to further training. The contrast with the traditional, highly didactic Ethiopian teacher is marked. The fact that the teachers are also fully committed to the school association, serve with parents on the school management committee and share in the collective labor also conveys a strong impression that, at least in Guraghe, things are turning around.

Teachers, none "certified," are confident in class and open to further training. They are also fully committed to the school association and share in collective labor.

The community dimension is very evident. The school management committee is active and pressing for the school to be expanded regardless of the implications for recurrent costs. Parents, teachers and students have taken the government's urging regarding education and production very seriously. The natural resources surrounding the school are already being put to good use. A sizeable school potato field is growing well. Nearby, a tree nursery will soon be in a position to market eucalyptus saplings—fast growing, straight and in high demand in the area. But it is clear that no matter how much effort the committee puts into local production, this will still not be enough to maintain the school at the present level, let alone expand it.

The second dimension to their fund-raising strategy enters at this point. The local people have a reputation for hard work and reliability. Many have

The school committee has set up a support committee based in Addis Ababa that supplements the schools' own fundraising efforts.

migrated to Addis Ababa to seek paid employment, and have done well. Equally, many retain their ties to their home area. The school committee saw an opportunity here and moved to set up a support committee based in Addis Ababa that supplements the school's own fundraising efforts. The Addis committee and the local school management committee plan together and show every sign that their immediate goal of establishing a full primary school will be achieved. The fifth grade is already full. Plans are in place for still further expansion both to complete the primary structure and to add a skills training center. In short, for the moment in Guraghe at least, self-reliance seems to be working.

Both support groups, in Guraghe and in Addis Ababa, are aware of the bigger challenge. Supposing, indeed, they were to complete the primary phase; this would not be sufficient in itself to prepare the young people of Guraghe for employment. Already, discussion has begun about a new project of basic skills training for out-of-school youth on school land. The unsolved issue remains what kind of skills will allow these young people either to slot easily into the Addis Ababa job market, or to transform the green hills of Guraghe into a real economic resource.

Discussion has begun about a new project of basic skills training for out-of-school youth on school land.

Looking at PIE overall in its final year[87] a remarkable range of creative action is displayed, all with the same theoretical core: that local organizations can be "reared" to be responsible for their social institutions and that with this kind of leadership, these institutions will endure. Save the Children, having managed the PIE project through its initial, experimental phases, sees the project's accomplishment this way: "PIE builds on the values and needs of children and their communities by working towards bringing education to the people rather than people to education."

PIE brings various stakeholders (communities, local NGOs and government) constructively together to devise community-based systems of affordable, quality, basic education that is flexible enough to fit the lifestyle of the respective community; develop relevant learning packages and design program activities. Among the creative solutions that have emerged are: "home schooling for girls in Somali region; integrating children with disabilities….in early childhood education; an NGO network for wider impact and policy influence; developing teacher support systems and active learning facilitation methods and creating community-government links at the local level to mobilize and sustain resources." [88]

> *Local organizations can be "reared" to be responsible for their social institutions and with this kind of leadership, these institutions will endure.*

By mid-2004, PIE's support system had reached 27 centers, with a total enrollment of 6,483 (48.5 percent girls). In 2003/4, enrollment in PIE-related primary schools increased by 18.5 percent. A distance education program for PIE trainers was launched. Support was increased for both BEN and the Oromia Education Bureau in its education planning. Many of the centers in the PIE-linked pioneer wave were financially autonomous agencies.

A school committee member teaches his children while a new school is being built.
Photo credit: Michael Bisceglie.

The One Love Schools 2001–2004

The picture is slightly different with the One Love Schools, created through a philanthropic act by Bob Marley[89] and friends to support basic education in Ethiopia. During his lifetime, Bob Marley had strong ties with Ethiopia through the Rastafarian movement. With funding from the Lurie Foundation, Save the Children became the implementing agency in selecting locations and mobilizing communities to construct schools and providing pedagogical backing for the teachers. Twenty One Love Schools are now operating in the Oromia and Somali regions, serving more than 5,000 students, almost 40 percent of whom are girls.

These schools directly address the issue of access. They make no claim to model development that leads to sustainability, as in the PIE Project. The notion here is much simpler: communities, with little prompting, will get together to build serviceable schools from local materials, find teachers, and maintain the facility at a basic level. Again, this is in line with the federal guideline referred to earlier.

The act of building and maintaining a school, would, it is assumed, be enough to guarantee its short-term existence. Its long-term existence would be brought about by Save the Children's efforts to raise the level of pedagogy through upgrading the teachers and thus the demonstrated performance of the children. Ultimately the local *woreda* would step in and cover the recurrent costs, especially once teachers had achieved the "certification" stage. Possibly the *woreda* itself might have sufficient resources to cover teachers' salaries. A critical element is whether Save the Children will have enough resources to continue to provide technical support to the teachers in these schools.

To some degree this challenge is being met, with the original connection between Save the Children and the Lurie Foundation being revived. As a tribute to Bob Marley's commitment to Ethiopia and to education, his son, Ziggy Marley, has maintained the original pledge made to Save the Children, that at least some of the proceeds of the Marley inheritance would be devoted to the support of these schools.

> The One Love project has been successful in linking woreda officials with their respective communities to design, plan, implement and supervise basic education activities, literally from the ground up.

The One Love schools provide a micro version of the Ethiopian Government's wish to test out the viability of community management and implementation, at *woreda* and *kebele* level. While the project is now drawing to a close, it is clear that in Oromia and Somali the project has been successful in linking *woreda* officials with their respective communities to design, plan, implement and supervise basic education activities, literally from the ground up. Not only have 20 low-cost primary schools been constructed that are now fully functioning, school management committees have also been trained in line with new national policy. Save the Children staff has conducted regular teacher support efforts that go well beyond organizing parents to construct a building. Currently the schools accommodate 5,089 students, 37.34 percent of whom are girls.

Given that Save the Children sponsorship[90] schools (see below) have shown what a relatively small additional flow of cash can achieve, the One Love

Schools' future looks promising as well. The sponsorship schools too have a modest, regular cash input covering teachers. The issue here is not so much the volume of funds, but a regular, dependable flow to support a long-term approach to training and upgrading.

Teaching in a classroom under construction.

Photo credit: Michael Bisceglie

Child sponsorship schools, 2001–2005: an internal funding mechanism

SC's child sponsorship program, a relative latecomer to Ethiopia, is fairly small. It supports nine schools (serving 2,431 students, more than 48 percent of whom are girls) in Woliso *woreda* in Oromia Region. These schools dovetail with the PIE and One Love schools. The design is basically the same including building materials used, although what the sponsorship school offers is more generous. The sponsorship program provides a more comprehensive package of services: classes with a better teacher/pupil ratio and trained teachers; a school health and nutrition program; clean water supply and sanitary facilities; the beginnings of an early childhood development program and an out-of-school program for youth. Here, too, there is a major contribution of community labor in the building of the schools.

> *The child sponsorship program provides classes with a better teacher/pupil ratio and trained teachers; a health and nutrition program; clean water and sanitation; an early childhood development program; and an out-of-school program for youth.*

Save the Children's international child sponsorship program ensures that modest but regular support funds flow to the Woliso Schools. This means that while outwardly the schools are very similar to other Save the Children efforts, there are two key differences on the inside. The sponsorship schools' generous teacher/pupil ratio (1/45) ensures a greater degree of child-centered education. The contrast even with BESO schools where ratios of above 1/100 still prevail is remarkable. Secondly, the sponsorship system makes it possible to provide learning and teaching materials, and, however modest, on-going classroom follow-up and frequent supervisory visits from Save the Children education staff. This creates a feeling on the part of the teacher that he or she is indeed supported and has someone to turn to when problems come up. The importance of this in rural Africa cannot be overstated.

The first five schools were modeled on the PIE schools; they were very low-cost, estimated at US $10,000 per unit though the actual cost was closer to US $15,000. This is still a rock bottom price for a school with five classrooms, benches and books for all students, two latrines, five teachers and regular professional supervision. As in earlier cases, the community contributed roughly 10 percent of the capital costs, mostly in labor and materials. The next wave of nine schools followed a slightly more expensive model (US $20,000—US $22,000 per unit) owing to an increase in teacher support.[91]

A class in session in a sponsorship school.

Photo credit: Michael Bisceglie

The positive learning climate in the sponsorship schools illustrates that with very little money, a rudimentary learning situation can readily be turned into a more positive one. There are many lessons here for the never-ending debate on what constitutes quality in basic education in Africa, especially in rural areas.

There is a critical lesson to be learned for all "aid" agencies looking to reduce the level of support for basic education to a minimum, yet maintain a sustainable model. It is clear that the cost reduction process can go too far and easily reach a stage where the educational experience itself may be threatened. With modest funds, the Save the Children sponsorship school can provide a decent desk, a modest supply of books and backing for teachers. Not much in itself, but for a school in Woliso District ten miles off the main highway along a muddy track and across two rivers, it is transformative.

The Pastoralist Education Project (PEP): 2002–2004

Save the Children's most recent innovative effort in basic education is the Pastoralist Education Project (2002–2004), an AID-funded, relatively small-scale effort aimed at meeting the needs of very in-accessible, cattle-herding and semi-settled groups. These efforts have been directed at different locations in the sparsely populated, but culturally and linguistically homogeneous Somali region.[92]

With very little money, a rudimentary learning situation can readily be turned into a more positive one.

The Somalis have herded cattle and camels through these lands for centuries. They have a very strong sense of identity bolstered by their powerful clan system and only in a few instances are beginning to adopt a more settled life-style. The political frontier between Ethiopia and Somalia has meant little to them in the past. Families passed across regardless of the alien notion of frontier. Today, with more tension along the border and Somalia still politically unstable, the tendency to move far afield in search of water and pasture is somewhat reduced. Indeed, the Somali pastoralist community now divides into pastoralists and agro-pastoralists: people who, when nature permits, may settle for a while and turn to some limited cultivation before again moving on.

Recognizing the special difficulties faced by mobile populations with regard to schooling, the purpose of PEP was to work with local people, especially local clan leaders, to bring opportunities for learning, increase understanding of the learning process among untrained teachers and, thereby, improve the environment for formal learning among pastoralist children.

Pastoralists need to have confidence that education will relate to their mobile lifestyle and recognize the realities of their culture.

Relating education to the pastoralist way of life has always been challenging. From the outset, it was understood that meeting these goals would require different delivery systems to fit the pastoralist way of life and that, given the strength of traditional leadership and the clan system, these systems could not be developed without community support. It was also accepted that traditional views of the "curriculum" would simply not work in this context and would have to be rethought. Pastoralists are not opposed to education but they need to have confidence that education will relate to their mobile lifestyle and recognize the realities of their culture.

An Ethiopian boy.

Photo credti: Jeffrey Gettleman

The focus of the Save the Children project is the Liben and Filtu *woredas* in the extreme south of Ethiopia. There is little tradition of formal education in the area other than Koranic schools[93] which concentrate on memorizing the Koran. Traditionally, teachers in Koranic schools were paid by parents once their students had demonstrably reached certain goals in the memorization process. Some elements of this system still persist today and have carried over into SC's attempts to complement the Koranic schools with more westernized forms of basic education.

The schools operate for the most part in the open air, in the shade of a tree. The teacher for the Koranic school and for the secular school can be one and the same person. The school day divides into Koranic and non-Koranic phases. On reaching the end of the time devoted to Koranic instruction in Arabic (itself somewhat flexible), the teacher simply switches to the secular curriculum in Somali, using tattered texts which have survived from previous, more settled days in Somalia. Materials in the Koranic school consist of ink made from charcoal and milk and an elongated wooden board on which passages of the Koran are written and recited.

The planners of PEP were presented with a very fluid situation. Part of the Somali community was clearly becoming more inclined to settle. During the recent drought, the population tended to cluster around food distribution points. The drought took a large toll on livestock, again reinforcing the tendency to cluster. With the return of good rains, however, many reverted to their previous nomadic or semi-nomadic living patterns.

While no single system of delivery could work in a situation like this, it has been possible to establish "permanent schools" which have the added effect, if well received by the local people, of strengthening the trend towards settling in one place. Eight such "permanent" schools providing basic education for more than 900 children were established, using the community self-help approach. Attendance was good in the wet season when the grass was up and feeding the livestock presented no difficulty. The test will come when the rains fade and the summer heat returns. And although efforts to revise the curriculum seem to have had mixed success, PEP did produce relevant materials on environmental science for lower primary grades and a resource book for teachers in Oromia PEP schools by actively involving the pastoralists and other stakeholders during the development process.

When the group is ready to move, the teacher, himself a pastoralist, stows the school's meager equipment on the back of a camel.

The strategy for permanent schools was best suited to semi-nomadic peoples. To reach the true pastoralists, two other strategies were introduced: the "shade" schools that serve the needs of semi-settled people and can be easily upgraded should the community be inclined to the "permanent" category; and mobile centers where the teacher, himself a pastoralist, joins a particular group as a full member. When the group is ready to move, he stows the school's meager equipment on the back of a camel. When the group moves, the "school" and teacher take to the road as well. It is estimated that the satellite and mobile centers cater for approximately 300 students. Overall, PEP reaches a total of 1,323 pupils, 27 percent of whom are girls.

The primary strength of the mobile school is the high degree of flexibility. Lessons lasting 2 to 3 hours take place mostly after the day's work by firelight, to accommodate students who are busy in the daylight hours with their traditional pursuits. Teachers ("uncertificated") are selected by the communities themselves. Community leaders have a major say in training, especially in deciding who goes for training and who has the opportunity to become a supervisor, traveling around visiting both the mobile and settled groups in the prestigious role of a teacher/coach. The clan leaders have also been involved in helping the project team develop a resource book and supplementary readers.[94] And local communities have committed themselves strongly to the work of the schools management committees, including being directly involved in environmental projects such as building water reservoirs and planting trees.

Pastoralist communities have committed themselves strongly to the work of the schools management committees, including being directly involved in environmental projects such as building water reservoirs and planting trees.

PEP is a small, low-budget enterprise seeking to respond to the educational needs of special groups in Ethiopia. Even so, PEP has followed the principles that are common to Save the Children education projects throughout the country and beyond. The community served is directly engaged in a management and design role, perhaps even more so in the pastoralist project than in other cases. PEP is an example where, but for the collaboration of the pastoralist community, the basic intent of the project—to devise a delivery system that would fit—could not have been achieved.

The engagement of the intended beneficiaries in aspects of the work other than the development of the delivery systems is particularly noteworthy in this case. The point is underlined that if this particularly hard to reach community is ever to be associated with modernizing education systems—and there is no necessary reason why it should be—then this will be achieved in large measure by its own co-operation and collaboration.

Financing innovative efforts

Ethiopia has been fortunate in recent years in its ability to attract both large-scale financing, primarily from the World Bank and USAID, and a range of NGO activities. Some of these are large-scale, some less so. All allow various creative individuals to pursue experiments within the newly devolved structure and to try and test new models of school and community engagement that fit within this devolved structure. For Save the Children, the BESO/SCOPE experience has been the major effort to move to scale but this would not have been possible without the crucial, smaller-scale funding, from private donors and community efforts, that made it possible to test some of these new models in practice.

The cornerstone is the Ministry of Education's 2001 guideline which boldly states: "…students are not required to pay tuition fees for the primary (1–8) and first cycle secondary (9–10) school education. The government has attached due attention . ….to reach out primary education to all by 2015."[95] In eliminating the economic obstacle to access, the guideline endorses a "rights-based" view of education and the central role of education in the political, social and economic progress of the country. At the same time, the tradition of self-help is acknowledged: "The government will provide the necessary support if the community, through its own initiative, builds schools and supplies education materials." In short, for strong practical reasons, little fundamental change is to be expected in the financing of education, with communities continuing to play a crucial role in educational expansion.

> Communities [must] continue to play a crucial role in education expansion.

However, the reformed system tried to address the issue of incentives to an unprecedented extent. The *woreda* would have access to a block grant from which operational expenditure (mostly salaries) would be met. In addition, the *woreda* is at liberty to reward outstanding performance or adjust contributions based on special needs. Schools could themselves make action plans to address their own priorities. The block grant may be complemented by funds generated by the school, over which the community has control. The strength of the block grant was its guaranteed nature. Funding would not arrive in small quantities on an irregular basis. The overall pattern of financing included the national budget, the school's own earnings, community support in cash or in kind, and support from non-governmental organizations and the private sector.

Teaching in a newly constructed classroom.

Photo credit: Michael Bisceglie

However, the need for continued sharing of responsibility for basic education is indicated by the low level of support provided by the Ministry's grant to the *woreda* and through it, to the schools. In this system, the early years are dangerously neglected and this under-funding of children in the first grades itself contributes to the dropout rate. This is perhaps the justification for the continued involvement of NGOs such as Save the Children in basic education in Ethiopia: the country on its own does not at present have the means to support a full-blown education system.

> *SC has developed a national network of non-governmental organizations in support of basic education nationwide.*

SC's national network of support groups

From the mid 1990s onwards, Save the Children has labored, drawing on a variety of funding sources, to develop the "right" form of basic education to fit differing contexts and resolve different problems in Ethiopia. In so doing, it has developed a national network of non-governmental organizations in support of basic education nationwide. This is in line with the national policy of sharing responsibility for basic education which in several instances has made inroads into the sustainability issue. Perhaps most importantly, School Management Committees are growing in confidence and willingness to confront on their own, or together with local government colleagues, what is needed to make schools take firm root in some of Africa's toughest situations.

All these different approaches share one feature: to be effective, each initiative must include in the planning, development and long-term implementation those community members whose children are the principal clients of any basic education initiative and upon whose success the prospects for Ethiopia's advancement rest.

A six-year-old girl with her exercise book.

Photo credit: Michael Bisceglie

Notes

[79] The introductory information has been adapted from the USAID RFA for Ethiopian NFE and adult literacy, released in June 2004.

[80] *"Learning for Life"- Save the Children's Experience in Alternative Basic Education in Ethiopia*, Save the Children Alliance, Sept.2002, p. 18.

[81] The gross enrollment rate is the proportion of all pupils/students in a particular level of education compared to the school-age population at that level.

[82] *"Improving Retention with a Special Focus on Girls,"* Ministry of Education with BESO, October 1999.

[83] Ministry of Education, Guideline, 2001 *op. cit.*

[84] Training Program Development under BESO II-SCOPE, USAID, Save the Children US, CARE, Creative Associates International, Addis Ababa, 2002.

[85] Private communication, BESO-SCOPE management, 28 May, 2004.

[86] *The Development of Primary Education in Ethiopia: Innovations and Lessons Learned Study,* USAID, Addis Ababa, 2000, p. 78 *et seq.*

[87] PIE funding terminated at the end of September 2004.

[88] Save the Children/USA, *Community-based Non-formal Basic Education Projects,* Addis Ababa, 2004.

[89] Bob Marley was a celebrated Jamaican pop singer, the father of reggae, a Rastafarian, with long-standing links to Ethiopia.

[90] Child Sponsorship is a fund-raising method employed by Save the Children and other agencies to build a close link between a child sponsored by a regular donation, usually from an individual or family. Most of the funding is used to deliver services to children, particularly in Education and Health. The strength of this approach is the commitment to reach children in need and the regularity and durability of funding.

[91] Private communication with Save the Children Africa Area director, May 2004.

[92] Part of the BESO-SCOPE Project is focused on Afar. This component while under Save the Children's general management is operated by CARE.

[93] In Liben *woreda* enrollment statistics are disturbing. The latest figures (1995) for enrollment in Lower Primary suggest a total of 15,636 children (7998 males and 9,638 females). In that year 5,645 males attended school and 2,569 females. This is supplemented by a small-scale effort directed at pastoralist children (964 males and 302 females).

[94] The Somali schools lack reading materials relevant to their circumstances. Yet the Somali people are outstanding tellers of tales. The project is beginning to grapple with the idea of recording Somali folk tales as children's story books.

[95] Ministry of Education Guideline, *op. cit.* p. 44.

References

Improving Retention, with Special Focus On Girls, Ministry of Education and Women's Affairs, Addis Ababa, October 1999.

The Development of Primary Education in Ethiopia-Innovations and Lessons Learned, study, USAID, Addis Ababa, May 2000.

Education Leadership, Organization, Community Participation and Financial Guidelines, Ministry of Education, Addis Ababa, August 2001.

Terminal Evaluation Report on Save the Children/USA Project entitled "Ethiopian Community School," Oromia Disaster and Preparedness Committee and Oromia education Bureau, Addis Ababa, July 2003.

Ethiopia Community Schools Terminal Report, Save the Children, Addis Ababa, 2003. September 2002.

Training Program Development under BESO II/SCOPE, Save the Children with CARE, Creative Associates International and US AID, Addis Ababa, undated.

Community-based non-formal basic education projects, Save the Children, Addis Ababa, 2004.

Save the Children/US Education Activities, Save the Children Ethiopia Field Office, Addis Ababa, April 2004.

Pastoralist Education Project, Save the Children Annual Report for Fiscal Year 2003, Addis Ababa, undated.

Alternative Basic Education in Pastoralist Regions, Ministry of Education, Addis Ababa, March 2004.

BESO-SCOPE Guji Zone, Save the Children, Nagele Field Office, April 2004, mimeo. *"Learning for Life"—Save the Children's Experience in Alternative Basic Education,* International Save the Children Alliance, Addis Ababa.

Chapter 5

Uganda, 1999–2005: Transferring to Government Control[*]

Bonita Birungi, Hadijah Nandyose, Fred Wood and Catherine Kennedy

Learning English at a Ugandan school.
Photo credit: Chad Stevens

---

[*] Lynn Murphy contributed to the early thinking and research in the development of CHANCE schools and to this chapter.

Education: a national priority

Community-based schooling has a long history in Uganda. Mission schools were established in the 1890s, and in 1924 the government opened the first secondary school for Africans. However, by 1950, the government operated only three secondary schools; three others were privately funded, and 47 were operated by religious organizations. After independence in 1962, many villages, especially in the south, built schools, hired teachers, and appealed for, and received, government assistance to operate their own village schools.

During the 1970s and '80s, the education system suffered the effects of economic decline and political instability. During the 1990s, the Museveni government set out to reestablish education as a national priority. With the 1997 Presidential Decree on Universal Primary Education (UPE), the government of Uganda attempted to provide education to all the children in the country. To aid in this undertaking, and as part of the wider decentralization process, the government shifted the focus of education from the national to the district level in order to bring education closer to the families it serves.

Uganda's UPE initiative faced several constraints in its attempt to provide universal primary education. Among these were a lack of physical, financial and human resources to cope with the sudden influx of new pupils. With the declaration of UPE, the number of children in school increased from 2.7 million in 1997 to 7 million by March 1999. The quality of education provided inevitably suffered as a result. At the same time, the rigid and formal structure of the education system continued to exclude large numbers of children. There were still many communities in various parts of the country whose children had little access to school and for whom the established system was not working well enough.

The rigid and formal structure of the education system continued to exclude large numbers of children.

Save the Children Federation, Inc. (SC) opened its office in Uganda in 1999 at the government's request to aid in the Universal Primary Education initiative. It is these constraints that SC addressed through the "flexible education" concept and the Child-centered Alternatives for Non-formal, Community-based Education (CHANCE). The program, which started as a pilot in Nakasongola District, is still ongoing.

CHANCE Community Schools:

1999–2003

The CHANCE project was introduced to provide access to quality primary, non-formal education to children from marginalized or disadvantaged groups.

The CHANCE project was introduced to provide access to quality primary, non-formal education to children from marginalized or disadvantaged groups, including fishing and pastoralist children, the rural poor, the geographically isolated, orphans and children affected by HIV/AIDS. In this context, the choice of Nakasongola is in itself interesting. One of several newly created districts in Uganda, it is situated in the geographical center of the country, on the northern edge of the Buganda region, on the Nile and Lake Kyoga. The district was formed out of Luwero District in the Buganda kingdom and consists of areas where government services have traditionally been at a very low level. In fact, Nakasongola is one of the historic "lost counties" cut from the Bunyoro kingdom in punishment for opposing British rule and has suffered from neglect ever since.

A CHANCE school in the village of Kibuye.

Photo credit: Chad Stevens

When CHANCE was launched, Nakasongola's population of approximately 150,000 comprised a mix of nomadic pastoralists, migratory fishing communities and farmers. The area was affected by both the bush war of the late 1980s and, to some extent, by the ongoing disturbances to the north. Poverty levels were very high and the district had some of the lowest literacy rates in the country.

Indeed, Nakasongola had some of the country's worst educational statistics for both attendance and retention. There were 39,879 children enrolled in the district. This was double the number of children enrolled prior to the introduction of UPE, taxing to extremes an already overburdened system. Moreover, although a large percentage of children were enrolled in school, many were unable to attend for more than half the school year because of their involvement in income-generating activities which contribute to the household economy.

There were 92 primary schools in the district, of which 57 received financial contributions from the government and 32 were self-financed, community-initiated schools. There were 696 teachers, of whom 275 were trained and 421 (about 60 percent) were untrained. Many teachers did not even have the O-level qualifications required by the government to be eligible for full teacher status, and thus for the in-service training aimed at upgrading their skills and qualifications. Of the untrained teachers, 113 were participating in existing teacher training schemes (35 in the nation-wide Teacher Development and Management Scheme and 78 in the Luwero District Teacher Education Program). However, funding for both was due to end at the end of 1999, with the training of the teachers half done.

The majority of the teachers (i.e., those who were untrained) were not receiving salaries through the government. And, as Nakasongola was a new district consisting of eight sub-counties, the district administration was thinly staffed with only one District Education Officer (DEO) for the entire district. Standard district staffing was expected to be one DEO, two Assistant DEOs, one District Inspector of Schools (DIS) and one Assistant DIS per sub-county.

Despite these difficulties, the government was committed to improving access to, and the quality of education for all children, with one objective being to incorporate hard-to-reach groups. However, much work was needed to overcome the obstacles hindering attendance and retention of pupils in existing schools, incorporate those children who had no access to education, and improve the overall quality of education.

The assessment indicated a need to incorporate more flexible, community-based options for the provision of primary education, which would take into account the specific constraints faced by the children.

SC's Uganda Field Office undertook a needs assessment to identify and seek solutions to the weaknesses in education provision in Nakasongola. The findings indicated a need to incorporate more flexible, community-based options for the provision of primary education, which would take into account the specific constraints faced by the children, as well as building the capacity of both the formal school system and the community-based schools. The outcome of the needs assessment was the "flexible education" concept and the CHANCE pilot project. Its operational style would demonstrate the much-vaunted flexibility of the community school approach in delivering quality basic education in diverse and remote settings.

Objectives and scope of the CHANCE pilot project

CHANCE is SC's district-level strategy of flexible education for addressing the quality of, and access to education for all of the children in a given district; in this case, Nakasongola. Ingo Muller of Church Development Service, Germany, described it this way: "CHANCE ... really serves the needs of these communities."

The CHANCE pilot project aimed to help the government reach groups of children who were left out of the available education system at the time, as well as increasing the quality of education provided through a flexible approach. From the start, CHANCE saw itself as a complement to what the government of Uganda was seeking to achieve

> *CHANCE saw itself as a complement to what the government of Uganda was seeking to achieve through its UPE decree.*

through its UPE decree. The pilot project was engaged in the district on three levels:

- community-based, self-help, non-formal primary education;
- capacity building for existing community-based, non-government schools; and
- capacity building for the formal, district-level education system.

In addition to the district-level project, SC would undertake advocacy, capacity building and coordination initiatives at the national level to build a foundation for a more flexible, nation-wide approach to education.

The concept of "flexible education" shares the same philosophy as the Partnership for Innovations in Education (PIE) project implemented by SC in Ethiopia: that education should be brought *to the people,* and not vice versa. Across the world, education systems tend to be rigid and inflexible in terms of schedules, subjects, relationships between teachers and students, examinations, etc. This is understandable, given the scale of formal systems, which are usually nation-wide and standardized. Those who fail to access or succeed in the formal system—including working children, drop-outs and the disabled—are viewed as problematic and too difficult for state systems to cater to, especially where resources are limited.

> *Minorities actually have access to better, albeit more expensive, education, with smaller classes, more active learning methodologies and more committed teachers.*

Non-formal education (NFE), with its more learner-friendly approach, is often seen as completely separate from the mainstream system. It is left to NGOs and community groups to fill the gaps and provide for those who cannot participate in the formal system. As a result, NFE provision is usually piecemeal and small-scale. Lessons learned regarding innovation and quality are rarely transferred to the formal sector. Consequently, it has often been found that minorities actually have access to better, albeit more expensive, education, with smaller classes, more active learning methodologies, more committed teachers, etc.

Help with the lesson.

Photo credit: Chad Stevens

SC in Uganda is promoting a shift away from the usual approach where government provides education through a large system and where those who do not fit in have to be lucky to find NGOs that provide a more flexible, accessible program. But since the Ugandan government was genuinely committed to UPE, the pilot was an ideal test case for SC to push the idea that all education provision should be seen as part of the government system. The majority of children can be catered to in normal schools, but separate facilities must be available for those whose circumstances do not allow them to fit easily into the mainstream; and all the outlets would be supported and supervised by MOES staff. In this way, good practice from either the "formal" or the "non-formal" components could be more easily transferred, giving larger numbers of children access to quality and innovation. In addition to this national-level advocacy, SC is offering a model for providing flexible, non-formal, community-based education in the Ugandan context through the CHANCE pilot project.

> The CHANCE design is based on the idea that the education system should fit the children's needs instead of making the children fit the system.

The CHANCE design is based on the idea that the education system should fit the children's needs, instead of making the children fit the system. CHANCE provides an inexpensive, high-quality, accessible education that complements the formal, school-based system. Experience in other African countries such as Mali, Ethiopia, Guinea, Malawi and Mozambique has informed the process. The intervention targets hard-to-reach children, especially those in the pastoralist and fishing communities, who are not participating in the existing UPE because the existing system is difficult to access.

A key element in the CHANCE design was the decision to keep the CHANCE curriculum broadly in line with the national curriculum. The differences were in the length of the school day; the local supervision of the school; the hiring and on-the-job training of so-called paraprofessional teachers and, later, supervisors who support a cluster of schools; and, critically, the school calendar and time-table.

The most vulnerable groups were targeted, including working children who contribute to the household income. Since such children cannot take the whole day off to attend school, learning hours are consolidated to provide shorter classes of 3–3½ hours a day. In acknowledgement of the children's responsibilities that could take them away from school, especially in semi-nomadic, migratory communities, seasonal and daily calendars were drawn so that the school year and school day could be planned around the children's duties.

Although UPE had been introduced, there were still costs attached to schooling which meant that children from poor families could not participate. The cost of a uniform or exercise book could keep children at home. Thus the project provides basic scholastic materials and textbooks.

Hard-to-reach groups of children have the same learning needs as the majority of children and do not need a separate curriculum. In an effort to achieve UPE, the government curriculum is used in order to provide an opportunity for children to transfer easily to the formal sector and even to higher education. However, additional subjects such as child rights and traditional local skills and occupations have been introduced by CHANCE to reinforce life skills development and contextual relevance.

Start-up of a CHANCE Learning Centre

The pilot started in March 1999 with 20 classes; another 20 classes were started in May 2000. By the end of 2002, the project had proved to be successful and was supporting 73 classes in Nakasongola District and 15 community-based schools in Luwero District with more than 2,000 children enrolled. The first batch that had started in 1999 had successfully completed the first three years of primary school and was in the 4th grade.

All these children came from disadvantaged backgrounds and would not otherwise have been attending school. Some children, from pastoralist and fishing communities, had found it difficult to

All these children came from disadvantaged backgrounds and would not otherwise have been attending school.

participate in UPE mainly because of the rigidity in the school year and the daily schedule. Others lived in low population-density areas, where the nearest formal school was too far to walk to. Others were too poor to pay the hidden costs of formal school—uniforms, notebooks and pencils. Fourteen percent of pupils were orphaned, while 5.25 percent admitted to being AIDS orphans. The actual total of AIDS orphans is probably much closer to the total percentage of orphans.

CHANCE school, Kibuye Village.

Photo credit: Chad Stevens

The 20 one-classroom centers had a maximum of 40 children each. The active learning approach was encouraged to engage children in the learning process. Group work, discussions, games, etc., are priorities, in contrast to traditional rote learning.

> *Group work, discussions, games, etc. are priorities, in contrast to traditional rote learning.*

SC invests its resources to ensure quality of learning rather than quality of buildings. Parents use locally available materials to put up shelters for their children. They construct traditional buildings like their homes that are affordable and easy to maintain. This provides a sense of ownership, but most importantly, it allows a low-capital, high-return education to begin.

Orientation meetings

Meetings are held at different levels with key stakeholders on education and child welfare, beginning at the district level with both political and technical leadership. At each level, lower level representatives are invited to participate. An orientation is given on the CHANCE concept, philosophy and design and a mapping session is carried out to identify areas of greatest need. Thus, at the district meeting, sub-counties are identified. At sub-county level, parishes are identified and at parish level, villages where the actual sites are to be established are identified through the same process.

Teaching at a CHANCE Learning Center.
Photo credit: Rick D'Elia

Village meetings

In the selected villages, meetings are held with all community members to share the CHANCE philosophy and brief the community about SC's work principles and values. A discussion is also held about impediments to education within that village, and what can be done to ensure that children come to school. The partnership roles of SC and the community in starting the school are clarified, and an action plan is drawn up to carry the process forward.

Working committees are elected by the community to start with registration and verification of the children, selection of three potential teachers, identification of the site, construction of the school or center and mobilization of the School Management Committee (SMC).

Follow-up meetings

Follow-up meetings are held after one to two weeks. In these meetings, various issues are discussed and, it is hoped, resolved before opening the center.

Registration, verification and selection of students

Parents are asked to accompany potential students for verification. Children who are eight years old and above, are not already enrolled in school and fall into the "other vulnerable children" (OVC) category are given first priority. Gender balance is also very critical in the selection of students.

Calendar drawing

Parents and children are mobilized to draw daily and seasonal calendars. These calendars determine how the school year will function.

Selection, constitution and role of the SMC

Communities play a vital role in Ugandan education. Parents value learning, and often make great sacrifices to obtain an education for their children. Hence, School Management Committees (SMCs) of nine to ten people, mostly parents, are set up to oversee the day-to-day running of the school. Members are volunteers from the community who have a vested interest in ensuring that their school is run properly.

The SMC is comprised of a chairperson, a vice chairperson, a secretary (teacher or teacher supervisor), a treasurer, an information secretary, a person in charge of children's affairs, a Local County representative, a representative of parents who have no children in the school and a representative, usually a head teacher, from the nearby formal school or education office. (Inclusion of the latter creates transparency and visibility, and the head teachers take some of the good practice back to their own schools.)

The procedure for selection of SMC members is as follows:

- Parents nominate three people for each of the nine posts and the best person is selected by the majority vote.
- Women are supposed to occupy four to five positions on the SMC.

After selection, the committee is given an orientation in SMC management skills, roles and responsibilities. Follow-up orientation meetings are also carried out annually. SMC members meet on a monthly basis to develop new ideas to improve the learning environment or address emerging issues. Their roles also include:

- Identifying and selecting the teacher as well as providing ongoing supervision of the teacher's work.

- Providing for leadership, representation and participation of parents in all meetings and school activities.
- Organizing, in conjunction with the relevant authorities, sessions with parents for planning, reviews, information-sharing, etc.
- Mobilizing the community to identify the learning space and construct and maintain school structures.
- Mobilizing the community to register and select children.
- Follow-up on school enrollments, attendance and drop-out cases.
- Ensuring that the learning environment includes proper sanitation and the provision of seats, where possible.

SMC training

School management and governance were new initiatives for communities. In areas where there had been no schools or previous PTA experience, it was critical that SC provide training, technical support and guidance to boost the confidence of SMC members.

Training was conducted for all SMCs at sub-county level. The objectives of the training were to enable SMCs not only to effectively plan and manage CHANCE schools, but to take the lead in developing a sustainability strategy for the schools. Topics for the training included basic management skills, gender relations, child rights, basic conflict resolution and problem identification and solution, among others. At the end of the training, each SMC developed an action plan for its school. Several SMCs were able to use their new skills and confidence to lobby at the local level for resources for their schools. For example, some centers acquired funds from the local council, raised through local taxes, to purchase benches for their schools. Others effectively lobbied their local council representatives and received funding for school improvement.

Several SMCs were able to use their new skills and confidence to lobby at the local level for resources for their schools.

Review meetings were also conducted to analyze progress. In these meetings, the CHANCE philosophy was reviewed vis-à-vis the current practices at the various centers. Ensuing discussions centered on how these principles, as well as best practices and lessons from other centers, can be further upheld and continuously shared with the wider community. In some centers, SMC members identified three pertinent issues to work on over a two-month period and drew up action plans. In the reviews, as in the training, SMC members from neighboring government schools participated to encourage interactions, appreciation, awareness and collective responsibility and to help bridge the gap between the formal and community school systems.

It was clear that the training paid off in increased confidence among SMC members. "When you conducted the training for us," said one SMC member at a CHANCE school in the village of Nakajooga, "we understood that we are the decision-makers. So as decision makers we have decided we need another class."

Teaching the digestive system at a CHANCE Learning Center.

Photo credit: Rick D'Elia

The role of Save the Children

For the most part, the role of SC consists of:

- support supervision—onsite and during teachers' meetings.
- providing scholastic materials.
- paying teacher stipends: 60,000shs (Equivalent to approximately US $33 per teacher per month).
- advocacy at the local and nation levels.
- capacity building sessions for teachers and parents, including teacher training.

SC staff capacity building

SC made it possible for its staff members to participate in several relevant trainings internally and externally to further equip them with the necessary skills to oversee and provide technical support to the teachers, SMCs and other entities that support the program. The staff members who were trained are expected to replicate the training or provide an orientation for the rest of the team. On other occasions the staff presents papers and discusses the project with other stakeholders.

Through these experiences the staff gathered many valuable ideas and insights, which they used to strengthen certain components of CHANCE based on SC's experience elsewhere or through learning from other interventions with similar objectives.

Teacher selection

Three people (male and female) are identified by a teacher selection panel according to following criteria:

- a local person who knows the language and is known by the people.
- respect from the community.
- commitment to children and education.
- must have secondary education.
- females are encouraged to apply.

The newly constituted SMC forwards representatives to the teacher selection panel who then participate in the selection interview. Results are shared with the parents as the selected teacher is introduced.

Basic teacher training

By the end of 2003, teacher training had been given to teachers who were conducting the initial 40 classes. The ten-day training focused on:

The training also provided first-hand experience of the child-centered approaches that would be emphasized in class.

- understanding what education is and what its purpose is;
- the CHANCE model and how it fits within the EFA goals;
- community mobilization for increased participation;
- child rights and gender issues in education;
- the Nakasongola perspective;
- what makes good teaching (principles, methods, aids, and plans);
- effective lesson planning and delivery; and
- classroom discipline and control.

Another important part of the training was "micro facilitation." Each of the trainees planned a lesson, which was conducted to demonstrate their newly acquired skills and knowledge. This was useful because each participant received support during feedback sessions on his or her style and approach. The training also provided first-hand experience of the child-centered approaches that would be emphasized in class.

Monthly trainings

SC was aware that support to the teachers and teacher supervisors was key to their motivation and to the quality of the project. Hence, district-wide, in-service training for teachers was also organized and conducted on a regular basis, at the end of each month. Sessions were organized depending on the needs identified during supervision visits, and as requested by teachers. Hands-on sessions and simulations were also designed as core activities during the monthly trainings. Immediate follow-up and supervision of concept practices were introduced in the monthly trainings at center level to support the immediate utilization of acquired skills and knowledge.

A class works out a problem at a CHANCE Learning Center.

Photo credit: Rick D'Elia

Soon after the basic training was completed, ongoing training was reduced to every second month. On alternate months, meetings were held at sub-county level. This allowed for more active participation, as the groups were smaller. These meetings take a problem-solving approach, sharing issues which have come up, and are sub-county-specific.

Topics include: orientation on special needs education; gender and child rights; enhancing reading and writing in the lower grades; materials development; use of the mother tongue; building confidence and motivation in the classroom; emphasis on positive discipline strategies; psychosocial issues in education; teaching English as a second language; reviewing teaching methods and relevant use of teaching and learning aids; early childhood care and education; practices and challenges in lesson planning and delivery; appreciative testing[96], marking and reporting.

Orientation for the new grades

At the beginning of every learning cycle, as teachers take on new grades and learners progress to the next level, a formal orientation is organized to discuss approaches to teaching different subjects to the new grade, the use of available textbooks and other instructional materials for maximum benefit and themes and topics to be handled in these specific classes.

Nakaseke PTC in-service teacher training program

In liaison with the District Education Office, SC supported the participation of 200 teachers in in-service teacher training at the nearest Primary Teachers' College, Nakaseke PTC. By the end of 2003, 80 of the teachers who upgraded their skills at Nakaseke PTC had taken the final year qualification exam and fully qualified as Grade 11 primary school teachers. Nakasongola District then took up this initiative and began lobbying for funds to support in-service training for another group of 600 teachers under a similar arrangement.

Cluster meetings

A cluster is a group of five to eight schools. Clusters meet on a weekly basis, with a cluster leader, or supervisor, as facilitator. They review the previous week's lessons and plan for the following week. Any issues that arise can also be dealt with immediately.

The teachers and cluster leaders, who often describe the learning centers and the whole program as a source of positive identity, achievement and pride, feel their work is rewarded with recognition and trust from their communities.

Cluster leader training and support

CHANCE teachers who show particular promise are selected to be supervisors or cluster leaders, given extra support and encouragement and detached to supervise five to eight teachers in clusters. These cluster leaders were SC's main point of entry into the community and had been promoted as a result of their commitment and ability. The cluster leaders' skills were upgraded over the years, with training in participatory, community based research (PRA), the REFLECT[97] approach, data collection and analysis, community mobilization, facilitative supervision and providing feedback.

The cluster leaders also participated in the national in-service teacher training with support from SC to enable them to gain full, qualified teacher status. The cluster leaders grew tremendously in capacity and confidence along with the project, and SC views them as a key community asset for the future. The teachers and cluster leaders, who often describe the learning centers and the whole program as a source of positive identity, achievement and pride, feel their work is rewarded with recognition and trust from their communities.

As the project progressed, three of the cluster leaders were promoted to Community Liaison Assistants because of their outstanding contributions, not only to CHANCE but to other programs as well. This enabled them to spread their expertise over a wider geographical region, and act as role models for the other cluster leaders.

Review meetings for cluster leaders were conducted bimonthly. In these meetings, feedback on performance was given and discussions took place on outstanding issues that relate to different clusters but that were not addressed by the training and mini-sessions conducted on other relevant topics.

Onsite support

While the bulk of on-site support visits were made by cluster leaders, SC project staff also worked alongside cluster leaders both on random check-ups, and when their support was requested. During lesson observation, the cluster leader or supervisor observes the atmosphere in the classroom, the teacher's attitude and behavior, their use of active learning methods and other skills or knowledge areas discussed in the trainings, as well as the teacher's actual delivery to fulfill the learning objectives. A feedback conference with the teacher follows to discuss areas of strength and provide suggestions for improvement. Where necessary, the supervisor carries out a demonstration lesson to provide the teacher an opportunity to see first-hand some of the methods being presented. Other activities during these visits include talking to children and SMC members, supporting meetings and reviewing records at the centre.

The support provided to teachers in their classrooms was further reinforced by initiatives to start a mobile reference section to provide extra materials for the teachers to work with, which they accessed during onsite visits or at cluster meetings.

Improving quality

The quality of the interaction between children and teachers was the feature most noted and commented on by visitors to the project. The insistence on respect for children was a major contributing factor to the quality of the experience for children and teachers. David Bruns, Education Advisor for USAID, wrote in an email in September 2002:

The insistence on respect for children was a major contributing factor to the quality of the experience for children and teachers.

"My strongest impression of our visit was the healthy, dynamic interaction between student and teacher. Students were not passive recipients of rote learning, but were engaged with the teacher and their peers in thinking and answering relevant questions. It was evident that these students were learning more in their shortened instructional hours than students in the formal system. At the end of our visit, we asked the students if they had any questions for us. We were surprised at the reaction as we spent the next 15 minutes answering all kinds of delightful questions from these engaged children. In sum, it is very evident that CHANCE instructors are receiving excellent in-service support and have developed a very participatory method of classroom instruction that will lead to good education outcomes."

A more conventional method of measuring the quality of children's learning involved administering the same year-end examinations to children in the project and to those in the formal school system. The performance of the children in the project was then compared with their counterparts in the formal sector. The CHANCE children continued to perform well compared to children in formal schools.

> *"In the CHANCE schools, the teachers' eyes are really shining. You can see they love their work."*

In September 2002, Naoki Yoshikawa, Education Program Advisor at the Ministry of Education and Sports, remarked, "In the formal schools the teachers' eyes are half dead. In the CHANCE schools, the teachers' eyes are really shining. You can see they love their work." [98]

The relationship of CHANCE schools to formal schools

The CHANCE project uses the Uganda national curriculum, thus providing children with the opportunity to transfer to the formal system and/or to continue with secondary education. Informal relations between CHANCE and the formal schools are often strong. Formal schools appreciate CHANCE as a complementary service provider and a source of new ideas rather than viewing it as a competitor. The head teachers on the formal school SMCs have often taken ideas from the CHANCE approach and applied them in their own schools. In some centers, when the teacher in the CHANCE school was sick for a week, the SMC approached the nearest formal school for assistance. It was agreed a part-time teacher from the formal school could come and teach at the CHANCE school, while the head teacher from the formal school covered some of his classes. Increasingly, teachers from the formal sector are participating in planning CHANCE schools, in CHANCE cluster meetings and in the sharing of textbooks with CHANCE schools.

Pupils at a CHANCE school work together to solve a math problem.

Photo credit: Rick D'Elia

Increasing access and participation: 2001–2005

Children's participation

The Ugandan curriculum becomes increasingly academic as it proceeds through the primary cycle. Yet if children are to develop, they need to actively participate and their interest in learning needs to be stimulated outside of the classroom and by their peers. To make the CHANCE curriculum relevant and the activities meaningful to children's lives, SC encouraged a number of interactions and initiatives at the center, or school, level. These include, among others:

- Visits between neighboring centers, especially at the cluster level, to facilitate the exchange of experiences and to enable children to interact with one another. Teachers organize the visits around discussions of certain topics or themes. This arrangement also provides an opportunity for the children to be exposed to other teachers and gives direct support to teachers, especially with subjects they are having difficulty teaching.
- Debates, both within schools and with neighboring CHANCE schools have also been organized to stimulate discussion on given themes. Teachers identify a theme and children are asked to research on it in small groups. Ideas are reconciled and a formal discussion or debate is conducted. These exercises further increase interaction among children

at neighboring schools, in addition to building the capacity of the children to express themselves.

- Home visits by children and teachers to sick or absent children, or to lobby parents to allow their classmates to come back to school, are instrumental in weaving stronger relationships among children, as well as in promoting a culture of caring and support.
- Story-telling hours and news hours are integrated into the day's activities. Every day, two or three children identify a story or a game they want to share with the class. They present it and at the end the class asks them questions. The news hour mainly focuses on children presenting to their friends what they heard or saw outside school, or at school, in the form of news. These activities help children increase their confidence, become more aware of their environment, work more collaboratively, and improve their reading and writing skills.

Children use at least one to two hours a week for extra-curricular activities. In most centers, children played traditional games like football and netball. Other activities include making their own local mats or seats; collecting thatch for their shelters; traditional activities like basket-weaving and rope-making; writing letters to other schools; establishing pen friends; holding elections (selecting leaders and/or voting for the best pupil of the week); working in school gardens and receiving practical lessons from agricultural extension staff.

> *Since the beginning of the CHANCE project, parents had been constantly requesting a literacy program for themselves.*

Adult literacy

Since the beginning of the CHANCE project, parents had been constantly requesting a literacy program for themselves. So, with support from USAID, adult literacy training was introduced in 2001. Forty teachers were trained in the REFLECT methodology and 943 community members enrolled to participate in the program, which has strong links to the CHANCE project.

For example, since many of the participants are parents with children in CHANCE schools, the adult literacy participants have sessions with their children once a week, an activity which SC plans to evaluate and then expand to other groups. Mini-training sessions using REFLECT for analysis by SMCs to increase the involvement of children and parents were also piloted. Textbooks in the local language (Luganda) that are used in CHANCE schools were introduced in the adult literacy circles, leading to greater impact. Field workers for the CHANCE program are part of the support structure. Experiences are borrowed from either project to complement and enrich the activities of the other, and CHANCE school shelters are used for adult literacy sessions and other community meetings.

School feeding and School Feeding Committees

The Global Food for Education Initiative (implemented by the US Department of Agriculture) complements the goals and objectives of the CHANCE project. In 2001 a school feeding pilot project was introduced to serve all the primary schools—formal and CHANCE—in two Nakasongola sub-counties, Lwampanga and Lwabiyata. These two sub-counties were chosen because SC research found that the children of the fishing communities there had the poorest nutritional status of the three livelihood groups in Nakasongola.

One student at a CHANCE school, Denis Bakobe-Kigingo, put it this way: "I want the hours spent in school increased because after eating, I have the strength and energy to stay and learn more and I am able to answer the teacher's questions. Before, I would think about home all the time." The program was later extended to all eight sub-counties except two.

Pupils study human and animal anatomy.

Photo credit: Rick D'Elia

> The school feeding program has had a positive impact on attendance and increased the number of hours children spend in school.

SMCs played a vital role in mobilizing and planning for the feeding. They helped to establish Food Committees and outlined their roles and responsibilities. With the experience from building CHANCE structures, SMCs supervised the construction of food stores in the beneficiary centers. The school feeding program has had a positive impact on attendance and has increased the number of hours children spend in school.

In addition, as part of the sustainability strategy, beneficiary schools were encouraged to start school gardens. Fifteen CHANCE centers were able to start gardens and run them for some time but most were adversely affected by the harsh weather conditions in the district.

Youth protection and development

Since most of the children in the older classes were already approaching their teens or adolescence, an Adolescent Reproductive and Sexual Health (ARSH) component was introduced to provide access to information and offer opportunities for discussion of ARSH issues at center level. To this effect, teachers were given an orientation on the basics of RH and discussions were held on how RH can be promoted focusing on the role of the teacher. All CHANCE schools were included on the mailing list of Straight and Young Talk, a local publication that addresses the sexual development issues of young people.

Support to community-owned classes

Due to overwhelming demand from the community, which could not be met with the limited resources at the time, 15 new first grade classes were started through community efforts in the course of 2002, bringing into the project an additional 262 children. The teachers were paid by their communities, and SC provided technical support. The teachers attended bi-monthly trainings and meetings, and met weekly with a cluster of neighboring CHANCE schools. SC staff and cluster leaders also made site support visits.

Integrating project activities with other interventions

"A major ... result of all the programmes has been the empowerment of whole communities.⁹⁹"

The CHANCE project, and particularly the SMC training, has been a catalyst for community action by creating and strengthening community networks around improving the lives of children. Individuals and communities have expanded their ambitions and their capacities and are taking action in many new ways.

By 2003, parents and SMCs had set up a total of 33 new classes. Confident of the CHANCE concept, methodologies and quality, communities have set up other classes next to the existing ones using the same SMC they have selected children and recruited and paid the teachers. The CHANCE schools are no longer a concern of a few parents with children in the school but are seen as a community asset. SMCs now include local influential people who see the benefit of the project. CHANCE school

> *The CHANCE project, and particularly the SMC training, has been a catalyst for community action. Communities have expanded their ambitions and their capacities and are taking action in many new ways.*

structures are seen as community buildings, and village meetings and other functions are often held there.

SMCs soon began looking at issues of sustainability for their schools, and forming groups for income-generating activities that could support the school in the future. Women have tended to take the lead in forming and running these groups. A number of initiatives have been considered: parents have planted plots of maize, potatoes and beans which they sell to pay a teacher for their first and second grade classes and to improve school infrastructure; some engage in poultry and pig-farming; others make and sell bricks locally (though this is traditionally a male occupation, women are taking the lead); women are also weaving baskets and mats; men are engaged in charcoal-burning, and intend to use part of the money raised to support the school.

Expansion into Luwero District

The CHANCE project was expanded to another district with populations similar to those of Nakasongola District.

SC entered into discussions with several other districts to select one as a partner for the expansion of CHANCE. Two meetings were held in Mukono District, and one visit was made to the CHANCE project by district education officials from Mukono. However, when it came to negotiating a Memorandum of Understanding (MoU), the district backed down on its commitments. SC decided to withdraw, and Luwero District was finally selected as the partner for the next phase. It was the district that was most enthusiastic about the project, and most willing to commit its own resources. Several meetings were held between SC and the District Administration, and Luwero District officials visited the CHANCE project twice.

After this series of meetings and visits, an MoU was developed. Initially, the district planned to submit the schools for acceptance onto the national payroll. This was already being piloted in Nakasongola, where the district had submitted 11 schools to be admitted onto the central payroll. However, the impact on those schools was found to be negative. SC decided to drop this requirement in the partnership with Luwero District until the Policy for the Disadvantaged, which would clarify the roles and structures of the partners, was in place.

SC agreed to provide technical support to enable these schools to become more like CHANCE schools in terms of flexibility and quality, so that they could draw in more marginalized children.

A new memorandum was therefore drafted and signed. As sustainability through government payment of salaries did not seem to be a viable option for the time being, it was agreed that SC would support existing community schools rather than start new ones. In these schools, communities were already paying the teachers. SC agreed to provide technical support to enable these schools to become more like CHANCE schools in terms of flexibility and quality, so that they could draw in more marginalized children. SC committed to train head teachers, teachers and School Management Committees, and to provide on-going support. The District agreed to provide scholastic materials, support and supervision.

Students work together at a CHANCE school.

Photo credit: Rick D'Elia

The district education officials and SC identified two Luwero District sub-counties, Ngoma and Kinyogoga, as the target areas for the project. These sub-counties are geographically isolated and inhabited by pastoralist populations. They are very similar to Nabiswera and Nakitoma in Nakasongola—arid, with low population density, limited public service provision and poor infrastructure. The district then helped SC identify all the community schools in the target area—there were 15—and arrange for provisional meetings. SC staff met with the head teachers of all the schools to explain the program, and to prioritize needs and plan accordingly.

> *Eighty-two teachers, 55 of whom had not had any form of training, benefited from SC's basic teacher training.*

Work started with the introduction of specific aspects of CHANCE in the 15 community schools with total enrollment of 2,721 (1,438 girls and 1,283 boys) children. In the course of the year, 82 teachers, 55 of whom had not had any form of training, benefited from SC's basic teacher training.

The first phase of training targeted 50 teachers from the 15 schools. The training covered children's rights, gender, community mobilization, the purpose of education, Education for All and Universal Primary Education, formal, non-formal and informal education, the basics of good teaching, teaching methods, classroom discipline and management, lesson planning, and teaching and learning aids. At the end of the training, teachers joined school teams to draw up an action plan to prioritize and plan for follow-up and the application of their new skills and ideas.

The schools were then clustered into three groups for support. Monthly meetings were held to review progress against the action plans, and to discuss any issues that arose. In all, 900 children benefited from improved quality education in the 15 schools.

Training of head teachers and SMCs was planned for the next year to enable them to perform better, to work together to increase the quality and accessibility of their schools programs, and to familiarize them further with the approaches and principles of CHANCE which have proved so successful in Nakasongola.

Sustaining CHANCE

Advocacy and capacity building for partners

Save the Children's work at all levels combines direct implementation with national and local advocacy. In this context, CHANCE continues to be used as irrefutable evidence of success in alternative education programming. In its experience-based advocacy, SC focuses on strengthening community groups and promoting partnerships between communities and government to help hard-to-reach children access quality education.

Community level-support to the formation of Literacy Committees

At the community level, teachers, field workers, SMCs, Literacy Support Committees and quality improvement teams now have a greater understanding of children's rights—especially the right to a quality education—and they collaborate to promote these rights.

> CHANCE continues to be used as irrefutable evidence of success in alternative education programming.

Eight Literacy Support Committees were formed, one for each sub-county, consisting of adult literacy teachers, CHANCE teachers, and SMC representatives. Team leaders at the sub-county level were selected to promote education initiatives and to raise awareness of the programs as often as possible within their sub-counties. The committees sent representatives to the district level to form the Nakasongola District Literacy Support Committee, which continues to work to promote literacy in the community. The committee handles issues of teacher motivation, raising the profile of educational programs in the district and acting as a link between the community and other partners on issues of education. The committee also disseminates information about the progress of the programs to local leaders on an annual basis.

Partnerships at the district level

At the district level, SC works closely with the district administration and local authorities to implement the CHANCE project. There are two main reasons for this: one is to ensure greater sustainability, the other is to raise awareness and to build capacity in the provision if flexible, quality education.

The Nakasongola District Administration took on recurrent costs such as teacher salaries and textbooks for 11 CHANCE schools. By end of 2003, 13 additional centers were being considered for receipt of the same. The District Inspector of Schools monitors quality in the CHANCE schools and administers formal end-of-year exams.

In the expansion to Luwero, the partnership with the district administration has been even closer from the beginning. A Memorandum of Understanding was signed under which the district was to provide textbooks and other materials to 15 community-based schools in the pastoralist sub-counties of Ngoma and Kinyogoga. SC provides technical assistance to these schools. In addition, SC continues to support the in-service training of untrained teachers in the district at the National Teacher Training College. SC also conducts an Education Forum, a quarterly meeting with the district education team aimed at sharing information and updating the district on current achievements and developments.

The national Policy for Basic Education for the Disadvantaged (NFE)

If Uganda is to realize quality primary education for all children, it is absolutely essential that it institute innovative, alternative education structures that reach out to the 13 to 18 percent of 6 to12-year-olds who are not now in school. In addition to CHANCE, some examples of other such programs in Uganda are Alternative Basic Education for Karamoja (ABEK), Basic Education for Urban Poverty Areas (BEUPA), and Mumbende Non-Formal Education (MNFE). In order to get all children in school, these kinds of programs must be taken to a larger scale, providing nation-wide coverage for those children for whom the formal structures of primary schooling are not a viable alternative. Research suggests that "… this will require new governance structures and new, large-scale partnerships with NGOs and other civil society representatives at community, regional and national levels." [100]

As many as 20 percent of Ugandan children are still not in school.

The government and the Ministry of Education and Sports (MOES) admit that as many as 20 percent of Ugandan children are still not in school, despite the introduction of Universal Primary Education (UPE) in 1997. They also acknowledge the value of the complimentary projects in the country, and have expressed a desire to expand the reach of these projects.

In this context, a Policy for Basic Education for the Disadvantaged was developed. The Director of Save the Children was a member of the national task force, together with other NGO representatives, donors and senior MOES officials. A draft policy paper was developed and debated many times, and district stakeholder meetings were also held. The paper was presented at the October mid-term review of the MOES.

SC's concern was that the policy needs to be flexible in order to ensure inclusivity and to allow a variety of actors—children, parents, NGOs and national bodies—to bring their varied expertise and contributions together to ensure that more children can join UPE. SC organized meetings for the Forum for Education NGOs in Uganda (FENU) to prepare a position paper on the subject, and took the lead in drafting it. SC also suggested that an appropriate

SC's concern was that the policy needs to be flexible in order to ensure inclusivity.

way to proceed is to draw up a general policy that is broad and inclusive, and that details should be worked out in a strategy document and implementation plan to be developed later. The strategy and work plan should be developed by all stakeholders after more participatory research with out-of-school children, and after an evaluation of existing complementary programs—of which there are currently five: CHANCE, ABEK, ACCESS (a non-formal primary education project supported by ActionAid in Mubende District), COPE (UNICEF's Complementary Opportunities for Primary Education initiative) and BEUPA—to establish what works.

However, given the process and the state of the policy at the time, SC had real fears that the policy would be too top-down and would actually be exclusive, resulting in even fewer real alternatives for disadvantaged children. Consequently, with SC as one of the steering members of the NFE working group, a coalition of all NGOs in the country implementing non-formal programs was born out of the work on the Policy for the Disadvantaged. The group is in dialogue with the MOES to try to convince them to support NFE in the mainstream funding process. Current related issues under debate include curriculum, NFE as an option for the war-ravaged areas in Northern Uganda and instructors' salaries, among others.

Working with FENU

SC is a member of the coordinating committee of FENU, a network of NGOs working in education with the aim of providing a thematic forum to address issues pertaining to access, equity, quality and sustainability of education in Uganda. FENU's objective is to ensure greater participation by the public in education policy, "linking people, policy and practice for a better education."

Once FENU was well positioned and visible within the national education agenda, one of its objectives was to set up district FENUs in five pilot districts. Nakasongola was one of the districts chosen, with SC taking the lead to ensure that the district-level forum got off the ground. After two meetings, the participants agreed that the district should establish an NGO Forum first, and then set up FENU as a sub-committee within it, to follow the model in Kampala.

Help from the teacher.
Photo credit: Chad Stevens

As a member of FENU, SC contributes to other policy debates, such as the review of the Education Sector Investment Plan (ESIP) and the Poverty Eradication Action Plan (PEAP), specifically lobbying for space for NFE. Through FENU, SC is an active member of the organizing committee for the activities of the Global Campaign for Education week which takes place in April. Activities have focused on raising awareness about the challenges disadvantaged children, particularly girls, face in accessing education. Press conferences that inform the public on the state of girls' education in Uganda convey the level of commitment of various actors to promote girls' education. Radio and TV talk shows hold debates and share insights on some innovations that have worked in promoting EFA. Articles with stimulating messages, written by girls, call for action. In addition, CHANCE was used to illustrate the benefits of NFE in promoting girls' education. The work of the CHANCE project in Nakasongola District was shared as a best practice and a solution that government could adopt in addressing the special needs and realities of girls' education.

> *CHANCE was used as a case study to demonstrate the cost-effectiveness of alternative education.*

Through FENU, SC has worked with VOICE International, another NGO, to contribute to a national study aimed at promoting dialogue and mobilization in Uganda and internationally on the "real costs of education" at a bigger forum of key actors in the education sector, including the government. CHANCE was used as a case study to demonstrate the cost-effectiveness of alternative education.

Phase-over of the learning centers to government

Phase 1: The Pilot Transfer of Eleven Schools

As part of the sustainability strategy, the running costs of CHANCE schools are to be gradually taken over by the government while the concepts of the CHANCE model are to be retained. Eleven CHANCE schools were identified for this pilot. However, the government was able to take over the costs but not the principles of CHANCE. Upon takeover, head teachers were appointed and old SMCs were replaced by new SMCs appointed by the district without consulting the parents. The school hours changed back to 8 a.m. to 4 p.m. and parents had no say whatsoever.

Since SC was still committed to providing technical support, orientation training on Non-Formal Education was conducted for the head teachers of the 11 schools. Subsequently, SC held meetings with the District Education Officer and the Education Advisor to the Ministry of Education seeking commitment and action to maintain the identity and delivery mechanisms of the 11 CHANCE schools. From the discussions it was clear that the district lacked the capacity in terms of manpower and time to follow up with the centers and hold discussions with the communities.

Although the new head teachers were oriented, they had no opportunity to apply the skills they had acquired. The barriers to access that had been identified in the beginning were reinstated. In the long run, the children failed to cope and began dropping out.

Documentation of the take-over of the 11 schools by government: lessons learned

A study conducted by David Sussman[101] between May and July 2003 provides some insight into the strengths and weaknesses of the current system and into the differences between non-formal and formal education programs. The study generated lessons that allowed for improvement and provided insights into the impact of the transfer processes of the CHANCE learning centers.

During the study, focus group discussions were held with parents, children, teachers and SMCs in six of the 11 schools that were taken over by the government. The selection of the six schools was made in accordance with the observed response to the merger's three format areas: full integration, half-and-half and separation but in same compound. Questions were tailored to generate perceptions on how the transfer was done, its consequences and options for the future.

A pupil at a CHANCE school.

Photo credit: Chad Stevens

It was found that the involvement of all stakeholders was paramount. In his report, Sussman highlighted that overall CHANCE was appreciated and that its success was tied to the provision of materials and teacher training. He further indicated that the communities' exp-

> It was found that the involvement of all stakeholders was paramount.

ectations for the future varied and that their opinions were mixed, indicating a need to clarify the prospects and direction of CHANCE. It was found that the involvement of all stakeholders was paramount and that communication about the transfer as well as the process had to be structured and given adequate time. He also emphasized that opportunities for modeling CHANCE exist and, especially where systems are maintained, the sharing of resources among formal and non-formal schools is inevitable.

Phase 2: Transfer of 15 centers to government-aided schools

In 2004, 15 CHANCE centers consisting of 41 classes were to be transferred to government-aided schools. The initiative was to be conducted in partnership with the District Education Office. For over a year now, there has been on-going dialogue between SMCs, SC and the Education Office resulting in the development of criteria for the selection of the 15 centers.

A number of issues are being considered. The higher grades have been selected because it was felt that older children would be able to walk the 3 to 5 km to school. The education office deliberately put up school facilities in the vicinity of seven of the centers to provide an opportunity for a school facility in the community to increase access once the transfer was carried out. Five of the centers in Wabinyonyi sub-county were included because of the presence of World Vision, which recently started implementing a sponsorship program within the government-aided schools in the sub-county and will be supporting some of the children as they are transferred.

The change to the government curriculum resulted in an increase of subjects from four to eight. Although CHANCE uses the government curriculum, only the core subjects are taught in order to work within the available time and calendar. The transfer would thus also be an opportunity for the children to benefit from the additional subjects currently being introduced in government-aided schools. These include Agriculture, Swahili, Religious Education, Physical Arts (a holistic approach to martial arts), Physical Education, Music and Arts and Crafts.

For the first term of these new schools, teachers will transfer with their classes for continuity but the children will also gradually have the opportunity to be introduced to other teachers. SC, in liaison with the District Education Office, will continue providing technical support to all the teachers in the schools to ensure that all concepts of CHANCE are not lost, that areas of merger are strengthened and desirable aspects copied. The head teachers in the schools will also have an orientation to prepare them to receive the children. Given that the head teachers of some of these schools belong to an SMC and at least three of the SMCs were trained, it is hoped that this will be sufficient to support the transfer.

SC continues to support 20 of the centers (with a total of 32 classes) that were not eligible for the transfer because they were in very remote areas, with no school within at least 5 km. Of these classes, 16 are upper classes to be supported for two years to allow them to complete the primary grades, and 16 are lower classes that also need to be supported for two years in order to attain the basic education level.

Lessons learned

Payment of teachers' salaries by the communities

Batches of three and four CHANCE schools were started by communities themselves. While Save the Children provided technical support, the communities paid the teachers. This was a positive sign because it showed that communities were now convinced of the quality of the education available, and were willing to support it with resources to a greater extent than when the project began. However, there were problems associated with the communities' payment of the teachers. From a practical perspective, parents cannot afford to pay very much. This leads to a high turnover among teachers who look for other opportunities. This means that there are always new teachers who have not been trained by SC. This has an impact on the education in three ways: lack of continuity for the children; teachers with low skill levels and teachers with low motivation levels. It also causes problems for the project in creating two tiers of teachers, with inevitable resentment from the lower paid. And it impacts negatively on data collected for the project. Because of financial and time constraints the project has not been able to train and retrain the constantly replaced teachers. This has raised the question of sustainability.

> *Communities were now convinced of the quality of the education available, and were willing to support it with resources to a greater extent than when the project began.*

The importance of positive discipline

"Both instructors and learners' evaluations of the programmes suggest why they have had such a fundamental effect on the communities. They emphasize the conducive practices of the programmes: friendly and supportive relationships between teachers and pupils, preference by both parties and insistence by management on learning rather than competing, practical, participatory, learner-centered teaching approaches and, above all, positive rather than negative discipline techniques."[102]

Community ownership

As the schools advance in terms of classes and scope, the communities also grow in skills, knowledge and control of the CHANCE schools. Community participation in the building of structures, identification and selection of teachers and children and monitoring of attendance and retention fosters a strong sense of ownership. Many decisions concerning the schools, such as the firing and hiring of teachers, are made at center level with less consultation from SC. Community cohesion has also increased. "This school has brought unity to our village," says

> *"This school has brought unity to our village."*

Harriet Nanyonga, a CHANCE parent. "We all work together in the school gardens and on the buildings for the sake of our children."

Conclusion

It is too soon to draw final conclusions on the new CHANCE. Certainly, despite some rough waters, the program has already achieved much. It has shown some capacity for scaling up with the accession of additional districts. And it has shown an ability to diversify into new areas of social crisis, notably the continuation of the HIV menace and conflict situations. For example, some components of CHANCE have been replicated in other educational programs: the outreach work in Kasese District, though brief, focused on linking education and psychosocial support for internally displaced persons (IDPs). The program has also worked with IDP children in Lwampanga District and has submitted a proposal to have some elements of CHANCE included in the Program for Emergency Education in the North.

With regard to the broader question of the place of community schools in Uganda, the government's 1994 White Paper on Education, with its accent on those who are left out, certainly opens the way to sharing the effort to work for solutions to the needs of special groups. Community schools, or centers, fit in with this scheme of things. This, perhaps, is as much as can be expected until the problem of disadvantaged groups is comprehensively dealt with and the focus of education renewal moves beyond access to quality of service.

Notes

[96] Appreciative testing is an approach to conducting assessments in a manner that helps all involved to value and participate in the assessments.

[97] REFLECT is an approach to adult learning and social change that fuses the theories of Paulo Freire with the methodology of participatory rural appraisal.

[98] This remark was made in an interview with Catherine Kennedy, Field Office Director, Save the Children Uganda, in September 2002.

[99] Ilon, Lynn and Kyeyune, Robinah, *Cost Evaluation of Complementary Basic Education Programs in Uganda* USAID report, 2002, p. 33.

[100] Steven J. Klees, Joshua D. Hawley and Victor Byabamazima, *Policy Options for Achieving Quality Primary Education for all Children in Uganda*—Draft Final Report. UNICEF and MOES, Uganda, 2002.

[101] Sussman, D. *A Study of the Transfer of the CHANCE Schools to the Ministry of Education and Sports in Nakasongola.* (Save the Children/Uganda, 2003) p. 2.

[102] Ilon and Kyeyune *Cost Evaluation of Complimentary Basic Education Programs in Uganda.* Creative Associates and USAID, 2002, p. 34.

Chapter 6

USAID and Community Schools in Africa: The Vision, the Strategy, the Commitment[103, *]

Yolande Miller-Grandvaux

The term "community schools" has been interpreted in many different ways. Here, the term is used to describe the paradigm of community engagement and participation in schools through the mobilization, sensitization, funding, training and capacity building of a representative and effective Parent Teacher Association (PTA). Community schools in this context refers to the multiple school models of community-managed schools, and the process of school-community engagement and empowerment developed by various NGO and PVO partners funded by USAID to improve basic education in Africa.

More than 5,000 community schools in Africa

USAID supports more than 5,000 community-managed schools through its African education programs in Benin, Ethiopia, Ghana, Guinea, Malawi, Mali, South Sudan, Uganda, and Zambia. These schools represent the fruit of an effort begun in the early 1990s on the part of USAID, national governments and international and national NGOs seeking to empower parents and communities to improve education in Africa.

A range of innovations appeared over the course of the '90s. USAID and its partner PVOs created a movement that not only increased access to education. It also prompted stakeholders and policy makers to consider how alternative modes of delivery could help countries educate *all* of their children, attain the goals of Education for All, improve student achievement and reach out to remote, disadvantaged populations.

There is no single model of community schools; no "one size fits all" approach to be found in USAID programs to improve community participation in schools in Africa. Indeed, USAID adapts its designs and strategies for

---

* The author's views expressed in this publication do not necessarily reflect the views of the United States Agency for International Development or the United States Government.

community schools to the context of the countries in which they operate. These designs and strategies evolved along with the host country's political and socio-economic development. Common USAID strategies and patterns are, nonetheless, apparent in different countries. Community participation does not develop linearly; it is chiefly determined by the socio-political environment in which a community must function. Nevertheless, in USAID's support to community schooling across countries, similar tensions, points of replicability and strategic trends are evident.

Given that almost all community-schooling programs in Africa supported by USAID are now at least a decade old, it is useful to look at the identifiable patterns and phases of implementation. This essay frames the presentation of case studies of Save the Children's community schools in Mali, Ethiopia, Malawi and Uganda supported by USAID (and other funders in certain cases). It examines the *why* and *how* of USAID-supported community schools, the strategies that were adopted and how they changed over time. It is a descriptive analysis that addresses the lessons learned by USAID to guide its strategic and programmatic decisions[104].

Why does USAID support community schools?

In the late 1980s, the USAID Africa Bureau received a congressional earmark to develop the capacity of African countries to deliver, on a sustained basis, quality and equitable primary education. These funds allowed USAID to participate in education reform on a large scale, starting with the launching of five new basic education programs between 1989 and 1991 in Ghana, Guinea, Malawi, Mali and Namibia, under a new Development Fund for Africa designed by the US Congress in 1987.

A comprehensive approach to African education had to focus on achieving greater quality, equity and access at the primary level.

Together with the World Bank, USAID force-fully promoted a "system-wide" approach to reforming African education. A comprehensive approach to the renewal of African education systems, it argued, had to focus on achieving greater quality, equity and access at the primary level. USAID intended to assist governments in building their institutional capacity to efficiently manage their education systems; USAID's approach emphasized host country leadership, ownership and sustainability. A systemic reform required that ministries of education and the sector itself be reorganized; that decision-making, financing and the improvement of education management and planning capacity be decentralized[105]. It targeted "reform of the education system by the system itself" [106].

Equity for girls' education

In the early to mid 1990s, USAID focused primarily on building institutional capacity and slowly introduced the concept of equity through girls' education[107]. The combined emphasis on gender equity and on the need to bring education systems closer to the beneficiaries naturally pointed to strengthening community support for schools at the local levels and improving the quality of education services. Supporting girls' access to school was thus a major component of USAID's education programs, particularly in countries where the gender gap was wide, such as Mali, Ethiopia, Malawi, Uganda, Ghana and Guinea.

In order to specifically accommodate girls—half the target population—rather than be an obstacle to their participation, the system needed to be changed and an enabling environment needed to be shaped.

Any effort to achieve gender parity in enrollment required that parents be sensitized to the multiple benefits of educating girls; to keeping daughters safe and close to their parents and to their communities; to adjusting a school timetable to girls' work at home, to adapting curricula to the needs and values of the community. In other words, in order to specifically accommodate girls—half the target population—rather than be an obstacle to their participation, the system needed to be changed and an enabling environment needed to be shaped.

In the mid to late 1990s, USAID's Africa Bureau further refined its understanding of the process of education reform. To guide its missions in the field, it developed the Education Reform Support Framework, which was published in 1997. The framework suggested that development assistance for education reform could be designed to help build the capacity of various actors, including indigenous NGOs and civil society organizations. Such organizations could work together to influence policy reform by empowering citizens to further their own interests and ultimately create networks and coalitions to support the policy dialogue. Many USAID missions had already been providing grants to international and national NGOs and PVOs to implement school-based development projects. The framework reinforced the idea that missions could create partnerships with civil society and governments to achieve access, quality and equity of education, and thus support education reform.

Development assistance for education reform could be designed to help build the capacity of various actors, including indigenous NGOs and civil society organizations.

Within the broader framework of Education for All, USAID Washington pursued the development of a policy reform and education sector support framework that was committed to three goals: school and community change; systemic reform; African ownership of and capacity for the reform process[108]. More specifically it was based on the promotion of community participation and the improvement of access to education, especially for girls, as well as quality and efficiency.

When NGOs such as Save the Children or World Education proposed their own innovative, community-based approaches to achieving these broader goals in Mali, Guinea, Ethiopia, Malawi and Benin in unsolicited proposals to USAID missions, they clearly matched and supported USAID's goals and theoretical approaches. USAID and NGOs have since maintained a fruitful partnership, mutually reinforcing each other's vision and strategies.

The role of NGOs

As governments were adjusting to receiving and relying on large donor funds, their institutional structures often could not meet the operating demands or even understand the approaches promoted by donor agencies. Governments often reacted with cumbersome bureaucracies, uneven levels of competence, and sometimes uncooperative administrative structures.

USAID was under pressure from Congress to produce results, to decrease or simply stop providing direct budget support to governments (as a case in point, USAID Benin withdrew its budget support in 1998). Hence, USAID missions tilted their decisions and programs towards working with communities through NGOs to foster school-level changes and reach out to local beneficiaries. By doing so, USAID programs were to gain in efficiency and sustainability while at the same time building the capacity of civil society as a whole.

Governments alone did not have the means or the capacity to deliver education services to rural communities that had no schools. NGOs were certainly best placed to do so: NGOs work at the community level, thus affecting social change where governments cannot; NGOs can represent and catalyze civil society, a key to democratization and sustainability; and NGOs are simply more efficient than government partners[109.] USAID's strategy in all countries in Africa, therefore, was to fund international NGOs such as Save the Children, World Education, Africare, World Learning, CARE and others to partner with and train national NGOs to build local capacity and assist parents in organizing and providing services to their own communities. Local development agents were funded and trained by international NGOs under contracts with USAID, leading the local organizations to play an increasingly important managerial and pedagogical role in schools. This, in turn, inevitably led to certain overlaps and frictions with government authorities.

Local development agents were funded and trained by international NGOs under contracts with USAID, leading the local organizations to play an increasingly important managerial and pedagogical role in schools.

Examples of role overlaps abound. One was in Malawi where Save the Children produced a teaching manual, and in Mali where Save the Children, together with its local partner NGOs, trained teachers and monitored their performance or provided the means for ministry inspectors to visit schools and teachers. In these instances, Save the Children was playing the controversial role theoretically assumed by pedagogical advisors to travel to remote schools to work with teachers on an individual or a cluster basis. Government officials in Mali and in Ethiopia challenged this role quite seriously and momentarily put projects in jeopardy. When local government authorities felt forced by donors to recognize NGOs as legitimate partners, they often resisted, thereby challenging USAID's preferential way of doing business through NGOs.

In many instances, however, this contentious overlap contributed to the improvement of education quality by providing teaching and learning materials that the government could not provide. The most striking example of positive outcomes is that the principle of using maternal languages as a medium of instruction, experimented with by Save the Children community schools in Mali, was later adopted into the national Malian curriculum.

Evolving issues and strategies

Quite naturally, USAID's support for community schools has been focused on different areas of interventions at different times. It started from an initial concern with getting children *into* school (access and equity) within a clear strategic reform framework. It then addressed larger issues related to the quality and relevance of education; to the diversity and acceptability—by parents, by ministries of education—of alternative delivery of education; to the blurring of the division between formal and non-formal education; to the basic financing of education; to the implications of EFA; and finally to USAID's strategic decisions related to sector investments. Many of these questions are still being discussed today. USAID, like its partners and the communities it is serving, benefits from its long experience in support of community schools.

> *The principle of using maternal languages as a medium of instruction, experimented with by Save the Children community schools in Mali, was later adopted into the national Malian curriculum.*

Hence, USAID community schooling programs can be said to have evolved in three phases:

- A first phase focused on access and quality within a strong systemic policy reform and capacity building framework.
- A second phase emphasized the quality and relevance of education at the school level within a decentralized framework based on a project approach.
- A third phase attempted to bridge the gap between formal education and alternative delivery of education services within a pluralistic national framework.

Phase 1: systemic reform to improve access and quality

From 1991 to approximately 1996, USAID supported different models of community involvement in Mali, Ethiopia, Ghana, Guinea, Malawi, Zambia, and Uganda. It focused on increasing access to primary education for the large majority of disadvantaged, out-of-school children, especially girls, by providing

Increasing access meant not only increasing enrollments but also ensuring that children stay in school.

education services to communities that governments could not reach. Increasing access meant not only increasing enrollments but also ensuring that children *stay* in school. Focusing on access through community participation during that first stage meant that parents primarily provided labor and funding to create or sustain their own schooling infrastructures and material inputs.

Over time, however, implementers and decision-makers were faced with difficult quality issues that required a new type of community involvement. Parents had to understand what quality of education meant to them and how they could influence it; that teachers needed qualifications and training; that curriculum and the language of instruction had to be made relevant to their needs; that relationships with education officials had to be established to obtain pedagogical support and be officially recognized. Both USAID and the implementing NGOs struggled with such needs and adjustments, which often ran contrary to their initial principles.

USAID's strategies in education thus focused virtually concurrently on access, especially for girls, *and* quality. Community participation was viewed as a way to meet the goals of increasing access, equity and quality, which still characterize all of USAID's education strategic objectives in Africa.

USAID's community schooling strategies were based on three factors. First, the outreach and decentralization of social services and the commitment to education were seen as the pathway to development by countries that had experienced major political upheavals and had replaced dictatorships with democracies. Second was the realization that although governments had committed to Education for All, none had the capacity or resources to meet the demand for education. Thus they had to pass the responsibility for education to communities to address their own needs. Third, the guiding principle, taken from the education agenda that USAID had been developing for its African programs, was that community participation is a key component to the success of systemic reform. All USAID missions embarked on programs that built on these factors.

The following four country programs illustrate the pattern adopted by USAID in this early phase.

Malawi

The guiding principle was that community participation is a key component to the success of systemic reform.

The USAID strategy in Malawi evolved slowly, first pursuing the goal of increasing access and equity within a national systemic reform framework, "rather than the rapid expansion of access[110], and eventually switching to a focus on quality. In 1991, USAID Malawi launched the Girls Attainment in Basic Literacy and Education (GABLE) project that focused on access, especially for girls, and systemic education reform. In 1998, it shifted its emphasis to the quality of learning with the Quality Education through Supporting Teaching (QUEST) project. GABLE reached out to communities by implementing a large mobilization program to educate girls and provide them with a relevant, gender sensitive learning environment. When, in 1994, a new democratic government suddenly decided to promote free primary education, USAID provided assistance with the many quality of education issues raised by the influx of 1.4 million pupils into the system.

Community participation, however, was not just a donor strategy. For one thing, the Ministry of Education had already intended to revive the school management committees that existed but were not functioning. Also, Malawi's Policy Investment Framework (PIF) called for community mobilization to increase the role of communities in improving school facilities and increasing attendance rates. The government of Malawi, however, had neither the means nor the expertise to generate grassroots community support for schools, especially at a time when at least 18,000 teachers were needed immediately.

USAID, therefore, favored the approach of emphasizing access *and* quality, and the strategy evolved from community mobilization through GABLE to community participation through QUEST. At the implementation level this translated into different community roles. Under GABLE the communities' role was limited to providing labor and funding[111]; under QUEST, communities addressed issues of learning and teaching, with the expectation that school-based quality interventions had the potential to influence education policy.

In 1994, USAID merged these strategies by funding innovative education management initiatives achieved through community involvement. For example, through Save the Children it funded 24 village-based schools. The village-based schools program trained school management committees and PTAs to manage local schools. The School Management Committees hired paraprofessional teachers and provided them with in-service teacher training and support; they involved the parents in construction and decision-making. High levels of community participation, well-prepared teachers and pupil-centered learning characterized these model schools[112]. USAID and its partners had progressively shifted their strategies and were now promoting grassroots participation to support higher-level education goals.

Mali

However, USAID's role and strategies promoting the development of community schools are best represented in Mali. USAID's Basic Education and Expansion Project (BEEP) is one of the best-known experiments in community participation in education in Africa. The community school component of the program implemented by Save the Children and the community involvement program implemented by World Education in the early to mid 1990s were the flagships of the USAID

High levels of community participation, well-prepared teachers and pupil-centered learning characterized these model schools.

Mali mission for more than a decade, and changed the African educational landscape.

Again, USAID's goal was to increase access in a country with abysmal enrollment rates and to improve quality through a systemic reform support framework. In 1992, Save the Children approached the USAID mission with an unsolicited proposal to fund a community schools project in the district of Kolondieba, based on the well known Bangladesh Rural Advance Committee (BRAC) model. USAID took this opportunity to help the new democratic government address the issue of access to education and assist with promising innovations that would help achieve the Jomtien commitment to Education for All.

Save the Children's intent was to encourage remote, rural communities to take charge of their own destiny by helping them provide a relevant education based on local needs and cultural values. As described in the other chapters of this study, communities built their own schools and recruited their own teachers (literate individuals from the community). The curriculum was learner-centered and used the maternal language as the medium of instruction. Schools were run on a flexible schedule to allow for children, and especially girls, to tend to their household chores. Success was immediate: in five years more than 651 community schools were built.

USAID concurrently funded another model proposed by World Education based on the premise that strengthening the capacity of communities through locally elected Parents' Associations (*Associations des Parents d'Elèves*, or APE) to democratically manage their *public* schools would lead to improved retention and quality of education[113]. In this case, all education inputs met national standards: the national curriculum was used, French was the language of instruction, and the teachers were civil servants. This model also spread quickly: within three years, APEs were actively involved in 340 schools.

All education stakeholders were taken by surprise at the rapid expansion of the community schools movement, the engagement of illiterate communities and the inspiring model of cultural and linguistic relevance offered by the Save the Children schools.

In 1997, USAID education, democracy and governance and health programs entered into another cooperative agreement with Africare to create and support additional community schools in the Segou region. By 2001, there were 81 of these community-managed schools.

All education stakeholders were taken by surprise at the rapid expansion of the community schools movement, the engagement of illiterate communities and the inspiring model of cultural and linguistic relevance offered by the Save the Children schools. USAID saw these innovations as a complementary form of systemic support to education reform that aimed to increase access and improve quality and equity in Mali. USAID's BEEP program focused on building institutional capacity at the central levels of the Ministry of Education;

community participation in school was one strategy among several to support the government of Mali.

In the case of the Save the Children schools, communities focused on access and expansion by creating schools and building infrastructure, and on quality by providing the resources to pay for educational inputs such as materials as teachers' salaries. In effect, communities and their local partner NGOs were assuming a new role, filling in where government had failed, meeting their own needs. Neither USAID nor the host country government claimed to have clear answers as to how to manage this new situation.

In 1994, policies were quickly drafted to give community schools the status of private schools. Resistance slowly built among education officials who saw NGOs empowered to act as educators and receiving per diems to do so, while they saw themselves as kept out of the system[114]. And since community schools were built with mud and clay, French was not taught and pupils were not in school for more than three hours a day, some feared that a parallel system of education was being created; that poor quality, discount education services were being offered. Other issues—not analyzed here—included the recruitment, status and certification of community school teachers, the sustainability of funding, the relevance of the curriculum, the distribution of

Communities and their local partner NGOs were assuming a new role, filling in where government had failed, meeting their own needs.

materials, and the official recognition of schools by the government. Yet, ten years after the beginning of the experiment, 1,665 community schools in Mali are receiving support from USAID, and other donors have been enthusiastically replicating the models in different regions of the country.

Guinea

A similar evolution in the direction of aid took place in Guinea. Until 1995, USAID Guinea had used budget support to fund the education sector under the Education Sector Adjustment Program (Programme d'Ajustement Sectoriel de l'Education (PASE). PASE 1 goals were to substantially increase primary school enrollment and expenditure for primary education. USAID/Guinea, in collaboration with other donors, used a systemic reform approach to build institutional capacity at the Ministry of Education.

Although sectoral management improved and enrollment increased, USAID was concerned that improvements in the quality of education were not taking place at the school level. The 1996 political and economic crisis and the Ministry of Education's inability to ensure the regular flow of resources to the education sector precipitated a strategic change for PASE 2. The focus switched from expanding access to designing a customer-driven program for education quality and equity that would promote change in schools while continuing to build capacity. USAID introduced the idea of working through local NGOs and

Parents' Associations, an approach partly inspired by the Mali and Benin experiences.

In 1997, USAID Guinea funded two pilot models that focused on increasing the participation of civil society in the primary school system by strengthening the institutional capacity of local Parents' Associations through grants to Save the Children and World Education. Save the Children went to remote parts of the country to help communities create their own schools. World Education worked with existing schools in the Mamou region to develop the capacity of Parents' Associations to manage government schools.

The endemic issue of teacher shortages in Guinea initially affected Save the Children. New schools were built by communities but teachers could not be found. Unlike in Mali and Malawi, the Ministry of Education insisted on controlling the quality of teaching by providing only trained and certified teachers who had gone through the government's approved training system. No para-professionals were hired and school authorities could not supply enough teachers to meet the demand. As a result, only one-third of the community schools had teachers. USAID reacted by shifting its focus from increasing access through the construction of community schools to addressing access, quality and equity issues through improved public governance of existing primary schools.

Ethiopia

As early as 1991, the Ethiopian Ministry of Education had stipulated that community participation would increase demand for education and would allow for resource mobilization for schools. However, the mandate was unclear and little implementation followed[115]. When USAID's Basic Education Sector Overhaul (BESO 1) program was initiated in 1994, the primary goal was to promote quality and access, rather than expand access by building infrastructure.

The Ministry of Education insisted on providing only trained and certified teachers. As a result, only one-third of the community schools had teachers.

As it had done in other African countries, USAID sought to build institutional capacity in the education sector to support reform. It funded various programs: teacher development, materials production, education planning and policy, financing and management. The community participation component of BESO, implemented by World Learning, was developed to change the learning environment in existing schools and ensure equitable access for girls. An incentive funding system was put in place whereby communities could apply for a grant to address what they perceived as their school's greatest needs.

Communities typically began by focusing on improving the physical condition of their schools; the concrete process and visible results empowered them. Subsequently they felt better equipped to focus on quality inputs leading to better student retention and learning. USAID Ethiopia is committed to innovation in the area of community participation and alternative education delivery by supporting different models of community schooling. In 1997 the Project for Innovations in Education (PIE), which USAID supported in partnership with Pact, the Banyan Tree Foundation and Save the Children, was developed to promote community engagement and self-reliance in education in Guraghe.

Phase 2: school-based quality and institutional decentralization

The challenges related to the quality of community schools and of community participation in schools are well known and documented[116]. They relate to such issues as poor teacher qualifications and competence, lack of supplies, insufficient resources to fund teachers' salaries and lack of teacher support and supervision. Indeed, the challenges faced by community schools are mostly a reflection of the conditions that affect national education systems.

These challenges partly explain the strategic changes made by USAID to the design of programs, with strong implications for the international and national NGOs implementing them. While systemic reform design largely relies on a cookie-cutter approach to capacity building and sectoral support across countries, community participation strategies had to be revised and redeveloped one at a time. In this second phase, from the mid 1990s to early 2000, USAID's strategic directions aimed at bridging the gaps between institutional capacity building and the quality of education systems at central levels, and community-based interventions at local and school levels. During this period, the political and institutional contexts were clearly shifting and the agency and its partners had to adjust their education strategies accordingly.

Decentralizing education quality

From the mid 1990s on, most African governments sought to decentralize their functions to regional or even local levels, based on the rationale that education decentralization would improve efficiency, equity, effectiveness and democracy. While for many governments and ministries of education this meant deconcentrating or delegating rather than decentralizing resources and functions, the emphasis was placed on bringing government structures closer to the constituents and potential taxpayers. Donors, including USAID, encouraged the decentralization of education services, and governments drafted policies to support the new trend.

USAID supported decentralization through the strategic objectives of its education programs as well as through those of its democracy and governance programs. As a result, it supported decentralized quality of education interventions such as training regional and local education authorities; promoting cluster-based teacher training; the local production of pedagogical materials; regional management of information systems; and funding for regional management units. USAID also provided funding for regional education authorities and regional management and operations. In Mali,

Ethiopia, Ghana and Malawi, USAID decentralized most of its education programming.

The same shift to a focus on the quality of services was taking place at the community school level. After communities had built, equipped and provided financial and managerial support to their schools, it seemed that the next natural step was to help them become involved in the quality of learning and teaching in school. In Ethiopia, after most communities used their grants to improve the physical infrastructure of their schools, they began to focus on student learning, teaching performance and school management. The move from access to quality was seen as natural, albeit complex. USAID programs in Mali, Malawi, Guinea, Ethiopia, Benin and Ghana, emphasized the quality of interventions— including effective teaching, continuous assessment, development of local pedagogical aids, learner-centered pedagogy, group learning, ability grouping and interactive curriculum modules.

After communities had built, equipped and provided financial and managerial support to their schools, the next step was to help them become involved in the quality of learning and teaching.

Communities began to monitor student attendance in class and drop-out and retention rates, to check on homework at home, to provide opportunities for girls to get extra-curricular assistance, to fund pedagogical advisors to supervise their teachers and organize mock exams for their pupils. In Ethiopia and Mali, the NGOs recruited and paid government officials to work as development agents or education facilitators with teachers.

The emphasis on quality paid off. Several student performance tests were conducted in selected countries. In Mali and Malawi, community school students consistently showed higher results than their counterparts in control groups. The community school movement was slowly changing the African educational landscape.

However, the quality of education in community schools was soon subsumed by two issues: the integration of community schools into the formal education system and the relationship with government authorities within the decentralization policy framework.

Integrating community schools into national education systems

When communities in Mali asked to integrate their community schools into the formal education system and to change the mother-tongue curriculum to French so that graduating 3rd graders could move on to 4th grade and eventually complete the primary school cycle, new strategies had to be developed. Parents who had created and sustained their local school wanted their children to be given the opportunity to join a public school and have equal access to the Malian education system. As Save the Children and USAID revised their strategies, the key factor to address was the quality of instruction.

Save the Children Mali responded by providing teaching and coaching support to teachers, upgrading their recruitment criteria (teachers had to be francophone and most francophones did not live in the villages; teachers' qualifications had to be upgraded to a 9th grade level) and working closely with the Ministry of Education to ensure that teachers would teach to the standardized curriculum starting in 4th grade and to the CEP test at the end of the six-year primary school cycle.

The government of Mali struggled with the serious issue of integrating non-public community schools into the system, first as a quality of education problem and second as a financing problem. Would the children have the necessary achievement levels to join the public school pupils who had learned to read and write in French? Should the teachers who always taught in Bambara receive the same pedagogical training as public school teachers? Communities could not afford to cover the cost of more than one or two teachers per year, nor could they sustain the level of economic engagement required for a full-fledged

> *Would the children have the necessary achievement levels to join the public school pupils who had learned to read and write in French?*

school with six grades and all ancillary materials. The Malian government, strapped for resources, acknowledged that it could not afford to finance community schools and balked.

Similar dilemmas arose in countries where the same models of community schools had been supported by other partners, such as the hundreds Schools for Life in northern Ghana (supported by Denmark) or the ACCESS centers of Ethiopia and Tanzania (supported by Action Aid) and Togo's village schools (supported by a French Catholic organization). In Guinea, the problem had been avoided by the Ministry of Education, which had insisted from the outset that USAID's community participation interventions not create a "parallel" system of community schools but rather work within the existing framework of officially recognized public schools.

The USAID Mali mission saw the integration of community schools as a major concern to which no immediate and clear solution existed. Full integration meant that government recognized these schools officially as a "public interest" service to which they would therefore allocate resources. The integration issue raised the question of the financial sustainability of schools, since neither the communities nor the government could fully support them. In 2000 USAID, the World Bank and Malian authorities joined forces, leading to an

> *Public monies from debt relief funds [would] be used to contribute to the salaries of non-public, community school teachers.*

agreement that public monies from debt relief funds be used to contribute to the salaries of non-public, community school teachers.

They also found an institutional answer to the issue of integration by agreeing to build "bridges" (*passerelles*) between public and community schools so that community school pupils could attend formal schools. This required children from community-owned schools to learn French, to function within the national curriculum, and also to travel far from home, all of which were initially seen as irrelevant and inappropriate to village life.

The communities' demand to have their schools integrated radically altered the original model of community school. Yet it kept its alignment with the communities' vision. At the policy level, the model challenged USAID and the government alike to ensure sustainability without taxing communities any further and without risking the loss of school ownership.

Regional and local government authorities were often reluctant to embrace community schools and to be held accountable by illiterate communities or NGOs that were stepping on their territories.

Decentralization and the devolution of authority

How did the community school model fit into the emerging progression of decentralization? USAID programs supported both. The process of decentralization taking place in most countries would, it seemed, help institutionalize community schools by supporting the local delivery of education services to remote communities. USAID engaged in policy dialogue with governments to make this happen. Several constraints, however, made the implementation of this complex process less smooth than hoped for.

First, in spite of decentralizing reforms, the allocation of resources and decision-making authority to regional and local entities did not occur in most cases for reasons already analyzed[117]. Regional and local government authorities were often reluctant to embrace community schools and to be held accountable by illiterate communities or NGOs that were stepping on their territories. At the same time, governments recognized that USAID strategies of working though NGOs and with communities had considerably contributed to raising enrollment rates, improved the quality of education, and increased private investments in education. The strategies of USAID and the NGOs provided evidence that governments could not attain Education for All goals by themselves.

Good policy should be grounded in effective practice that can in turn inform the policy framework.

Second, USAID's difficult and idiosyncratic contractual practices contributed to a lack of policy coherence needed to support or institutionalize community-schooling innovations. Good policy should be grounded in effective practice that can in turn inform the policy framework. However, USAID's education programs typically rely on a multitude of implementing partners who often manage their components independently of each other because they are governed by the approach and deliverables stipulated in their contracts or cooperative agreements. There are no compelling reasons for partners to invest in the synergies, partnerships, networking or sustainable interactions that would anchor decentralization in practice and thus further the community schooling approach[118].

Third, the project-based assistance pattern adopted by USAID tends to weaken the traditional cohesion of education programs based on joint institutional reform support and community empowerment. The programming tensions between central and regional support to government structures, and between government support and community/NGO support have never been analyzed. Tensions are also created by the very nature of an approach warrants empowering communities—a non-education input—to produce an education output, *i.e.,* quality of learning and higher achievement, USAID's project-based approach to funding education activities has in some instances had a negative impact on promising community schooling innovations.

> *There are no compelling reasons for partners to invest in the synergies, partnerships, networking or sustainable interactions that would anchor decentralization in practice and thus further the community schooling approach.*

Finally, in some cases such as in Guinea, USAID considers community participation programs as of "indirect" rather than "direct" benefit to the government, which implies that community participation cannot be of benefit to the formal education system[119].

By the end of the late 1990s, several questions had arisen: What kind of partnerships, between governments and other constituencies, should be developed to sustain community support to schools? Should USAID invest in building the capacity of civil society rather than that of government? Can institutional reform and community schooling be mutually reinforcing endeavors that will ensure the integration of new modes of education delivery and management into the formal education system?

Phase 3: reinforcing bilateral support and multiple partnerships

USAID's strategy for community school programs shifted in the early 2000s. First, the community participation model was significantly scaled up to increase geographic coverage. Second, USAID now mainly supports two community managed school models: one that builds the management and governance capacity of the Parents' Associations in existing public schools and one that empowers communities to create and own schools that provide an alternative and flexible model for educating marginalized children. Third, USAID strategies focus on inclusiveness: the new programmatic directions bring together central, formal education authorities and local communities through partnerships and federations of civil society organizations networking in favor of education.

Scaling up

In the early 2000s, USAID missions in Guinea, Benin, Mali, Malawi, Ghana and Ethiopia decided to scale up their community school participation activities. In 2001, USAID Benin asked World Education to expand its Parents' Association

The rapid scaling up of USAID programs is provoked by the widely acknowledged links between quality of education and community engagement.

training program from one region to the whole country, increasing from 50 schools to 1,300 in a year. In Guinea, recognizing that primary schools had visibly improved through the active management of Parents' Associations, USAID also made the decision to expand. The number of community-managed schools rose from 250 in 1991 to 738 in 2004. Ghana expanded its community participation program in 2001 to include 389 communities. In 2003 it supported the training of 10,600 Parents' Association representatives from 2,656 schools, helping them acquire the relevant skills and knowledge in school management procedures and activities. In addition, 220 National Service persons were trained to serve as community facilitators to help achieve maximum community involvement in primary education at the grassroots. In Malawi, the USAID 2001–2005 strategy is committed to expansion by adding four more districts to QUEST.

This pattern of rapid scaling up across USAID programs has been provoked by the widely acknowledged links between quality of education and community engagement (all annual reports from USAID missions in the early 2000s state that community participation had a system-level impact warranting the geographic expansion of the approach) as well as by ongoing pressure from Congress to produce large, quantitative results.

USAID's new strategies to scale up can only succeed with strong support from governments and from the institutionalization of community school management practices. USAID-funded PVOs systematically include government staff in their community participation and management training, so that education officials are in a position to conduct community empowerment activities in the schools that they monitor. Government and NGO staffs collaborate to develop and implement teacher training programs. Community schools negotiate the provision of pedagogical materials with local education authorities. Thus, the expansion has been carried out in partnership with, and through, government representatives—something that was inconceivable seven years ago. The USAID scaling up strategy, therefore, reinforced the creation of partnerships based on a principle of inclusiveness.

The expansion has been carried out in partnership with, and through, government representatives—something that was inconceivable seven years ago.

Current models

USAID currently supports two main community schooling models:

- One model, based on the Save the Children community schools innovation in Mali, aims at providing relevant, community-owned learning opportunities to disadvantaged target groups. Communities create, build and manage their own schools; the curriculum is made relevant and the timetable is flexible in order to accommodate all children; instruction is in maternal languages. This model targets specific groups of vulnerable children in countries such as Zambia[120] where the number of AIDS orphans has destabilized the system; in Southern Sudan, which has war-affected populations to educate; and in remote, nomadic areas of Ethiopia. Such alternative systems are seen as the only hope for providing a minimal package of education to vulnerable children.

- The other model, inherited from the World Education experiment, seeks to increase the participation of civil society with the formal primary education system. Here, programs are developed to reinforce Parent's Associations so that they can participate more actively, effectively and meaningfully in the management of their children's schools. In the 2000s, the approach has evolved from the local training level of school-based Parents' Associations to regional levels whereby Parents' Associations are trained to organize networks and federations. In addition to building management skills, USAID programs provide federations of Parents' Associations with the advocacy skills needed to make their demands known to the government and to negotiate with decision-makers.

Partnerships

After a decade of fairly successful experiments and accomplishments in community participation in schools, governments, donors and NGOs all recognize the need to partner and collaborate to ensure the provision and quality of education. USAID missions no longer ponder whether to invest in NGOs or government capacity; which community schooling model to adopt or whether to fund regional versus central entities. In this third phase of development, USAID strategies of inclusiveness tend to build bridges between central and local government structures, between gov-ernment and communities; to reconcile the grassroots communities it supported through its community school programs with the central authorities supported through the systemic reform framework. The middle link is an increasingly organized, federated process of negotiations and collaboration to achieve common education goals.

USAID strategies of inclusiveness tend to build bridges between central and local government structures, between government and communities.

Partnerships are complex, labor intensive, costly and ever-changing. But they are shaping the integration of the community schooling paradigm into the formal education system. On the one hand, governments now demand more quality control over the management of schools; yet they have also accepted the need to partner with NGOs as the only way to achieve universal primary education in their countries, as long as this remains within a standardized framework. The creation of School Management Committees is a case in point. These equivalents of school boards consist of school staff members who work together with the demo-

> *Partnerships are shaping the integration of the community schooling paradigm into the formal education system.*

cratically elected Parents' Association. At the local level, the quality component for the new strategic objective in Malawi, for example, is linked to yet another slight shift: to focus on the empowerment of School Management Committees as well as Parents' Associations and to dialogue with the authorities[121]. Roles are still controversial. However, governments in instances such as Mali, Malawi, Ghana and Benin have agreed to contribute to school expenses or community school teachers' salaries.

On the other hand, USAID strategies support both community based organizations and government structures by fostering dialogue among constituencies and establishing networks and channels of communication between communities and authorities and with each other. In Malawi, USAID has helped to position the Centre for Creative Community Mobilization (CRECOM) as the education NGO that can have a seat at the policy table. In Mali, USAID phased out its support to the Save the Children village schools in 2003, but the inclusiveness trend is clear: the new education program includes a strong bi-lateral support program with the government and promotes community participation in school clusters comprising public schools, community schools and *medersas*. All are geared to benefit from government educational inputs while retaining communal and community-based practices and prerogatives.

> *The last decade has seen the emergence of a dynamic set of formal and alternative education models that have promoted a process of continuous transformation for communities.*

Presently, USAID's renewed emphasis on bilateral support through systemic education reform and capacity building to improve the quality of education still governs its education programs. Yet USAID has over time expanded its support to the regional and local levels, aligning its strategies in most cases with decentralization policies that have affected the funding of decentralized structures. USAID's current strategies also aim to foster new partnerships among a multiplicity of civil society partners and to promote the acceptance of different delivery models within an agreed national, decentralized policy framework.

Perspectives

The last decade has seen the emergence of a dynamic set of formal and alternative education models that have promoted a process of continuous transformation for communities around, and beyond, their schools. The line between non-formal and formal education has been blurred and USAID's trend towards inclusiveness has con-

> *Communities' governance of schools affects not only education; it also strengthens constructive social and democratic behavior.*

tributed to showing that alternative delivery mechanisms can, indeed, coexist with formal systems to ensure wide access to equity and quality of education.

In all the cases discussed here, the trend shows USAID education programs moving towards inclusiveness, recognizing that alternative systems of delivery can cater to minority and special needs children and still feed into a national education system; that governments can contribute their share of funding and support to relieve the financial burden placed on communities; that communities' governance of schools affects not only education; it also strengthens constructive social and democratic behavior.

The context in which USAID is operating is in flux. Fewer resources for education and better endowed sectors have created a need to consolidate resources while exploring the potential of multi-sectoral approaches. In fact, a strategic pattern is currently emerging at USAID: it aims a con-solidating strategic objectives such as health with education programs. Certainly the trend towards consolidating education programs with other sectors, particularly within the context of HIV/AIDs or conflict, is likely to accelerate and to propel the principle of inclusiveness to the forefront of the agency's thinking.

> *Community schooling pioneered by USAID and its partner NGOs has evolved from being an approach to becoming a development strategy.*

Patterns and trends have emerged over time and across education programs in Africa. Community schooling pioneered by USAID and its partner NGOs has evolved from being an approach to becoming a development strategy. USAID has progressively integrated the lessons learned from implementation into its strategic vision and has adapted this vision to each country context. In each case the learning process resulted in an informed and intentional change of strategy, consistent with USAID's vision of support to education systems.

Interviews with USAID education officers conducted for this paper have made it clear that the commitment to retain community schools, or rather community engagement in schools, is a key component of all education programs. Several USAID programs are asking the question: where to take the current commitment? An evaluation of best community school practices and lessons learned across countries needs to be carried out to further inform future strategies. This will not be enough, however. In light of current international violence, conflict and the HIV/AIDS pandemic, donors and governments

An evaluation of best community school practices and lessons learned across countries needs to be carried out to further inform future strategies.

realize that the needs and aspirations of uneducated populations must be systematically addressed, often one community at a time, and that this entails a long-term commitment. The next strategic challenge for ministries of education across Africa and for USAID as a donor may just be how to manage a multiplicity of models of education delivery within a unifying vision, in systemic collaboration with a multiplicity of actors and partners. The macro education context may temporarily be of help: Education for All, the Fast Track Initiative[122] and the Millennium Development Goals add to the list of partners that have already joined forces to pursue what communities did at their own level and with their own limited resources. That being the case, we can count on communities to show the way.

Notes

[103] The opinions and findings presented in this publication are those of the author and do not necessarily reflect the views of USAID.

[104] A review of strengths and weaknesses of community schools was conducted in the *Literature Review of Community Schools in Africa*, Yolande Miller-Grandvaux and Karla Yoder, USAID Africa Bureau, Washington, 2002.

[105] For a comprehensive history of the systemic reform approach to education reform in Africa, see *Education Reforms in Sub-Saharan Africa: Paradigm Lost,* Jeanne Moulton, Karen Mundy, Michel Welmond and James Williams. Greenwood Publishing Group December, 2002; also see *Basic Education in Africa: USAID's Approach to Sustainable Reform in the 1990s,* Joseph DeStefano, Hartwell Ash and Karen Tietjen, 1995.

[106] *Overview of USAID Basic Education Programs in sub-Saharan Africa III.* (USAID, Washington D.C., 1999) p. 13.

[107] Wolf, Joy. *Analysis of USAID Programs to Improve Equity in Malawi and Ghana's Education Systems* (1995).

[108] Overview of USAID Basic Education Programs in sub-Saharan Africa III, USAID, Washington, 1999, p. 13.

[109] *Evolving Partnerships: the Role of NGOs in Basic Education in Africa*, Miller-Grandvaux Yolande, Michel Welmond, Joy Wolf, USAID, 2002.

[81] *Paradigm Lost*, p. 25.

[111] cf. Wolf, p. 43.

[112] Miske, Shirley, and Amy Jo Dowd: Teaching and Learning in Mangochi Classrooms: Combining Quantitative and Qualitative Information to Study Twelve Primary Schools in Malawi. (Creative Associates International, Washington D.C., 1998).

[113] This approach was not readily accepted by USAID. It met with some resistance in Mali and elsewhere. In Guinea, for instance, "World Education faced on-going difficulties in persuading USAID of the value of their community participation activities as a means to improve education quality." DeMarcken, Natasha: *This Vast Field of Partnership: a Study of Community Participation to Improve Basic Education in Guinea.* (University of Minnesota, 2003) p. 143.

[114] For an in-depth study of the role of NGOs in Mali, see *Evolving Partnerships: the Role of NGOs in Basic Education in Africa*, Washington, 2002 and in *Le rôle des ONG dans l'Education au Mali*, Brehima Tounkara, ROCARE, Bamako, 2002.

[115] *Paradigm Lost*, 163.

[116] *A Literature Review of Community Schools in Africa*, Miller-Grandvaux, Yoder, USAID, 2002.

[117] For the most recent analysis, see *Education Decentralization in Africa: A Review of Recent Policy and Practice,* Gershberg, Alec Ian, and Donald R. Winkler. Washington D.C., World Bank, 2003. www1.worldbank.org/publicsector/decentralization/Feb2004Course/Background%20materials/Winkle.doc

[118] Ash Hartwell and Mitch Kirby, Malawi TDY trip report, February 2001.

[119] DeMarcken, 149.

[120] A program is currently being implemented by USAID in more than 600 community schools in partnership with UNICEF.

[121] USAID Malawi. *Triennial Review Report, Country Strategic Plan FY 2001–05.* (Lilongwe, October 2003).

[93] The Fast Track Initiative (FTI) is a partnership of developing countries and donors created to help low-income countries achieve the Millennium Development Goal of Universal Completion of Primary Education by 2015.

References

Brehima, Tounkara. *Le rôle des ONG dans l'Education au Mali.* (ROCARE, Bamako, 2002)

DeMarcken, Natasha. *This Vast Field of Partnership: a Study of Community Participation to Improve Basic Education in Guinea.* (University of Minnesota, 2003)

DeStefano, Joseph, Ash Hartwell and Karen Tietjen. *Basic Education in Africa: USAID's Approach to Sustainable Reform in the 1990s.* (1995)

Gershberg, Alec Ian, and Donald R. Winkler. *Education Decentralization in Africa: A Review of Recent Policy and Practice.* (World Bank, Washington D.C., 2003) www1.worldbank.org/publicsector/decentralization/Feb2004Course/Background%20materials/Winkle.doc

Miller-Grandvaux, Yolande and Karla Yoder. *Literature Review of Community schools in Africa.* (USAID Africa Bureau, Washington D.C., 2002)

Miller-Grandvaux, Yolande, Michel Welmond, and Joy Wolf. *Evolving Partnerships: the Role of NGOs in Basic Education in Africa.* (USAID, Washington D.C., 2002)

Miske, Shirley and Amy Jo Dowd, *Teaching and Learning in Mangochi Classrooms: Combining Quantitative and Qualitative Information to Study Twelve Primary Schools in Malawi.* (Creative Associates International, Washington D.C., 1998)

Moulton, Jeane, Karen Mundy, Michel Welmond, and James Williams. *Education Reforms in Sub-Saharan Africa: Paradigm Lost.* (Greenwood Publishing Group, December 2002)

USAID. *Overview of USAID Basic Education Programs in sub-Saharan Africa III.* (USAID, Washington D.C., 1999)

USAID Malawi. *Triennial Review Report, Country Strategic Plan FY 2001–05.* (Lilongwe, October 2003)

Wolf, Joy. *Analysis of USAID Programs to Improve Equity in Malawi and Ghana's Education Systems.* (1995)

Chapter 7

Supply-Side Education: Africa's Home-grown Schools

Joe DeStefano

Ten years ago I first visited the district of Kolondieba in Mali. At that time, Save the Children was three years into its pilot initiative helping villagers start and run their own schools. Inspired by the experience of BRAC in Bangladesh, Save the Children was eagerly challenging many of the basic assumptions about access to schooling in Mali: Was access to basic education a supply rather than a demand problem? Could rural villagers organize and run their own schools? Could those schools, using locally recruited teachers with very limited formal schooling, actually provide quality education? As early as 1994–95, the experiences in Kolondieba, as well as in many other countries, were already indicating that the answer to these questions would be "Yes."

Community schools in 17 countries worldwide

The ensuing decade has seen community schools like those supported by Save the Children expand in Mali as well as in other countries where similar efforts were being piloted. No formal count of the total number of community schools exists, but we can easily identify 17 countries (seven in Africa) where community-based models for providing education are serving significant numbers of children.[123]

Can alternatively provided schooling spur improved, long-term development strategies and education sector policy within countries? Yes.

As such large numbers of children attend schools started and managed by their own communities and/or by non-governmental actors, it becomes increasingly possible to ask, "Can village-based or community schools have a national impact on access to education? Can alternatively provided schooling spur improved, long-term development strategies and education sector policy within countries? Can this experience also have a profound and lasting effect on how the international community approaches the goals of Education for All?" All indications are that the answer to these questions is also, "Yes."

This paper justifies the "yes" answers provided above and explores several issues raised by the community school experience around the world. First, I will consider the impact of community schools in increasing access and completion of primary school. Second, I will discuss their influence on the shape and behavior of the public sector. Third, I will explore how community-based strategies and active non-governmental provision of schooling fit into the global context of Education for All and, in particular, the Fast Track Initiative. Fourth, I will discuss how two areas of education sector policy—finance and decentralization—need to respond to the experience of community schools.

The impact of community schools: access

The past two decades have seen a growth in the non-governmental provision of public education. Many of these community-based schools started out as distinct initiatives funded through bilateral donor projects, non-governmental organization initiatives, private voluntary contributions, or other in-country, local efforts. In some instances, these projects have grown to the point of making major contributions to meeting a country's Education for All objectives.

A million children attend 35,000 non-formal, primary schools run by BRAC in Bangladesh. In Ethiopia, 350 community schools enroll approximately 30,000 students. Some 370,000 learners make use of 2,800 interactive radio instruction centers in Honduras, and some 30,000 use 250 similar centers in Zambia. The *Escuela Nueva* in Columbia now reaches over 1 million pupils in 20,000 schools.[124]

In Mali, more than 2,400 community schools enrolled 231,000 children in grades one through six in the 2002–03 school year. Overall, community schools enrolled 12 percent of the 7- to 12-year-olds in the country. They accounted for a 27 percent increase in access to primary school in Mali, raising the national public sector Gross Enrollment Rate (GER) from 44 percent to 56 percent (when private schools and *medersas* are added in, Mali's overall GER now reaches 67 percent).[125] Hence, at the national level, community schools represent an important contribution to the goal of Education for All in Mali.

However, the impact of community schooling can really be seen in the sub-regions where non-governmental initiatives were concentrated during the last decade. For example, Figure 7.1 shows that in seven of the 15 *academies d'enseignement* (sub-regions) in Mali, the percentage increase in access due to community schools exceeded the national percentage increase of 27 percent. In the sub-regions of San and Sikasso, community schools contribute 58 and 56 percent increases to the GER. (Save the Children schools are concentrated in Sikasso.)

Community schools provide access to basic education in areas and for populations routinely underserved by the formal system of public schools. This is by design and by necessity: rural areas are unserved by most public services. The opportunity to launch community school projects presents itself precisely because of the inadequacy of the formal public sector supply of basic education for certain populations. Community schools organize supply in ways that overcome the constraints faced by the public sector and therefore redress those inadequacies.

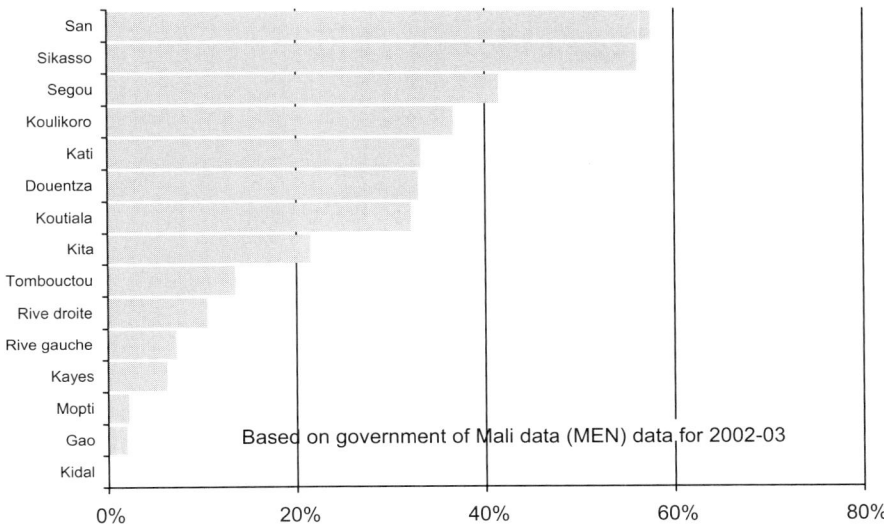

Figure 7.1: Percentage Increase in GER from Community Schools in Mali.

In Mali (see Figure 7.2), community schools have disproportionately reached rural children. One quarter of the children attending primary school in rural Mali go to community schools.[126]

The experience of community schooling has demonstrated that communities previously poorly served in terms of access to education can work with non-governmental actors to organize the supply of basic education. *Escuela Nueva* serves more than half of Columbia's rural areas. Guatemala has 1,300 *Nuevas Escuelas Unitarias* reaching the rural, indigenous Indian population. Community schools in Zambia in part target HIV/AIDS orphans. Community organized schools in Northern Pakistan provide access for 53,000 girls.[127]

The impact of community schools: completion

Access is one thing. Do these schools also ensure learning? Data on learning outcomes for primary school students, whether in community schools or in public sector schools, are scarce. Data that are available indicate that community schools are more effective in terms of assuring completion of school. In Guatemala, the *Nuevas Escuelas Unitarias* (NEU) have posted completion rates double those of other unitary primary schools that were not implementing the NEU program.[128] In Colombia, learning outcomes for students in the areas served by NEU are superior to the outcomes in the rest of the country.

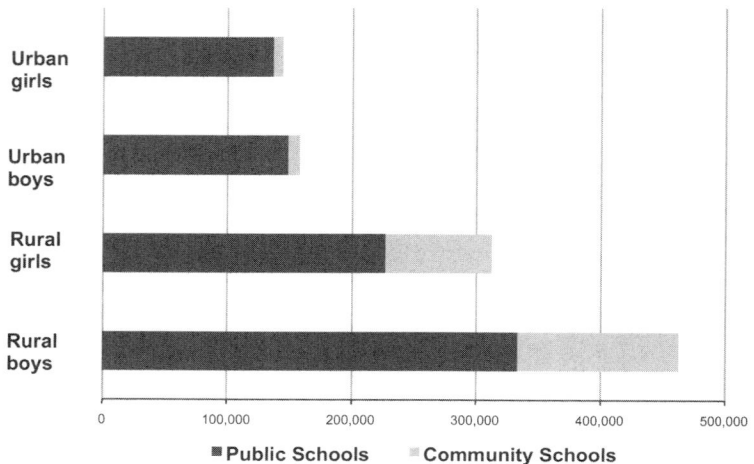

Figure 7.2: Urban and Rural Community Schools in Mali as Compared to Public Schools.

In Northern Ghana, the School for Life program condensing three years of primary school into a literacy-focused, nine-month program has seen 60 percent of its students go on to fourth grade in public schools, compared to a 46 percent survival rate to fourth grade for students attending the first three years of public school. School for Life is run by a local Ghanaian NGO with support from Danish non-governmental organizations. Most recent available data indicate that these schools are four to five times as cost-effective as the first three years of public school.[129] The schools supported through the Community Girls' Schools project in Baluchistan, Pakistan have contributed to decreased dropout and increased completion rates, almost tripling the number of girls going on to middle school in seven years.[130] Community schools in the Sikasso region of Mali are estimated to be 1.3 to 1.4 times as effective as public schools at producing 12-year-olds who make it to sixth grade.[131]

> *Data indicate that community schools are more effective [than public sector schools] in terms of assuring completion of school.*

The impact of community schools: policy

In addition to directly helping to organize places in school for underserved populations in developing countries, community schools, perhaps just as importantly, have influenced the basic education policy of governments.

The policy impact of large-scale community schooling is evident, for example, in government recognition that community-based approaches are viable complements to the formal public education system. In Mali, the government now includes community schools in all its official education statistics, whereas only a decade ago, the government did not even recognize these schools as viable entities. Through concerted effort on the part of the NGO community and USAID, a legal framework affording official status to community-initiated schools was developed and put in place in Mali. In Egypt, following the pilot efforts of UNICEF in Upper Egypt, the government and external funders have set up mechanisms for systematically transferring the lessons learned and best practices in UNICEF model community schools to regular public schools.[132]

The policy impact of large-scale community schooling is evident in government recognition that community-based approaches are viable complements to the formal public education system.

In addition to including community schools in their national statistics, governments have also shared some of the cost burden associated with operating these schools. Some models, like the community girls' schools in Pakistan or the schools supported by World Education in Mali, relied on government financing of teachers by design. Communities in Baluchistan identify and recruit teachers to work in their girls' schools. After initial training and a three-month trial period, the government recognizes these teachers and places them on the public sector payroll.[133] In other cases, governments have either taken over some of the financing of community schools or have begun promoting community-based supply models as features of public sector schools. Mali affords an example of the former. During the last three years, as part of a debt relief program, the Malian government has been able to provide a monthly stipend (25,000 FCFA) to approximately 5,000 community school teachers.[134]

Governments have also shared some of the cost burden associated with operating these schools.

Government recognition and partial funding of community schools implies at least a tacit, if not explicit recognition of the viability of less qualified teachers. In almost all cases, community schools have relied on locally recruited teachers with less than the nationally required level of education. Often, locally recruited teachers have minimal formal schooling—lower secondary, primary, or in some cases even less. What they lack in formal pre-service qualifications, however, they make up for in willingness to serve in a given place (often an area of the country where it has been difficult to place teachers, one major reason why the population in those areas is underserved in terms of access to basic education). Greater ongoing interaction and support

Greater ongoing interaction and support through the use of non-governmental intermediaries enables less qualified individuals to serve successfully as lower primary school teachers.

through the use of non-governmental intermediaries also enables less qualified individuals to serve successfully as lower primary school teachers. Recognizing community schools and paying their teachers represents a significant policy shift for the education sector, one that may hold the most promise for overcoming the supply bottleneck caused by inadequate numbers of qualified personnel willing to serve as teachers in remote areas.

Curriculum

Many of the community school projects and models being implemented around the world share a few common approaches to curriculum. Community school models often rely on a drastically reduced curriculum, focused primarily on reading and basic math. The Schools for Life in Ghana best illustrate this. By reducing the curriculum to a focus on literacy, they are able to provide the equivalent of a public school third grade education in just nine months.

> *By reducing the curriculum to a focus on literacy, they are able to provide the equivalent of a public school third grade education in just nine months. Perhaps most important is the use of maternal languages in the early primary grades.*

Perhaps most important is an emphasis on the use of maternal languages in the early primary grades. This is probably the single greatest factor that allows locally recruited teachers to be successful in the classroom. The intercultural, bilingual education program in Guatemala targeted the Mayan-speaking population, which had traditionally been poorly served by public schools using Spanish as the sole medium of instruction. The community schools supported by Save the Children in Mali relied on instruction in Bamanakan in the first three grades of primary school. The Schools for Life in Ghana also make use of the local language.

In Guatemala and Mali, government recognition of the success of these curricula and of the use of local languages has led to their inclusion in national, long-term sectoral development strategies. As illustrated by the Mali case, the *Nouvelle Ecole Fondamentale*, the centerpiece of the government's ten-year education strategy which begins instruction in the maternal language and then introduces and eventually switches to French, was based in large part on the Save the Children community school model.

> *Less qualified, local teachers who are hired and monitored by the community or by a local NGO show up and teach much more frequently than their officially more qualified colleagues in the public schools.*

Almost all developing countries struggle with teacher attendance and performance when teachers are assigned to work in the least desirable (poorest, most remote) regions of a country. Less qualified, local teachers who are hired and monitored by the community or by a local NGO show up and teach much more frequently than their officially more qualified colleagues in the public schools. A combination of more contact hours, a reduced curriculum, and instruction in the maternal language could easily explain how community schools, even using teachers with minimal formal schooling, can obtain results comparable to formal public schools.

Admittedly, formal public schools in most developing countries are obtaining miserable results, especially for the poorest people living in the least developed parts of the country. And, just as effort is directed at improving the public schools in a country, initiatives are needed that seek to dramatically improve what community-based models are able to achieve. The important thing to note is that improved community-based approaches to basic education would require decidedly different kinds of efforts and actors. The international community and the world-wide movement to achieve EFA need to recognize and take into account exactly what these differences entail and what they imply for how development assistance is structured.

Community schools and the global movement toward EFA

Fifteen years after its initial proclamation in 1990, achieving Education for All remains a major challenge for many countries. Progress has been made towards providing universal access to primary education, but 104 million children were still out of school in 2000.[135] In fact, providing adequate places in school to accommodate all of a country's children is only one aspect of achieving education for all. Available data show that in 11 countries, only half of the children who enter first grade persist through fifth grade. In another 15 countries, between 60 and 75 percent of the students survive through fifth grade. For these countries dropping out of school is as large a problem as lack of access.[136]

> *Initiatives are needed that seek to dramatically improve what community-based models are able to achieve. Improved community-based approaches to basic education would require decidedly different kinds of efforts and actors.*

Education systems the world over have been expanding to accommodate growing populations of school-age children. However, in the least developed countries of the world, typified by sub-Saharan Africa, growth in access in the last decade has barely kept pace with population growth.[137] The 1990s delivered severe shocks to the political, economic and social stability of many developing countries. Political strife derailed the development of too many countries in sub-Saharan Africa. Added to the problems brought on by armed conflict, and indeed exacerbated because of it, is the HIV/AIDS epidemic. Large percentages of the population across southern Africa are stricken. The impact is felt in terms of the children whose families are ravaged by sickness and death, leaving them less able to attend school. It is also felt increasingly in terms of the numbers of teachers who become sick and die each year.

The nature and structure of international development assistance will go a long way in determining whether countries will be able to meet the challenge of

162   *Community Schools in Africa: Reaching the Unreached*

expanding access and improving quality under current political and economic conditions. The international community remains committed to EFA and the last few years have seen a movement towards greater coordination and mobilization of budgetary resources for countries demonstrating good governance and good policies. A tool for targeting resources to those countries is The Education for All Fast Track Initiative (FTI). FTI focuses on achieving universal primary completion for boys and girls by 2015 and explicitly links increased donor support for primary education to recipient countries' policy performance and accountability for results. FTI focuses policy dialogue in each country around an indicative framework of clear education benchmarks relating to service delivery, student flow, system expansion and system financing. When a country succeeds in developing a sectoral plan that responds to these benchmarks they become eligible for additional, coordinated donor funding.

FTI explicitly links increased donor support for primary education to recipient countries' policy performance and accountability for results.

The funding shortfall

In June 2002, 18 countries were initially eligible for FTI support, and an additional five with large out-of-school populations were offered technical support to prepare plans for achieving universal primary completion. By January 2004, 12 of the original 18 were officially endorsed for incremental financial support through the FTI process. Later that year, the World Bank agreed to make eligible all low-income countries with a poverty reduction strategy and an agreed education sector plan, increasing the number of eligible countries from 18 to about 40. The challenge, as FTI defines it, is to ensure the commitment of funds necessary to support all those countries that are making progress towards universal primary access and completion by 2015. According to World Bank estimates, overall external financing for primary education in low-income countries will need to increase from just over $1 billion per year to about $3.7 billion per year through 2015.[138]

External financing for primary education in low-income countries will need to increase from just over $1 billion per year to about $3.7 billion per year through 2015... [This] is not likely to occur.

The need to contribute significantly more external assistance to help low-income countries invest in developing their own human resources is obvious. Equally obvious is the recognition that such an unprecedented increase in external financing is not likely to occur. In fact, the track record of the FTI to date in "closing the financing gap" is poor. The first ten countries to meet FTI criteria as of 2003 received commitments totaling $207.7 million for three years, $118.7 million less than what the donors themselves identified as the necessary external contribution to fund those countries' strategies.[139]

Too much emphasis on public sector reform

Also troubling is the FTI over-reliance on sectoral reform and expansion as the essential strategies for reaching the populations and areas that education systems currently are failing to serve. As laid out in Achieving Universal Primary Education by 2015: A Chance for Every Child,[140] the FTI approach is based on rigorous research into the financing and policy frameworks associated with countries that have track records of achieving universal, or near universal, primary completion. The FTI's "indicative framework" uses that research to establish targets for such policy levers as the percentage of public resources allocated to basic education, teacher salaries, student-teacher ratios, and spending on inputs other than teachers.

The explicit assumption is that if a policy environment consistent with the indicative framework is put in place, and if governmental will is demonstrated by mobilizing the lion's share (90 percent) of the necessary resources to implement that framework, then external funders will contribute the remaining resources. It is also assumed that amounts that in many countries would constitute a significant increase in resources for basic education would then be managed well enough to expand provision and improve efficiency (in terms of producing primary school completers) in ways that have never been accomplished in those countries. After making the case for this approach, the authors point out that better management of resources is as much a challenge as mobilizing them.[141] Saying that this challenge requires attention to capacity building and institutional support does not overcome the inherent limitation of a public sector-centric approach to universalizing access and completion. To their credit, Bruns *et al* do state that they "assume a public sector responsibility for *financing* the bulk of primary schooling, but not necessarily public *provision*."[142]

Including non-public education strategies and actors

One could argue that FTI needs to go a step further and work to develop the specific ways in which non-public provision of schooling can figure into country education sector strategies for reaching EFA. We can ask whether the experience of large-scale community school projects can help the international community think differently about how those additional resources could be used. Most importantly, community school projects have shown that it takes a combination of efforts and actors to successfully provide basic education to populations poorly served by the current systems.

Community school projects have shown that it takes a combination of efforts and actors to successfully provide basic education to populations poorly served by the current systems.

In case after case, community schools have been successfully organized because they relied on several actors. These include,

Government policy needs to make a decided shift away from administering and enforcing a single supply model and move towards a pluralistic approach.

but are far from limited to, the national system of education, communities themselves, local NGOs, international NGOs, local and national education authorities, and providers of external assistance. To take advantage of these kinds of experiences, government policy needs to make a decided shift away from administering and enforcing a single supply model and move towards a pluralistic approach. Simply put, if the prevailing model for basic schooling continues to fail to meet the needs of specific segments of the population, then as a matter of public policy, the government needs to seek out and encourage the development of other models, drawing on other resources and capacities—or on alternatives that have proven their efficacy.

In an FTI context focused on budgetary support for government-led, sectoral investment strategies, the pluralism inherent in the community school experience argues for including the negotiation of complementary roles and responsibilities within a sectoral framework. Education sector policy needs to explicitly create

Education sector policy needs to explicitly create space and mechanisms for public-private interaction and collaboration.

space and mechanisms for public-private interaction and collaboration. For example, in El Salvador the government contracts directly with local NGOs to support schools. In Honduras, the government contracts for the running of education centers for lower secondary education. Numerous other examples exist: South Africa has moved to school-based funding and school-level governance and management; school-based management has long been the norm in Australia; charter schools in the U.S. run by private entities receive direct allocations of funds from state education authorities.

If donor countries operating within the framework of FTI are going to funnel their resources through national education budgets, then it becomes even more important to develop policies and procedures that will allow the public sector to enter into, and manage, relationships with non-governmental actors, be they international or local NGOs, or communities themselves.

If donor countries are going to funnel their resources through national education budgets, then it becomes even more important to develop policies and procedures that will allow the public sector to enter into relationships with non-governmental actors, [including] communities.

Experience indicates that ministries of education are often unwilling to cede so much control and authority to local or non-governmental actors; or, when they are willing, they are usually inexperienced and need to develop new systems and modes of operation in order to be able to make those relationships work effectively. This includes collaborating on developing alternative approaches to teacher recruitment, teacher support, curriculum, school management, and community-school interaction. It can also include contracting for services, allocating and disbursing government funds to private entities, setting up mechanisms for oversight and accountability, and collecting sound and consistent information.

In addition to various types of public-private interaction, community schools in many instances have modeled inherently decentralized systems of schooling. NGOs have worked directly with communities and with local governments and education authorities to run their community school projects. The relationships at the local level are, in fact, a big contributing factor to what makes

The relationships at the local level are in fact a big contributing factor to what makes community schools able to operate and flourish.

community schools able to operate and flourish. The highly centralized systems of administration and management that are the norm in most low-income countries can gain a lot from looking at how decentralization has worked in the context of some large-scale community school projects. In the case of Mali, for example, this has even included local authorities creating mechanisms for generating resources for basic education. (Villages decide to allocate a fixed percentage of the revenue generated from cotton sales to support their community school). Control and decision-making authority are what make it possible to raise and use resources effectively locally, as well as to monitor teacher and school performance. Surveys of one group of community school management committees in Mali found that more than three-quarters of them regularly assured student and teacher attendance. In addition, they raised and spent, on average, US $159 per school.[143]

Experience has not demonstrated how to ensure that the teaching and learning that goes on in community schools is not just minimal, but in fact can rise to a level that can assure the completion of primary school and the attainment of life-long literacy and numeracy.

Community schools as features of education sector strategies

Community school projects have amply demonstrated that, by mobilizing local initiative, non-governmental actors, and decentralized capacity, it is possible to create opportunities for basic schooling that are more responsive to the needs of the populations living in areas largely unreached by the formal public sector. What the experience has not demonstrated is how to ensure that the teaching and learning that goes on in community schools is not just minimal, but in fact can rise to a level that can assure the completion of primary school and the attainment of life-long literacy and numeracy.

As discussed above, the global community working to support EFA should take into account some of the lessons from the community school experience. Most notably, education sector programs must encourage and accommodate roles for the full range of actors needed to successfully run schools. From a practical standpoint, this implies dramatically different capacity on the part of the public sector and improved capacity on the part of the private sector. For example, NGOs may have the experience and on-the-ground presence required to effectively engage communities and parents and help them set up the necessary structures to open and operate schools, and to do so using proven participatory methodologies. Rare are the government officials who have these tendencies, let alone these skills. On the other hand, government officials would have important roles to play in negotiating relationships, translating those relationships into contractual obligations, and then monitoring the fulfillment of the terms of those contracts (roles that were played by funding agencies when community schools were promoted through projects).

> *[There is a need for] dramatically different capacity on the part of the public sector and improved capacity on the part of the private sector.*

Decentralization efforts usually focus more on building the capacity of local education authorities to administer state-run systems. That would need to shift to building the above kinds of capacities and, in fact, forgo the direct running of the education system. A variety of approaches must be deployed to meet the variety of needs that exist across communities. This means that education authorities must abandon the prevailing administrative imperative of assuring consistent delivery of a single supply model. This will not occur without significant investment in a changed framework and new set of capacities, at the central ministry level, but more importantly throughout the decentralized education administration system.

Missed opportunities in Mali?

For their part, private non-governmental actors need to build their capacity to implement projects and to assure high levels of quality. This also implies that non-governmental agencies need to think more broadly about their roles within developing countries. If NGO provision of schooling is going to be progressively incorporated into the public education system, then NGOs can no longer define their mission as filling the space left vacant by lack of government services. They need to think critically about how their actions can in fact enhance and extend public sector capacity.

> *NGOs need to think critically about how their actions can in fact enhance and extend public sector capacity.*

The experience of USAID and Save the Children in Mali may, in fact, illustrate a missed opportunity to make this kind of shift in government-NGO relationships.

If the community school movement in Mali can be said to have successfully demonstrated an alternative approach to opening and running primary schools, it can also be said that it has failed at addressing what was identified as an issue as early as 1995.[144] At no point in the experience of Save the Children in Sikasso was the issue of government funding for community schools addressed. During the course of ten years of experience, it should have been possible to experiment with different funding mechanisms and arrangements that would have allowed the ministry to define ways to allocate funds to community schools that would not subvert the local governance and management that are at the heart of the model.

> *At no point in the experience of Save the Children in Sikasso was the issue of government funding for community schools addressed.*

Recently, Mali has negotiated a debt relief program that frees up resources to be used to pay a monthly stipend of 25,000 FCFA to contractual teachers, including 5,000 community school teachers.[145] While this provides some resources for community schools it also raises several questions: For how long will the central government be committed to paying community school teachers? Is the expectation that eventually responsibility for teacher salaries will revert back to the local SMCs, or do government long-term financial plans include continuing to pay community school teachers? If not, given the fact that SMCs were struggling to meet the requirements of paying their teachers 3,500 FCFA per month, how will they assume responsibility for this much higher stipend? Furthermore, the funds for the stipends are being allocated through the local education authority, not through the SMCs themselves. This risks severing the employer-employee relationship between SMCs and their teachers.

Another opportunity that may have been missed in Mali was to demonstrate how to set quality standards related to student outcomes and how to construct the means to more systematically monitor those outcomes. An Education for All strategy that includes multiple actors promoting a plurality of schooling models cannot rely on input-dependent standards of quality: class size, textbook ratios and the presence of furniture. Outcome measures—the percentage of students completing primary school; the percentage meeting measurable standards for language and math proficiency—would better serve a system deliberately pursuing multiple approaches to providing basic schooling. The capacity of NGOs, local communities and local governments to use outcome-based systems of accountability would also need to be included in sector development strategies. School self-assessments in Namibia, School Performance Assessment Meetings in Ghana, and report cards in Brazil are some promising examples of how a decentralized system of outcome-based accountability can work in developing countries.

The next step: higher quality

The lesson of community schools is that basic education can be organized through different approaches that rely more on local and non-governmental

> *The next decade should focus on how to use sector investment strategies not only to accommodate and expand community-based schooling but also to ratchet up the quality of community schools.*

actors than on the formal system. The challenge of community schools is: can these kinds of efforts be incorporated into the sector investment programs that draw the bulk of government and external financing and attention? What case examples are showing is that community schools do make significant contributions to achieving EFA, primarily by targeting the populations and areas least served by the formal system. Community schools are also modeling more democratic, inherently decentralized approaches to providing schooling. They have yet to prove whether they can deliver high quality instruction. The next decade should therefore focus on how to use sector investment strategies not only to accommodate and expand community-based schooling but also to ratchet up the quality of community schools.

Notes

[123] Mali, Ghana, Ethiopia, Malawi, Uganda, Chad, Zambia, Egypt, Bangladesh, Pakistan, Indonesia, India, Columbia, Guatemala, Honduras, El Salvador, Peru.

[124] USAID. EQUIP 2 Project, Policy Brief: Achieving EFA in underserved regions. (2004).

[125] Ministère de l'Education Nationale Mali. *Annuaire des statistiques scolaires de l'enseignement fondamental, 2002–2003.* (Government of Mali).

[126] *Ibid.*

[127] USAID. *EQUIP 2 Project, Policy Brief: Achieving EFA in underserved regions.*

[128] Chesterfield and Fubio. *Cost Effectiveness Study of Nueva Escuela Unitaria and Intercultural Bilingual Education.* (AED BEST Project, 1997).

[129] Schools for Life data were gathered by the EQUIP project from the implementing NGOs in Ghana and compared to government costs for primary schooling as put forth in Ghana's official FTI strategy.

[130] USAID. *EQUIP 2 Project, Policy Brief: Achieving EFA in underserved regions.*

[131] This is based on analysis of the percent of net 12 year old enrollment in sixth grade compared to overall enrollment in all grades of primary education for community and public schools. Since many community schools do not include a full primary cycle, this analysis probably greatly underestimates the effective contribution of community schools to net sixth grade completion.

[132] Farrell, Joseph. *The Egyptian Community Schools Program: Case Study.* (Ontario Institute for Studies in Education, University of Toronto, December 2003).

[133] Ogrady, Barbara. *Teaching Communities to Educate Girls in Balochistan.* (AED, 1994).

[134] EFA-FTI progress report 3-26-04.

[135] UNESCO *EFA Monitoring Report* 2003.

[136] *Ibid.*

[137] *Ibid.*

[138] EFA-FTI progress report 3-26-04.

[139] Global Campaign for Education. *Briefing Paper: Education for All Fast Track: The No-Progress Report.* (September 2003) p. 6.

[140] Bruns, Mingat and Rakotomala, World Bank, 2003.

[141] *Ibid,* p. 15.

[142] *Ibid,* p. 9 (italics in original text).

[143] Save the Children. *Annuaire statistique des programmes éducation et santé et nutrition scolaire du cercle de Kolondieba* (2003–2004).

[144] DeStefano, Joe. *Community-Based Primary Education: Lessons Learned from the Basic Education Expansion Project in Mali.* (USAID, 1996).

[145] World Bank. *Education for All—Fast Track Initiative Progress Report.* (March 2004) p. 13.

References

Chesterfield and Fubio. Cost Effectiveness Study of Nueva Escuela Unitaria and Intercultural Bilingual Education. (AED BEST Project, 1997)

DeStefano, Joe. Community-Based Primary Education: Lessons Learned from the Basic Education Expansion Project in Mali. (USAID, 1996)

Farrell, Joseph. The Egyptian Community Schools Program: Case Study. (Ontario Institute for Studies in Education, University of Toronto, December 2003)

Global Campaign for Education. Briefing Paper: Education for All Fast Track: The No-Progress Report. (September 2003)

Ministère de l'Education Nationale Mali. Annuaire des statistiques scolaires de l'enseignement fondamental, 2002–2003. (Government of Mali)

Ogrady, Barbara. Teaching Communities to Educate Girls in Balochistan. (AED, 1994)

Save the Children. Annuaire statistique des programmes éducation et santé et nutrition scolaire du cercle de Kolondieba (2003–2004)

UNESCO EFA Monitoring Report 2003

USAID. EQUIP 2 Project, Policy Brief: Achieving EFA in underserved regions. (2004)

World Bank. Education for All—Fast Track Initiative Progress Report. (March 2004)

Chapter 8

What's Next for Community Schools?

Jordan Naidoo

Meeting the present and future educational needs of individuals, communities and national and global economies is a momentous task. It will require far more than short-sighted tinkering with existing educational modalities. In an era of shrinking funding,[146] improved planning and administrative and managerial efficiency alone cannot ensure that educational opportunities will be available to all, especially to those who are hard to reach: children affected by HIV/AIDS;[147] orphans and vulnerable children; mobile populations, and those affected by on-going conflict and other crises across the world.

Moreover, while the decision to send children to school is strongly influenced by economic, social and cultural contexts, it is also affected by the terms on which schooling is made available, and by its quality. These "supply-side" issues, such as costs, distance to school, the availability of school facilities and school quality have a significant impact on access, participation, and learning outcomes.[148] Simply increasing resources will not guarantee greater access to, and improvements in, public education systems. Nor will it address the needs of communities in remote, poor, or disadvantaged areas. Entirely different approaches to educational provision, management, and governance are required.

New thinking in education challenges the concept of a "one-best-system" hierarchy, emphasizing instead the value of hybrid models of organization. The idea is that more hybrid, loosely coupled educational systems can capture the advantages of centralization and coordination produced by hierarchy, while at the same time

> A mix of complementary learning opportunities that include community schools is necessary to supplement public education systems.

harnessing the benefits of more decentralized provision and management of education.[149] From this perspective, it becomes clear that a mix of complementary learning opportunities that include community schools is necessary to supplement public education systems. Indeed, only by adopting such hybrid, or pluralistic, delivery systems can we hope to meet EFA goals and provide access to quality education for the more than a hundred million children who currently do not attend school.[150] Thus, a continuing role for community schools and other complementary models becomes even more vital, when one considers that the real challenge of EFA is not simply to provide access for those children not in school but also to create competencies and improve learning achievement.

Multiple actors, models and strategies

Community-based schooling and other complementary approaches have been successful because they rely on a variety of actors outside the national system of education: communities, local and international NGOs and other providers of external assistance. To take advantage of these kinds of expertise, government policies need to shift away from a single-supply model to a more pluralistic approach based on multiple models and strategies, drawing on resources, capacities and alternatives whose efficacy has been demonstrated.[151] At the same time, community-based efforts should not relieve governments of the political and financial responsibility for ensuring the right of every citizen to access an education appropriate to his or her needs. Community schools and local empowerment should not be used as a cover for governments to shift responsibility for providing adequate resources to meet their obligations to EFA.

Government policies need to shift away from a single-supply model to a more pluralistic approach based on multiple models and strategies.

The benefits of community schools

Usually characterized by the community contributing resources to, and participating in the management of schools, the value of community schools in providing access is generally undeniable. Whether as spontaneous, community-established schools (for example, the *Harambee* schools in Kenya) or community schools supported by international agencies (either intended to integrate ultimately into the state system or operating as an alternative to the state system), they offer an environment where teachers, students, parents and other community stakeholders see themselves as part of a community and deal with issues of learning, diversity, governance, and community-building on an intimate level.

Save the Children's experiences from Mali to Haiti[152] provide ample evidence that community schools increase access to education, especially for girls and other marginalized groups; that they are more relevant to local development needs and conditions; that they are more cost-effective than public schools in providing comparable, if not better, instructional services for less money; and that they have positive outcomes in terms of increased student achievement, greater teacher accountability and improved governance.

Key factors for the success of community schools include:

- reducing distance between home and school;
- the motivation of communities and other stakeholders;
- innovation and flexibility that address local needs;
- providing an appropriate curriculum in local languages;[153]
- drawing on and developing local capacities, including recruiting teachers familiar with the local environment at lower cost (with lower qualifications) and encouraging the recruitment of local female teachers;
- learning from previous experiences;
- the presence of external catalysts such as local, national and international NGOs, government agents and the private sector;
- consistent financial inputs;
- good communication and participation strategies.

What is the ultimate role of community schools?

The ultimate role of community schools is not completely clear. Is it to mainstream learners into the formal education system, or to develop an alternative, parallel delivery system? Save the Children's experience with community-based schooling suggests that adopting an either/or position with regard to these questions is not very useful. Clearly, we cannot simply apply a single, uniform school model throughout a country or even, for that matter, throughout a program.

Community schools increase access, are more relevant, more cost-effective and have positive outcomes in terms of student achievement, teacher accountability and improved governance.

This, then, leaves the issue of the degree of variation and flexibility versus fidelity to the original design. Over time, as experience from Mali to Malawi demonstrates, Save the Children has tended to implement the model in such a way that many of its schools are expected to make the transition into the "formal" government system. In these cases we still face the challenge of figuring out how to ensure the "operational integrity" of the community schools and how to retain the key features that contributed to their efficacy in the first place.

On the other hand, there are instances where community schools will, and should, remain outside the formal government system. This may be necessary especially where particular groups (defined by gender, ethnicity, age, etc.) face multiple barriers to learning, such as time, space, circumstance, conflict and emergencies. In these cases, community schools will need to adapt to meet the needs and circumstances of different environments, including religious and cultural environments, rural/urban environments and ethnically hetero-geneous environments. It is clear, therefore, that there needs to be some reconceptualizing of the notion of community schooling within a new, multi-faceted system of diverse and interconnected learning communities, institutions and spaces, which attempts to go beyond the artificial boundaries of formal and non-formal education.

The challenge for those supporting the community school, be it NGOs or even governments, is how to encourage the community to reflect on its own existing and emerging learning needs and practices and translate this reflection into social change. As we begin to strengthen the role of community schools in meeting the challenge of providing for the education needs of the world community, we need to monitor, evaluate and understand community schools better, taking into account dimensions of time and change. We at Save the Children see this review as a first step toward facilitating further dialogue around the role and design of community schools and other local participation initiatives. It is our intention that additional research will be forthcoming, including forms of participatory research by community and school stakeholders and the development and dissemination of integrated and comprehensive guidelines for the planning, design, and maintenance of different models of community schools. Some dilemmas and issues[154] arising from our initial reflection are explored below.

> *The challenge is how to encourage the community to reflect on its own existing and emerging learning needs and practices and translate this reflection into social change.*

Defining communities in the context of community schools

Community participation in education is seen as a way to increase resources and ensure that they are used cost-effectively; to improve the accountability of schools to the communities they serve and to respond to local needs. Hence, community participation tends to improve equitable access, retention, quality and performance in schooling.

Nevertheless, there is a need to reflect more critically on the nature of participation, and on how we define "community." Different degrees of participation may be apparent, from "pseudo-participation" involving community members' use of a service and their contribution of resources, to their "genuine participation" in decision-making. The degree of participation can vary among communities as well as among different members within communities.[155] Communities are complex and culturally diverse entities, not limited to geographical space and not necessarily bound by common interests, concerns, and goals. Thus, the "community" does not always represent a homogeneous group of people, devoid of power relations. Indeed, the promotion of community participation may fail to acknowledge the multiple ways in which local power is reinforced.[156]

While "community" has a vast number of definitions,[157] it commonly suggests membership or exclusion based on geography, ethnicity, gender, overlapping networks of relationships, commitment and generalized reciprocity, shared values and practices, collective goods, and duration.[158] Community schools, which generally reflect some of these characteristics, can be pivotal sites for drawing on a "spirit of community" as a means to extend participation in decision-making to support access to quality education.

Yet there are many sites where issues of membership, shared values, relationships, mutual commitment and duration (i.e., a community's longevity) apply weakly, if at all. In such instances, token participation based on a consultative process where participants are informed of, and expected to accept, decisions that have already been made,

> *Community schools can be pivotal sites for drawing on a "spirit of community" as a means to extend participation in decision-making in support of access to quality education.*

passes for authentic participation. For example, school management committees may mirror existing social divisions, with women not attending meetings or remaining silent when they do.[159] This is not to say that community participation in educational provision, management and decision-making should not be promoted, but rather to note that it is a complex tool that can be manipulated in multiple ways to varying effect.[160]

Clearly, there needs to be more critical reflection on the development priorities of the various sub-communities, NGOs, government and other groups involved in setting up and maintaining community schools, without assuming that the community as a whole is committed to the educational development project at hand. Thus, we must consider more seriously such questions as:

- How does the community perceive the school? e.g., as their own, the NGO's, the government's, or someone else's?
- What value does the community attach to the education that their children receive from this school?
- How does the community school link to, and contribute to, the development of local institutions, relationships, processes, culture, and knowledge systems?
- How are these local institutions, relationships, processes, culture, and knowledge systems reflected in the content, learning interactions and management of the community school?
- What is the specific nature of participation in the community schools? i.e., management, planning, financing, teaching/learning, curriculum design, etc.?
- Who participates in the decision-making processes and in what ways?
- Who facilitates the community participation process?
- Is the development of individual and community participation in society the focus of the school or is the development of the school the focus of community participation?

These questions become ever more urgent as communities face increasing socio-economic pressures, the demands of national standards, examinations and equivalency qualifications, and transitions into government systems.

Meeting the access challenge without sacrificing quality

Recently, quality interventions have tended to more away from a limited input-process-output model to encompass a results model, focusing on measuring the extent and nature of what children learn in school, and the program components that are most likely to produce desirable learning outcomes. Community-based schooling and other Alternate Basic Education (ABE) initiatives are beginning to follow a similar trajectory with an increasing emphasis on quality beyond mere access.

SC's community schools experience suggests that the quality of learning in community schools is at least as good, and often better, than the quality in government schools.

SC's community schools experience suggests that the quality of learning in community schools is at least as good, and often better, than the quality in government schools. For example, in SC's Mali community schools, pupils' scores in French and Math were equivalent to those in government schools, and these results were mostly due to school-related factors.[161] Students in the CHANCE schools in Uganda outperformed their counterparts in the government schools, and they accomplished this in a nine-month (instead of 12-month) school year and a shorter school day.

This review indicates further that: in addition to changed teacher behavior, teacher attitudes and beliefs are critical to what happens in the classroom; that change takes time; that programs need to address organizational conditions within and in relation to the school, including school leadership, management and supportive community participation. In order to keep the focus on quality outcomes, whether one is talking about formal school systems or community-based schools and other ABE initiatives, successful programs need to:

- empower teachers and administrators;
- engage families in their children's education;
- connect schools and communities;
- improve academic performance by fostering students' health;
- teach a core curriculum;
- provide relevant capacity building for parents, community stakeholders, educators and administrators.

Ensuring gains in gender equity

All the world's regions have striven to enroll more girls in school. During the 1990s, the number of girls in primary school increased faster than the number of boys. The rate of girls' enrollment in sub-Saharan Africa's primary schools has more than doubled since 1960, to nearly 70 percent. However, girls in the region remain far more likely than boys to never attend school or to drop out early. And worldwide, 58 million of the estimated 103 million primary-age

> *Gender discrimination [in education] remains a pressing, unsolved, global problem.*

children who are out of school are girls, which indicates that gender discrimination remains a pressing, unsolved, global problem.

Community-based schooling and other ABE initiatives address some of the problems that disproportionately affect girls' educational opportunities. These include, for example, fear for girls' safety when schools are a long way from home; the demand for girls' domestic work; and the lack of female role models in schools and the community.

However, to ensure that gains in gender parity are not eroded, community schooling models must employ strategies that are sometimes at odds with the larger system. For example, the practice of stipulating that 50 percent of those enrolled should be girls (employed by Save the Children in Mali) may be necessary in contexts where gender imbalances in enrollment are severe. Yet in instituting such measures, we would be remiss if we did not continue to investigate the reasons for girls' non-enrollment or withdrawal, and ensure that those households that are already suffering significant hardship and cannot afford to keep girls in school are not penalized further by, for example, having to pay fees and the cost of school materials.[162]

While community schools offer a means to ensure gender parity in education enrollment, a number of other steps should accompany future initiatives in order to promote broader transformation of gender roles in the community. As we adapt curricula and school organization to suit local cultural and economic practices, we need to guard against reinforcing discriminatory gender roles and responsibilities rather than attempting to address and transform them. For example, the school day is sometimes structured around girls' domestic chores, without questioning whether it is appropriate for girls to take on the bulk of this work, rather than promoting the view that the work should be more equally distributed between boys and girls. Accordingly, as we strengthen the role of community schools and other forms of ABE, we

> *Each additional year of girls' education strengthens their ability to delay marriage … to earn more and to improve their health and self-esteem.*

need to raise awareness within communities, including training school committee members, parents, and other community stakeholders on how to encourage girls' participation in education, without ignoring the broader issue of gender relations.

Another challenge in relation to gender is to recognize that extending equal educational opportunities to girls in their early years is but a first step in the empowerment of women. Primary education is essential for girls, but should not be the ultimate goal. Limiting the focus to access to primary education makes it difficult for children to integrate into the state system after completion of the initial cycle in a community school. There is a danger that a two-tier system is created in which those attending community schools are marginalized from the state system, while only those attending school at higher levels have access to job opportunities. Each additional year of girls' education strengthens their ability to delay marriage, a strategy that is critical to the survival and well-being of children, to the use of family planning, and to women's ability to earn more and to improve their health and self-esteem. The option of looking ahead to secondary school is an incentive for girls to attend and perform well in primary school, and reassures families that their investments will pay off.[163]

Managerial and financial implications

Experience and research indicate that many community schools serve children better than public schools in much of Sub-Saharan Africa. In studies of community schools in Ghana, Mali and Honduras as part of USAID's EQUIP 2 Program, Joe DeStefano found that Ghana's School for Life and Mali's Community Schools were more cost-effective than public schools—even though their unit costs were higher. Educatodos (Honduras) has both a higher completion rate and much lower costs[164] than public schools.

Save the Children's own experience, as borne out by the case studies in this book, offers a number of economic arguments in support of community schools and suggests that it is fiscally responsible to establish these schools to supplement public schools. The Save the Children US-supported CHANCE schools in Uganda, for example, are acknowledged by Ugandan government officials and others as a high-quality, inexpensive basic education program, recognized for its positive impact on educational access and performance, as compared to the formal educational system.

Save the Children's experience suggests that it is fiscally responsible to establish community schools to supplement public schools.

Many critics of community schools, however, are of the view that they are not much more cost-effective than public schools, and that they place an unnecessarily heavy burden on already disadvantaged communities. Indeed, there is a need to confront questions of cost-effectiveness more broadly, rather than simply looking at the cost of infrastructure and learning materials. We need to take into account start-up costs (including design costs), on-going operational costs (including external management by NGO personnel), payment and training of teachers and facilitators (including on-going school and classroom support to teachers beyond formal training sessions) and cash and in-kind inputs from communities. Community schools invariably require greater contributions from the community than government schools that serve wealthier areas. In Mali, for example, school management committees mobilize resources for school construction and teacher salaries from the community. Although construction costs and teacher payments are lower than in government schools, the fact that they are met by the community rather than by the government can sometimes be perceived as outweighing the benefits of community schools.[165]

In addition to the greater capacity and resources provided by NGOs like Save the Children-US to help establish and maintain community schools, increasing parents' involvement adds additional inputs of private time and effort. Yet private costs other than fees (such as uniforms, learning materials, and loss of labor) are often not included in an accounting of the costs and benefits of community schools, and they should be. These costs may be considerable and may limit the participation of some parents, thus undermining quality improvement efforts that depend on greater community participation. But these very investments may contribute to the success of community schools, especially when communities themselves, as well as donors, have a vested interest in seeing that community schools succeed. Successful community schools tend to have a motivating vision that is sharply defined and that includes a clearly articulated purpose and statement of desired results. So, even if we factor in all the costs, many studies indicate that community schools may, in fact, be more cost-effective than public schools.

> *Community school initiatives must confront the issue of what happens to their learners after they leave the community school.*

There is a need to define learning achievement more broadly, to include achievements in math and language and other tests, the transition of students to higher levels (for example, to junior secondary schools and beyond), and their participation in the formal and non-formal labor markets. Community school initiatives must confront the issue of what happens to their learners after they leave the community school, either through graduation or dropping out.

Other issues that must be considered in assessing the effectiveness of community schools include the extent to which these schools are incorporating new ideas that are emerging around learning, such as lifelong learning, multiple intelligences, flexible learning, collaborative learning, etc., as well as the schools' ability to adapt to and generate change.

Community schools and decentralization

The majority of education systems have, until recently, been managed through highly centralized bureaucracies, with most functions carried out directly by the central Ministry of Education (MOE) or by officials posted at the regional or district level acting on detailed instructions from ministry officials at the national level. During the 1990s, however, many countries began to implement changes in the way education is managed by decentralizing functions and resources, diversifying service delivery modes, and transforming roles and

Community schools are a part of the larger trend toward decentralization.

responsibilities within the central MOE and at regional, district, and school levels. Community schools, at least in their current manifestation, are in some ways a part of this larger trend toward decentralization. Interest in participation and community schools—often based within the NGO community—is becoming a part of the participatory discourse and of the official aims and objectives of governments and international development agencies.

Despite the considerable support for—indeed, the near universality—of decentralization policies, there are on-going debates about their impact. There is also ambivalence about which way to go, resulting in flip-flops or swings from top-down to bottom-up emphases.[166] Given that community schools are becoming more and more entangled in a process that is often a morass of confusion, there needs to be some clarification of the relationship of community schools to broader decentralization efforts and to the multiple forms of district- and school-based governance and management that decentralization entails. Whatever the rationale for decentralization, it implies a "principle of complementarity" and the notion of multiple actors working together towards Education for All. This suggests that decentralization does not imply abandonment by the state, but rather a change in the role of the state.[167] Therefore, careful consideration of the balance between formal education (working through host governments, formal schooling and sector-wide approaches, or SWAps) and non-formal interventions and alternatives to traditional schooling, including the role of NGOs, unions, voluntary groups, etc., is required.

District Education Offices and similar decentralized education management structures will differ significantly in the ways in which they relate to community and to "regular" government schools; in the amount of autonomy they allow them; and in the support they provide. Although not every district will employ the same set of strategies to support its schools, be they government or community schools, it is expected that community schools will be allowed greater flexibility to create programs that fit local needs. Within such a model the DEO should be a facilitator, providing activities and resources to all schools under its jurisdiction as they design and implement their programs. One of the dilemmas that DEOs face in such situations is how to accommodate school autonomy while ensuring compliance with national, state or provincial regulations.

We need to pay attention to how we work with communities in establishing and running schools and to the links between these schools and the larger process of decentralization, as well as to the role of stakeholders beyond the immediate "communities." Community schools should continue to be the locus for the provision of education and other services to marginalized communities. However, there needs to be change from the developmental practice that aims to produce limited, localized spaces of empowerment, to a practice aimed at thinking about relative levels of empowerment within local, regional, and national networks.

Indeed, reshaping linkages *beyond* the local community, and strengthening broader participatory processes and stocks of social capital may be a key determinant of the long-term success or failure of these schools. It also serves as a means whereby marginalized communities can command *enough* power to challenge structural inequalities (whether based on class, gender, or ethnicity) in their countries, beyond their own immediate locality. Through such an approach, community schools can become part of "longer-term projects and reshaped political networks that embed within themselves a more inclusive discourse of development, and a fuller sense of citizenship."[168]

> *Community schools can become part of "longer-term projects and reshaped political networks that embed within themselves a more inclusive discourse of development."*

Rethinking sustainability

Sustainability has many meanings, but the financial meaning is becoming the central focus in development. While some public finance analyses suggest that governments should indefinitely fund public goods and activities that generate positive results, advocates of sustainability emphasize local "ownership," and interventions that only require start-up funding, which can then be maintained locally without external support.[169] The focus on financial sustainability is partly motivated by opposition to indefinite development assistance "hand-outs."

While financial sustainability is certainly a desirable goal, it may be difficult to achieve as currently conceived. Although external development assistance cannot be expected to fund community schools into eternity, given the extreme poverty of many of the communities where these schools are established, it is naïve to expect those communities to take on the financial burden of operating the schools. Such communities can, and do, contribute a variety of resources but the overall operational costs, and in particular, budgets for the payment of teacher salaries, may have to be drawn from national public funds and/or external sources. Sudden withdrawal of external support may prove costly. While communities may be able to maintain the infrastructure and govern the school by drawing on local resources and labor, providing on-going curriculum support without external help may be impossible. While perhaps necessary under current circumstances, reliance on school fees and other forms of community funding is not desirable in the long term. If access to primary education comes to depend on the ability of a family or community to pay, then only the better-off can get a quality education, while the poorest will be left even farther behind. Relatively more advantaged communities served by government and private schools are not expected to pay for schooling. Why, then, do we expect impoverished communities to do so?

The advocates of sustainability are correct in saying that many development projects will fail if donors simply fund capital inputs and then leave. Yet the solution is not to create an illusion of sustainability, but rather to accept the reality of the need for continued subsidies for development projects, and to ensure that the necessary stream of funds for maintenance is available.[170] Securing the gains made through community schools, whether integrated into government systems or as stand-alone institutions, requires continuing commitment and support from government and development partners in both policy and financing, until the returns to the household and national economy materialize.

Scaling up innovative practices

On the supply side, various donors and international NGOs have invested heavily in a variety of interventions intended to increase access to schooling and/or to improve the practices of teachers, pupils and other education stakeholders. In many SSA countries, a number of community school programs (both integrated and alternative models) supported by different NGOs, co-exist. These are often small-scale, localized pockets of effective educational innovation, operating in areas under-served by the state system. In one sense or another, they represent "demonstration" projects designed to generate concrete information about good educational and pedagogical practice.[171] As we come to recognize more fully the enormity of the dual challenges of EFA access and quality, there is an increasing demand for system-wide expansion and improvement. Hence, external providers are being challenged to scale up such projects—implementing them more widely, more deeply and more rapidly than in the past.

The process of scale-up has usually consisted of a replication model characterized by a one-way flow of information and mandates from external providers or districts to schools and teachers. Success is determined by fidelity of implementation at multiple sites and failure is attributed to teachers not supporting the effort. But scaling up means more than merely replicating structures. The process of developing and scaling up education reforms is iterative and complex, requiring cooperative interactions among program developers, policymakers, and school authorities. How each group addresses their tasks and interactions will vary according to design, context, and resources. Perhaps most important, the actors must align policies and infrastructure into a cohesive network of support to sustain effective practice.

Save the Children's experience with community schools reaffirms what has been demonstrated in a number of education reform initiatives world-wide, namely, that *parent and community engagement* is essential. Clearly, successful provision of quality education is about local answers and widespread participation among stakeholders. Teachers, parents, and students should all take part in the design, development, and implementation of solutions aimed at improving their specific educational situation. At the same time, SC's experience indicates that successful innovation will not take place of its own accord: learning has to be facilitated, endogenous answers have to be obtained, institutions have to be built, technical capacity has to be transferred, information has to be gathered, and political-economic strategies have to be pursued.

Actors must align policies and infrastructure into a cohesive network of support to sustain effective practice.

These conditions, however, highlight a central contradiction when we speak of efforts to scale up and replicate successful innovations. Attempting to replicate the innovation itself (i.e., take it to scale) *inevitably* violates some of the very conditions that render certain innovations successful in the first place. The fact is that people's educational aspirations, needs, and contexts differ from place to place. Accordingly, what works in one location won't necessarily work in another. And even in those instances where an "outside" innovation addresses some of the specific needs and aspirations of a particular location, its fate is still precarious, for unless there is widespread ownership of the innovation (a factor largely engendered through the development of local solutions), chances are it will not become a permanent feature of that location's educational landscape.

Instead of replication of specific innovations, it is the *conditions which give rise to the innovations in the first place* that should be replicated. By doing so, not only do we improve the prospects that successful education projects will go to scale, but we also create an environment that will spawn multiple innovations and promote significant knowledge-sharing. What is needed, then, are the tools, techniques, structures, mechanisms, and institutions that can:

1. help generate widespread demand for quality innovations;
2. facilitate an informed, localized deliberation over the substance and character of education delivery, management and outcomes;
3. create a policy environment that is hospitable to quality education for all, and
4. safeguard ongoing, learning-driven change.[172]

Successful scale-up efforts have four properties: widespread implementation, deep changes in classroom practices, sustainability, and a sense of ownership of new practices and policies among teachers and school leaders. This last characteristic of a successful scale-up effort is particularly important. Without a shift in ownership, schools and communities must rely indefinitely on external providers to sustain the core practices of the school, a financial relationship that cannot be sustained over the long term. Hence, reform efforts must take into

While we may not be able to bring community schools per se to scale, it is possible to recreate the conditions that make them successful in other parts of the system.

account a set of core tasks that include: developing and providing support for implementation; ensuring high-quality implementation at each school site; evaluating and improving the intervention; obtaining or providing financial support; building organizational capacity; adapting to local contexts; and sustaining the reform over time. Instead of popping programs into schools, innovators should respect the resource limitations, values, and other conditions that already exist in schools.[173] Thus, while we may not be able to bring community schools *per se* to scale, it is possible to recreate the conditions that make them successful in other parts of the system.

Transitioning to government systems

The strategy of transitioning community schools into the larger government system has positive and negative implications. The value of the strategy in terms of sustainability, and of ensuring that governments fulfill their obligations as the primary provider of public education, is obvious. In addition, for educational quality improvement initiatives (such as community schools) to have broader impact, there is a "crying need to go to scale—that is, to transform the whole system."[174]

However, one needs to consider the impact of this on the quality of the community schools themselves and on the larger system. In many countries, the entire system is seriously deficient, with school infrastructure being inadequate, the most basic teaching materials (pencils, paper, chalk, textbooks) in short supply, and teachers poorly trained, supervised and monitored. As community schools are drawn into such an environment, the challenge is to ensure that they retain the operational integrity that accounted for much of their success in the first place.

Successful learning outcomes in community schools result, to some extent, from the idea of learning for community advantage and drawing from "funds of community knowledge." It is not surprising, therefore, that syllabuses and curricula in most community school initiatives have been designed so that teachers can facilitate the connection of students with subject matter drawn from an exploration of their world. Where they use the public education curriculum, it is usually in a condensed form, and includes additional content more closely relevant to the realities of students' lives. As community schools are transitioned into government systems, continuing to base learning on "community knowledge" does not have to be in conflict with the standardized syllabus requirements of government schools. It can supplement them. As part of the process, it is important that ministries and departments of education and teacher education programs develop appropriate pedagogies and curricula that enable students to access, record and learn from and through community funds of knowledge.[175] A balance must exist to ensure that students who go on to government schools acquire the content knowledge and appropriate skills to participate in those settings, and are not disadvantaged in their attempt to acquire formal qualifications.

The notion of operational integrity is particularly important to ensure continuing access and participation of marginalized populations. For example, while girls in urban areas are almost as likely as boys to be enrolled in school, the same cannot be said for girls in rural, remote areas. In these contexts the special features of community schools that provide safe, easy access while taking into account cultural and other local considerations ensure that girls are also enrolled. As these schools become part of larger government systems, measures must be instituted to ensure that such features are not lost; else the gains with regard to closing the gender gap may be short-lived.

> *As community schools are transitioned into government systems, continuing to base learning on "community knowledge" does not have to be in conflict with the standardized syllabus requirements of government schools.*

As schools are integrated or transitioned into the formal government system, leading to the financing of teachers at the central level but allowing local communities to start schools, unforeseen outcomes can occur. In Kenya, for example, these have included the construction of too many small schools; excessive spending on teachers relative to non-teacher inputs; and the setting of school fees and other school attendance requirements at a level that deters some (particularly the hardest to reach) from attending school.[176] At the same time, while more schools are constructed over time, there may be significant areas where school construction lags behind, unless there is coordinated planning involving government, NGOs, communities and other relevant stakeholders.

When we consider the transition of community schools to government systems, there is a need to be more creative in how we visualize the mainstreaming of community-based schools and other ABE initiatives, given that it is more important to replicate successful practices across schools than types of schools *per se.*

> *It is more important to replicate successful practices across schools than types of schools per se.*

One interesting strategy involves a clustering approach to share resources and organize activities for participants from a cluster group comprising a mix of community and government schools. Such variations on mainstreaming community-based education initiatives have been successfully implemented, for example, in Pakistan by the Aga Khan Foundation (with funding from USAID) working with a network of six local NGOs; in Haiti by USIAD/Haiti and its partners, and in Tigray, Ethiopia by the Relief Society of Tigray (REST).

In the Pakistan case, schools are organized into clusters for the professional development of teachers, but cluster divisions are also used for other activities, such as community campaigns and advocacy efforts and related health interventions. The six local NGOs implementing this program include DEO officials in their training and advocacy activities. Clustering has facilitated resource mobilization for education activities in program schools, as well as for nearby schools, by targeting key local decision-makers in a given geographic area.[177]

In Haiti, where private, non-public schools (operated by religious institutions, NGOs, communities, and individual proprietors) account for more than 80 percent of primary schools, the school system is highly fragmented, and schools in close geographic proximity hardly ever work together. Yet even in this fragmented system, a cluster school approach, with education programs for school directors, pedagogic teams, and PTAs, together with related support and monitoring in classrooms, was successfully implemented by USAID/Haiti and its partners. All schools in a cluster were granted equal status, fostering real change in relationships at the school and community levels.[178]

> *[We need to] broaden our thinking about how we conceptualize the "mainstreaming" of community-based education initiatives into government systems.*

These examples of transitioning, or systemic mainstreaming, beyond the absorption of one school at a time into the government system, suggest a need to broaden our thinking about how we conceptualize the "mainstreaming" of community-based education initiatives into government systems.

The role of NGOs: supporter, implementer, and intermediary

In many countries, NGOs have been key instruments for boosting state efforts to achieve EFA goals. Although the role of NGOs and their relationship to the state and to donors varies among different countries, a mix of international and local NGOs are involved in education service delivery, and in lobbying and advocating for educational reform world-wide.

Despite the obvious challenges in coordinating different implementers and sources of funding for basic education delivery, few governments or NGOs would deny the necessity of partnership in order to address EFA goals. In fact, most governments need, and often seek, the involvement of NGOs in various projects that require personnel and logistical support which governments themselves cannot provide. Through their community-based programs, many NGOs generate resources or bring

> *Governments can provide an enabling environment to support community-based initiatives.*

them into the community, mobilize people, and provide services to fill the gaps left by the normal delivery system of the government. They supplement official services, reaching out to sections of the society and geographic locations where government provision is inadequate. At the same time, governments can provide an enabling environment to support such community-based initiatives.

Clearly, there is a need for the continued involvement of NGOs in education activities. NGOs tend to enjoy greater access to communities than government officials, and have staff that is more committed, experienced, and sensitive to local needs, thus allowing them to function better as intermediaries than government agencies. This does not occur by magic. Rather, it is a by-product of the NGOs' need to perform well vis-à-vis both donors and the communities they serve in order to survive. In some contexts, NGOs help build bridges between donors, governments, and communities, and in others, they act as the voice of the suppressed conscience and, especially, help visualize societies and relationships among individuals and groups according to more egalitarian and ethical rules and assumptions.[179]

However, their multiple obligations—to communities, governments and donors—are not without complications. Serving mostly low-income populations, it is obvious that NGOs cannot generate sufficient revenues from such groups. In the last decade, international NGOs have gained greater support from external bilateral and multilateral agencies, and greater recognition from national governments, requiring them to oscillate between actions based on ethical convictions and local needs and the dictates of assistance providers and host country governments.

At a local level, national, regional and local NGOs and community-based organizations (CBOs), including federations of grassroots organizations, cooperatives, trade unions, and other stakeholder groups, can be valuable partners in ABE initiatives requiring broad participation. However, while the need for local NGO and CBO involvement in education support activities is undeniable, the relationships between communities and NGOs and/or the MOE, and their respective obligations and responsibilities, are not always clear. The relationship of NGOs to client communities may be affected by political or ethnic alignments, state regulation and other local influences. Therefore, if community school models that rely on NGO involvement at various levels are to have a greater systemic impact, questions such as the following need to be clarified: Are NGOs integral representatives of communities, are they outsiders or are they intermediaries? How do different types of NGOs/CBOs position themselves within the MOE-community relationship?

As we confront these and related questions, it is important to recognize that NGOs (international, national or local) may vary greatly in capacities, in the extent to which they ensure beneficiary participation, and in the kinds of relationships they develop with various stakeholders. At one extreme are NGOs (usually international but also national) whose orientation and competence are very similar to the private sector firms with whom they compete for contracts in project implementation and service delivery. Such NGOs may be efficient as service deliverers but are oriented to meeting the requirements of bureaucratic funding agencies and are unlikely to use genuinely participatory processes. At the other extreme are participatory NGOs that see themselves almost exclusively as enablers and capacity builders and refuse to compromise their objectives or independence by collaborating in official programs. Then there are some which emphasize "bottom-up" planning, combining strong technical expertise with effective institution building at the community level.[180]

Whatever their orientation, NGOs have a responsibility to align their support for community schools with DEO, district-wide, regional or national activities and policies. Only then can we expect coordinated programs intended to meet the needs of schools across a district, which is vital if systemic change is to occur. NGOs also have to make concerted efforts to reach agreements with DEOs to provide curriculum and instructional programs at community schools as well as at government schools. At the same time, in order to encourage NGO linkages and expansion and replication of successful NGO-initiated and directed programs, government agencies need to consider scaling down in terms of decentralizing and building flexibility and micro-variability into their operations. This not only pushes decision-making closer to the populations most affected (and is, in this sense, a more participatory way of working) but also makes it easier to work with regional and local NGOs.[181]

> NGOs have a responsibility to align their support for community schools with DEO, district-wide, regional or national activities and policies.

Future work on community schools and complementary provision

In order to inform a better understanding of community schools and a dialogue on complementary provision of quality education opportunities for all, we propose a number of activities,[182] outlined below. Central to these activities are collaborative efforts to form and support research and advocacy working groups and networks within countries and regionally, consisting of interested institutions and individuals, and ensuring a significant voice for those involved in community schooling on the ground.

Participatory research involving local communities, educational practitioners, administrators and policy makers, donors, and the research community will help counter "the monopoly of information"[183] and the dominance of received solutions and "pronouncements of trained experts over the discourses of ordinary people."[184] Such research must be carried out in such a way that different stakeholders (including students, parents and teachers), community organizations, and other grassroots advocates participate more fully in the development of knowledge, policy and practice in

> Research must be carried out in such a way that different stakeholders (including students, parents and teachers), community organizations, and other grassroots advocates participate more fully in the development of community-based schooling.

community-based schooling and other forms of complementary education provision. A more participatory, collaborative process of action research, stressing unity among research, practice and policy will provide not only a different base for expertise and a knowledge that comes from people and communities. It will also reinforce broader, more authentic forms of participation in education decision-making. In addition, it will guard against a polarization where researchers become either uncritical cheerleaders of community schools or rabid critics who are not prepared to accept the proven merits of much community-based schooling.

In addition to research and connected learning experiences, advocacy needs to be built around other elements that help forge successful community schools: a motivating vision, community partnerships, and strategic organization and financing. This may involve engaging communities more broadly, using data to define results and achievements, and promoting such practices as:

- the involvement of school communities more directly and explicitly in curriculum decisions;
- on-going professional development for teachers; facilitators and school leaders;
- integrated in-school and after-school learning experiences;
- support for broad-based local coalitions and sustainable partnerships to advance, develop and sustain community schools;
- developing local technical assistance capacity to support community schools, and,
- funding streams to support a community schools strategy.[185]

It will also be necessary to:

- identify, gather and share documentation with local communities, educational practitioners, administrators and policy makers on related, ongoing projects dealing with community-based schooling and other forms of complementary or alternate provision from different parts of the world.
- develop, test, and apply methodologies for analyzing the costs and cost-effectiveness of complementary approaches to providing access, completion, and learning to target populations.
- engage in the process of building strong working relationships with those involved in conceptualizing, designing, researching, and implementing community schools and related projects.
- advocate to ensure that sector-wide plans explicitly include complementary approaches—in terms of the populations they will serve and the resources that will be required.

- work with national stakeholders to identify underserved areas and populations (i.e., sub-national tracking of EFA) and help develop policies and strategies for targeting resources to those regions and populations.
- help to develop strategies to ensure that community schools become more oriented towards community learning and become resource centers that serve not only the learning and development needs of children, but also encourage or support the learning of adults and out-of-school youth in the community.
- facilitate research on how community schools may utilize the technological potential available in our constantly changing, "*glocalized* world."[186] More work is needed on how various technologies can be integrated into the community school model to enhance learning opportunities, flexibility, community participation, access to resources, communication, and sustainability.
- help develop mechanisms that allow sector funding to flow to non-governmental providers.
- work with multiple partners to support the development of appropriate government capacities to fund, administer, and manage a multi-faceted, loosely-coupled system of education provision.

Conclusion

We see this book as a start to an initiative for further conceptualizing and strengthening the idea of community schools as a complementary component within a multi-faceted education system. Within this system, governments, NGOs, foundations, religious entities and other community organizations, as well as the private sector, will provide formal and non-formal learning opportunities. Indeed, better understanding of community schools and other complementary programs for providing quality basic education for all, including underserved populations, may contribute more to meeting EFA goals than another round of large-scale, sectoral investment strategies.

> *Better understanding of community schools and other complementary programs for providing quality basic education for all, including underserved populations, may contribute more to meeting EFA goals than another round of large-scale, sector investment strategies.*

This is not to say that resources, reforms, and capacity are not needed. In fact, research on complementary models will help clarify what resources are needed and show how they can be invested and managed more effectively. This research and the dialogue that it generates can help identify appropriate policies that promote complementary and alternative approaches to providing basic education. It can also demonstrate how combinations of different capacities—governmental and nongovernmental, centralized and decentralized—can be mobilized, organized, and and reinforced.[187]

We at Save the Children-US regard this book as a basis for continuing dialogue among the various stakeholders on the practices and outcomes of community schools, thus helping to contribute to the overall effort to provide access to quality, lifelong education for all. Continuing to support and advocate for community schools is consistent with Save the Children's goal that children learn and develop to their full potential and that our interventions be responsive to the needs, interests and aspirations of individual learners and their local contexts and communities. To support these holistic notions of education and development, Save the Children actively seeks to strengthen and use multiple channels to ensure that all children have access to quality education.

Notes

[146] In real terms, education aid to developing nations has decreased by 30 percent in the past decade, and only eight of the world's 148 developing nations committed a fifth of government spending to education. (UNICEF, State of the World's Children 2004).

[147] The high prevalence of HIV/AIDS is affecting the efficiency and the supply of teachers, rapidly increasing the number of orphans and affecting girls in particular. It has enormous financial impacts and an effect on access and quality of education.

[148] UNESCO (2003). EFA Global Monitoring Report 2003/4: Gender and Education for All—The Leap to Quality. UNESCO: Paris and UNESCO (2004). EFA Global Monitoring Report, 2005: Education for All—The Quality Imperative. UNESCO: Paris.

[149] William Lowe Boyd and Robert L. Crowson (2002). The quest for a new hierarchy in education: from loose coupling back to tight? Journal of Educational Administration, 40 (6), pp. 521–533.

[150] Estimates by UNESCO, UNICEF, The World Bank and others range from 103 to 120 million.

[151] Joseph DeStefano (November, 2004). Meeting EFA: Lessons from Complementary Approaches. Washington, DC: EQUIP2, Academy for Educational Development, and USAID. (Draft—Cited with permission of the author.).

[152] In addition to the Community Schools in Africa, Save the Children-US also supports over 40 Community Schools in Haiti. Many of the features of its Community School model are implemented in the formal government schools and formal and non-formal Early Childhood Development programs with which it works in some 20 other countries.

[153] In the Mali Community Schools the language of instruction for at least the first three years would be the children's native tongue (Bambara) rather than French, so that real learning could take place from the outset. This also permitted villagers to serve as teachers, since many more persons in Kolondièba are literate in Bambara than in French. The possibility that some of the younger children might seek to enter the formal system after three years meant that the Village School would have to include intensive French lessons as an optional part of its third year curriculum.

[154] This section draws on questions and issues raised in: UNESCO (1997), Transforming Community Schools into Open Learning Communities; Rethinking Community Schools; Conceptualizing Open Learning Communities. http://www.newhorizons.org/trans/international/unesco_openlrn.htm#prob.

[155] Pauline Rose (2003). Communities, gender and education: Evidence from sub-Saharan Africa—Background paper for 2003 UNESCO Global Monitoring Report. http://portal.unesco.org/education/en/file_download.php/557aa4c1cc008d3a0807fc336b40c 3edCommunities,+gender+and+education.+Evidence+from+sub-Saharan+Africa..doc

[156] Wolf, J., Kane, E. & Strickland, B. (1997). Planning for Community Participation in Education, Washington DC: Office of Sustainable Development, Bureau for Africa, USAID.

[157] Hillery reviews 94 definitions of community and suggests that this is not an exhaustive list.—Hillery, G. A. (1955). Definitions of community: areas of agreement, Rural Sociology, 20, pp. 111–123.

[158] Thomas Erickson (1997). Social Interaction on the Net: Virtual Community as Participatory Genre. Proceedings of the Thirtieth Hawaii International Conference on System Sciences, January 6–10, 1997, Maui, Hawaii.
    http://www.pliant.org/personal/Tom_Erickson/VC_as_Genre.html

[159] Pauline Rose (2003). Community participation in school policy and practice in Malawi: Balancing local knowledge, national policies and international agency priorities. Compare, 33(1), 47–64.

[160] Dana Burde (May, 2004). Weak State, Strong Community? Promoting Community Participation in Post-Conflict Countries. Current Issues in Comparative Education, 6 (2).

[161] Miller Grandvaux and Yoder (2002).

[162] MacNeil, James (2004).Theory and Practice of Community Participation in Schooling. Paper presented at the North East, Comparative International Education Conference (CIES), George Washington University, Washington, DC.

[163] Save the Children (2005). State of the World's Mothers 2005: The Power and Promise of Girls Education. Westport, Connecticut: Save the Children.

[164] School for life is over three times as cost-effective as government schools in Ghana at producing a grade three completers. And, when tested, 81 percent of School for Life students demonstrated that they could read and calculate well. Community schools in Mali have higher unit costs than government schools, but they also have better rates of completion—67 percent compared to 56 percent—and higher pass rates on the primary cycle completion exam: 41 percent compared to 43 percent. Unit costs in these schools are 57 percent higher than in public schools, but the cost per completer is only 31 percent higher and the cost per learning outcome is only 10 percent higher. Educatodos is almost five times as cost effective as public schools at producing a grade six completer. For grades seven to nine, Educatodos has both a higher completion rate and much lower costs, making it 15 times as cost effective as the public system at producing a grade nine completer. Joseph DeStefano (November, 2004). Meeting EFA: Lessons from Complementary Approaches. NW, Washington, DC: EQUIP2, Academy for Educational Development, and USAID. (Draft—Cited with permission of the author.).

[165] UNESCO (2003). EFA Global Monitoring Report 2003/4: Gender and Education for All—The Leap to Quality. UNESCO: Paris.

[166] Jordan Naidoo (2005 forthcoming). Education Decentralization in Africa: Great Expectations and Unfulfilled Promises (Chapter 4, pp. 122–154). In David P. Baker Alexander W. Wiseman (Eds.) Global Trends in Educational Policy, Volume 6 in the International Perspectives on Education and Society Series. Elsevier Science, Ltd.

[167] De Grauwe, A., Lugaz, C., Baldé, D., Diakhaté, C., Dougnon, D., Moustapha, M., & Odushina, D. (2005). Does decentralization lead to school improvement? Findings and lessons from research in West-Africa. Journal of Education for International Development, 1(1). Retrieved April 22, 2005, from http://www.equip123.net/JEID/articles/1/1-1.pdf

[168] Williams, G. (2004). Evaluating Participatory Development: tyranny, power and (re)politicisation. Third World Quarterly 25(3), 557–579.

[169] Kremer and Miguel, 2004.

[170] Michael Kremer, Sylvie Moulin, Robert Namunyu (April, 2003) Decentralization: A Cautionary Tale (Work in Progress) http://www.povertyactionlab.org/papers/Decentrali-zation%20Cautionary%20Tale.doc

[171] Healey, F. H., & DeStefano, J. (1997). Education reform support: A framework for scaling up school reform. Retrieved May 18, 2005, from: http://www.seisummit.org/Downloads/aspd/EducReformSupport.PDF

[172] Healey and Stefano (1997).

[173] Thomas K. Glennan, Susan J. Bodilly, Jolene Galegher, and Kerri A. Kerr (eds.) (2004). Expanding the Reach of Education Reforms:

[174] Fullan, M. (1999). Change Forces: The Sequel. London: Falmer Press. pp.. (72–3).

175 Power, Anne and Robert Waters (2004). Envisaging classroom learning with the qualities of community learning: For the public good.
http://www.aare.edu.au/04pap/wat04160.pdf

176 Kremer et al, 2003.

177 USAID/EQUIP 1 (2004). Releasing Confidence and Creativity (RCC): Building Sound Foundations for Early Learning in Pakistan. Downloaded May 26, from: http://www.equip123.net/docs/e1TPD_PakistanProfile.pdf

178 USAID/ EQUIP1 (April 2004). Cluster schools and Teacher Professional development. EQ Review, 2 (2). Downloaded January 2005, from:
http://www.equip123.net/EQ_Review/2_2.pdf

179 Nelly P. Stromquist (November 15, 1998). NGOs in a New Paradigm of Civil Society. CICE 1 (1). Downloaded: May 27, 2005 from:
http://www.tc.columbia.edu/cice/articles/ns111.htm

180 The World Bank (1996) The World Bank Participation Source Book—Appendix 2—Working Paper Summaries: Participation and Intermediary NGOs. Washington, DC: The World Bank. Downloaded May 28, from: http://www.worldbank.org/wbi/sourcebook/sba210.htm

181 The World Bank (1996).

182 A number of these activities are substantially adapted from Joeseph Destefano (2004). Meeting EFA: Reaching and Educating Populations. In "Panel Presentation: Underserved Areas," CIES, March 22, 2005, Stanford University: Palo Alto, California. They are further informed by discussions with the author.

183 Habermac, J. (1979). Legitimation crisis in the modern society. Communication and the Evolution of Society. Boston: Beacon Press.

184 Foucault (1980). Power/knowledge: Selected interviews and other writings. New York: Pantheon.

185 Martin J. Blank, Atelia Melaville and Bela P. Shah (2003). Making a Difference: Research and Practice in Community Schools. Washington, DC: Coalition for Community Schools.http://www.communityschools.org/CCSFullReport.pdf

186 'Glocalization,' means 'a global outlook tailored to local conditions.' It sums up the inter-relations of the global and the local, and the notion that globalization is not simply linking already existing localities together, such that the integrity of each place is invaded and subjected to the homogenizing effects of global culture. Rather it also involves a deliberate reinforcing of heterogeneity by re-production of locality from within the locality itself as a way of taking advantage of the global patterns.—Ronald Robertson, "Glocalization: Time-Space and Homogeneity-Heterogeneity," in Mike Featherstone, Scott Lash and Ronald Robertson (eds), Global Modernities, (London, 1995).

187 Joseph DeStefano (November, 2004). Meeting EFA: Lessons from Complementary Approaches. Washington, DC: EQUIP2, Academy for Educational Development, and USAID. (Draft—Cited with permission of the author).

Index

Action Aid, 145
Africare, 136, 140

Bangladesh. *See* BRAC
Basic Education and Expansion Project
    (BEEP). *See* community schools
Benin. *See* community schools
BRAC, 6, 12, 140, 155–156
Brazil. *See* community schools

CARE, 136
CHANCE. *See* Uganda
civil society. *See* community schools
Colombia. *See* community schools
community mobilization, 7, 40, 49, 58,
    67, 69, 79, 113, 1515, 123, 139, 150
    See also under specific country entries
community schools, 1ª8, 133–193. *See*
    also under specific country entries
  access, 176
  Basic Education and Expansion
    Project (BEEP), 139–140
  benefits, 171–173
  Benin, 133, 135–136, 144, 148, 150
  Brazil, 167
  CHANCE, 102–132, 176, 178
  civil society, 142, 147, 149, 150
  Colombia, 158
  community-based organizations
    (CBO), 187
  community mobilization, 139 (*see also*
    under specific country entries)
  curriculum, 160, 161
  decentralization, 143–147, 165–166,
    179–180

defining community, 174–175
Education Reform Support
    Framework, 159
Egypt, 6, 159
El Salvador, 164
Ethiopia, 3, 7, 142, 148, 156, 185
financing of, 178, 181
funding gap, 162
future of, 171–191
Ghana, 148, 150, 158, 160, 167, 178
Girls Attainment in Basic Literacy and
    Education (GABLE), 138–139
girls' education, 134–135, 138,
    158–159, 176–178, 185
Guatemala, 157–160
Guinea, 141–142, 148
Haiti, 185–186
Honduras, 156, 164, 178
impact: on access, 156–158; on
    completion, 157, 158; on policy,
    6, 26, 31, 158, 159
integration, 144–147
Kenya, 5, 7, 172
local ownership, 4–5
Malawi, 3, 5, 138–139, 148, 150, 151
Mali, 3, 5–7, 139–141, 148, 150, 151,
    156–160, 165–168, 179
Namibia, 167
NGO role, 136–137, 186–188
non-public education, 163–165
Pakistan, 157–159, 186
parents associations, 140–142,
    148–150 (*see also under specific*
    country entries)
partnerships, 148–150

Programme d'Ajustement Sectoriel de l'Education (PASE), 141
phase 1, 137–143
phase 2, 143–147
phase 3, 147–150
quality measures, 176
QUEST, 5, 139 (*see also under main entry*)
rationale for, 134
research, 188–189
role of, 173–174
scaling up, 148, 182–184
school management committees, 5, 7, 150, 165 (*see also under specific country entries*)
South Africa, 164
success factors, 173
sustainability, 133, 135, 181–184 (*see also under specific country entries*)
systemic reform, 134, 136, 138, 139
Tanzania, 4
transition to government systems, 184–186
Uganda, 176
Zambia, 149, 156, 158

democratization, 3, 12, 140

Egypt. *See* community schools
El Salvador. *See* community schools
Ethiopia, 75–100
    Banyan Tree Foundation, 85, 143
    Basic Education Network, 86, 88
    Basic Education Structural Overhaul (BESO), 78, 142
    BESO II-SCOPE, 80–84
    block grants, 96–97
    child sponsorship schools, 91–93
    community mobilization, 78, 89
    dropout rate, 76, 97
    enrollment, 76, 89
    food crisis, 82–84
    girls' education, 7, 76, 79, 80, 89, 91, 95
    Guraghe People's Self-Help Development Organization, 86–89
    Lurie Foundation, 90

mobile populations/schools (*see* Pastoralist Education Project *under entry below*)
NGO network, 97
One Love Schools, 89–91
PACT, 85
parents groups, 79, 81, 84
Pastoralist Education Project (PEP), 93–96
Project for Innovations in Education (PIE), 85–91, 142
school management committees, 85, 90, 92, 97
sustainability, 85, 90, 92, 97
training, 80–84
USAID, 78, 82, 85, 96

Fast Track Initiative, 152, 156, 162

Ghana. *See* community schools
Girls Attainment in Basic Literacy and Education (GABLE). *See* community schools
gender equity. *See* girls' education
girls' education. *See* community schools; *also under specific country entries*
Guatemala. *See* community schools
Guinea. *See* community schools

Haiti. *See* community schools
health, 5, 18, 40, 42
HIV/AIDS, 2, 50, 53, 55, 56, 62–64, 69, 102, 132, 151, 157, 161, 171
Honduras. *See* community schools

integration, 8, 30, 38. *See also* community schools (transition)

Kenya. *See* community schools

local language. *See* maternal language

Malawi, 37–74. *See also* community schools
    Chichewa, 40, 43, 45–47, 61, 64, 66, 67, 69
    community mobilization, 40, 67, 69
    costs, 43, 52
    curriculum, 46–48

dropout rate, 41, 42, 51, 59, 68
education trainers, 57, 58, 60, 65, 69
Free Primary Education declaration,
    37, 38
girls' education, 40, 54, 61, 66
integration, 43
Malawi Institute of Education (MIE),
    51, 52, 61–64
MIITEP (Malawi's Integrated In-
    Service Teacher Education
    Program), 46, 57
Primary Education Advisors (PEAs),
    40, 44, 45, 49–52, 54, 55, 57, 58,
    60 (*see also under main entry for*
    QUEST)
PTA, 41, 42, 58–60
QUEST (*see under main entry*)
school committees, 41, 42, 58–60, 63,
    67–69
teacher certification, 38
teacher recruitment, training, and
    payment, 39, 40, 42–44, 50
teacher supervision, 45–46
Teachers Union of Malawi (TUM), 60
USAID, 38, 39, 46, 48, 49, 50, 51
Village-Based Schools, 38–69
Mali, 9–35. *See also* community schools
    costs, 12, 14, 21–24
    decentralization, 28, 30–32
    dropout rate, 24
    evaluation, 27
    enrollment, 10, 12–14, 16, 31
    French language, 12, 18, 20, 21, 24–26
    girls education, 10, 12–16, 20, 24,
        27, 29
    local language, 12, 14, 18, 26, 31
    Nouvelle École Fondamentale, 6, 26, 160
    quality, 12, 14, 25, 31
    school management committees, 12,
        15–16, 32
    Sikasso region, 10, 18, 23, 30, 31
    sustainability, 28, 30, 32
    teacher retention, 29–31
    teacher selection, training, supervision,
        19–21, 26
    USAID, 11, 21, 24–26, 28–30
maternal language, 137, 140, 149, 160,
    161
Millenium Development Goals, 152

Namibia. *See* community schools

One Love Schools. *See* Ethiopia

Pakistan. *See* community schools

QUEST, 5, 46, 48–69
    community capacity building, 51, 59
        59–60
    community development assistants
        (CDAs), 51, 58
    curriculum assessment, 61–63
    handbooks, 69, 73–74
    impact: on pupils, 64–66; on teachers,
        66–67; on communities, 67–68,
        national, 69–70
    Improving Educational Quality
        project, 51, 62–64, 66
    mentor teachers, 54–55, 57, 58, 60,
        63, 65
    primary education advisors (PEAs),
        51, 65
    results, 51–52
    teacher training and support, 54–59
    term initiatives, 59–60, 68

Redd Barna, 49

Schools for Life, 145, 160
school management committees. *See
    under specific country entries*; community
    schools
South Africa. *See* community schools
sustainability. *See under specific country
    entries*; community schools

Tanzania. *See* community schools

Uganda and the CHANCE Schools,
    101–132. *See also* community schools
    adult literacy, 119
    AIDS orphans, 102, 108
    capacity building, 104, 105
    clusters, 115–116
    design, 107
    disadvantaged populations, 102, 107,
        125–126
    enrollment, 103, 108

expansion to other districts, 122–124
Forum for Education NGOs in
    Uganda (FENU), 126–128
flexible education, 102, 104, 105
girls' education, 125, 127
lessons learned, 128–130
literacy support, 124
PTA, 111
quality, 116–117
relation to formal schools, 117
Save the Children's role, 112–116
school feeding, 120–121
school management committees,
    109–110, 123
sustainability, 111, 121, 122, 124–128,
    131, 134, 136
teacher selection and training, 113–116

UNICEF, 10, 49, 69, 126, 159
USAID, 133–153. *See also under specific*
    country entries
    Africa Bureau, 134–135
    community schools (*see* community
        schools)

Village-Based Schools. *See* Malawi
VOICE International, 127

World Bank, 29, 38, 96, 134, 145, 162
World Education, 135, 136, 139, 140'
    142, 148, 149, 159
World Learning, 136, 142
World Vision, 130

Zambia. *See* community schools